POLITICIZED MICROFINANCE

Money, Power, and Violence in the Black Americas

When Grameen Bank was awarded the Nobel Peace Prize in 2006, microfinance was lauded as an important contributor to the economic development of the Global South. However, political scandals, mission drift, and excessive commercialization have tarnished this example of responsible and inclusive financial development. *Politicized Microfinance* insightfully discusses exclusion while providing a path towards redemption.

In this work, Caroline Shenaz Hossein explores the politics, histories, and social prejudices that have shaped the legacy of microbanking in Grenada, Guyana, Haiti, Jamaica, and Trinidad. Writing from a feminist perspective, Hossein's analysis is rooted in original qualitative data and offers multiple solutions that prioritize the needs of marginalized and historically oppressed people of African descent.

A must read for scholars of political economy, diasporas studies, social economy, women's studies, as well as development practitioners, *Politicized Microfinance* convincingly argues for microfinance to return to its origins as a political tool that fights for those living in the margins.

CAROLINE SHENAZ HOSSEIN is an assistant professor in the Department of Social Science as well as a member of the Centre for Feminist Research and the Harriet Tubman Institute for Research on Africa and Its Diasporas at York University.

Politicized Microfinance

Money, Power, and Violence in the Black Americas

CAROLINE SHENAZ HOSSEIN

UNIVERSITY OF TORONTO PRESS
Toronto Buffalo London

Toronto Buffalo London
www.utppublishing.com
Printed in the U.S.A.

ISBN 978-1-4426-4820-3 (cloth)
ISBN 978-1-4426-1624-0 (paper)

♾ Printed on acid-free, 100% post-consumer recycled paper with vegetable-based inks.

Library and Archives Canada Cataloguing in Publication

Hossein, Caroline Shenaz, 1971–, author
Politicized microfinance : money, power, and violence in the Black Americas / Caroline Shenaz Hossein.

Includes bibliographical references and index.
ISBN 978-1-4426-4820-3 (cloth). – ISBN 978-1-4426-1624-0 (paper)

1. Microfinance – Political aspects – Caribbean Area. 2. Microfinance – Social aspects – Caribbean Area. 3. Microfinance – Caribbean Area – History. 4. Blacks – Caribbean Area – Economic conditions. 5. Blacks – Caribbean Area – Social conditions. 6. Caribbean Area – Economic conditions. 7. Caribbean Area – Social conditions. I. Title.

HG178.33.C37.H68 2016 332.09729 C2016-901493-2

This book has been published with the help of a grant from the Federation for the Humanities and Social Sciences, through the Awards to Scholarly Publications Program, using funds provided by the Social Sciences and Humanities Research Council of Canada.

University of Toronto Press acknowledges the financial assistance to its publishing program of the Canada Council for the Arts and the Ontario Arts Council, an agency of the Government of Ontario.

Funded by the Government of Canada
Financé par le gouvernement du Canada

This book is dedicated to the memory of my paternal grandfather from (Tiger Bay) Guyana, Mahboob Hussein, who encapsulates the business people I write about in this book, and my Grenadian-born maternal great-grandmother, Maude Gittens, a susu *banker in Trinidad who held on to an African tradition that continues in the Caribbean.*

For Shayan and Amba

Contents

Figures and Tables

Figures

Tables

Preface

Many community economic development programs whose goal is to help the poor appear to be succeeding. But what about those economic programs that fail to meet the needs of their target groups? Since its inception, microfinance has been very much part of the social economy, or third sector (that is, the sector made up of non-governmental, civil society, and other not-for-profit organizations like charities, self-help groups, and cooperatives).[1] But well-intentioned academics and practitioners often deploy microfinance in ways that undermine indigenous banking systems – systems that could help reform the social economy into one that it is truly inclusive and that helps those in need. As one of my interviewees from this study – "Pimp Juice," a twenty-four-year-old carwash owner – explained to me:

> The government and man in di bank fulling dem own pocket(s) and its dem wit money who run tings. Nobady sit back and let one people [Black people] get by … dem left wi [African-Guyanese] in jail. (Translation: Government officials and microfinance staff persons, and other bankers, are the ones who are in charge and help each other [This statement infers there is fraud.]. No one in the bank will help African-Guyanese. They would rather see them in jail.) (24 April 2010, Tiger Bay, Guyana)

This expressed view is shared by many low-income borrowers in the region, who see professionals within formal financial programs that target the poor misusing these funds in ways that reinforce unequal power dynamics, cultural bias, and social exclusion of the African diaspora. Black people's experiences in microfinance can thus be summed up by the concept of "politicized microfinance."

The story of the social economy is often told within a European framework by the people who embody that cultural origin. I contend that the microbanking concept pre-dates European cooperative development in the Western world (Gordon-Nembhard 2014; Du Bois 1907). Van Staveren (2015) also defines money as social relations, and argues that it is a very old system that has helped people resolve conflicts. People of colour were pooling money and engaging in collective banking institutions centuries before microfinance came into being (Hossein 2013a). Yet the literature makes little or no mention of this contribution. As a Black woman who has worked in economic development for a decade in Africa and the Caribbean, I am uniquely positioned to study the revival of microfinance. Microfinance's meteoric rise in popularity was pioneered by people of colour in the global South who had lived experience of their people's access (or lack thereof) to finance. Banks in the developing world, especially in countries with a history of enslavement and colonization, have been helping local elites (many born out of the colonizing project of miscegenation) advance their own projects, installing them in positions from which they can manipulate economic resources targeted for the poor in ways that sustain unequal societal structures (Mintz 2010). While commercialization dominates this global (re)invention of microfinance, myriad other players are engaged in the microbanking arena, and their methods and values differ from those of commercial lenders.

Microfinance's advocates *and* its critics tell a generic story of commercialization, while failing to examine intersectional identities and the people who run these programs. With my research, I want to tell the story of microfinance as it affects Black people. This story does not gloss over bias and exclusion in microbanking, but it does place the institution in a historical and colonial context. Microfinance has unfolded in many countries in a highly politicized manner.[2] In this book, I use the concept of "politicized microfinance" in two distinct ways that have particular meaning for the African diaspora. First, in the negative cases in this study, the concept of politicized microfinance refers to the "Big Men" who, through clientelist politicking and partisanship, further oppress the entrepreneurial poor in the marginalized urban areas around the capital city. This type of microfinance, politicized and managed by local elites, adheres to rhetoric and forces people into unequal social systems. Ferguson (2001) speaks to the "anti-politics" in aid regimes that deliberately scrubs people's voices from economic programs, rendering them depolitical. Kamat (2002) makes the important point that we need to consider the social class of those who lead development from within official development agencies and of those in grassroots organizations in India.

The second mode of politicized microfinance I consider aims to create alternative money systems that can bring about social change (Gibson-Graham 2003, 2006; Ardener and Burman 1996). In the effective cases in this book, politicized microfinance requires the people in charge of this resource to be politically conscious – to take on the role of conscientious activists. Indeed, in the case of Haiti, microfinance staff go so far as to take on deadly risks to make money available to excluded groups. This form of banking is not about inserting people into unjust systems, but about reforming the current system. Politicized microfinance in this way becomes a form of liberation – a concept that resonates with the Black diaspora, who recognize the different forms of politicization.

The reader should thus be well aware that "politicized microfinance" takes these two forms – and, of course, that it is the latter form that needs to be activated if economic programs are to truly address social exclusion (Galabuzi 2006). In this book, I examine the various forms of politics that intervene in the lending process, using an intersectional analysis of race, class, and gender; this will reveal that the "neutrality" of microloans is a myth. Microfinance, in reality, is highly politicized: a tool designed by the very people in charge to either instigate or mitigate exclusion.

No one tells the story of how indigenous African banking systems have persevered in spite of modernity, or of the many local banking systems that operate alongside more formalized economic programs but are not counted as part of the microfinance industry. This absence is strange, given that collective banks provide financial services to millions of excluded people around the world on their own terms. The politics of collective action is a major aspect of the Black diaspora experience (Gibson-Graham 2006). Within the Caribbean region, indigenous African money systems focus on the voices of the oppressed to create social and economic power in poor urban communities. This book aims to fill the gaps in the literature on Latin American and Caribbean studies on the subject of microfinance, and at the same time to examine the social economy of the African diaspora. No one else has examined the opportunities and constraints in access to microcredit based on intersectional identities of race, ethnicity, and gender. Indeed, few books on the social economy focus on the economic development of Black people. In response, this work will focus on microfinance as an intervention, on its part in the social economy, and on its impact on people of African heritage in a specific cultural context – the Caribbean region.

Sidney W. Mintz (2010), the great Caribbeanist, compellingly argued that the Caribbean peoples can be referred to as the Black Atlantic. African peoples forced to the colonies in the Caribbean region experienced unimaginable horrors under slavery and colonization for centuries with the sole purpose of modernizing Europe. Unlike larger countries like Brazil and the United States, the societies of the small Caribbean countries have been intensely affected by enslavement as a result of their size (Mintz 2010). The experiences of colonization and slavery continue to have a profound impact on the lives of African descendants in the Caribbean and on Afro-Americans in the Western Hemisphere.

My ultimate goal in *Politicized Microfinance* is to reveal the need to "politicize" microfinance. As I outlined above, microfinance can take two forms: oppressive (see Jamaica, Trinidad, and Guyana cases) or socially activist (see Haiti and Grenada cases). The call to "politicize" microfinance so that it becomes more socially conscious forces economic development practitioners and academics to change how they examine economic and financial development programs for marginalized people of colour. A movement toward socially conscious economics means that social economists must think about alternative business paradigms that centre on marginalized groups and confront systemic oppression. Gibson-Graham (1996; 2006) has also called for the politics of collective action and notes the cooperative nature of such economies in political terms. However, the social economy, designed as a place to "help," too often becomes a neutral site that fails to react against oppression. The social economy can in this way become a hiding place where the privileged elites can join in the process of replicating unequal systems that further harm those already at the bottom.

The microfinance or microbanking sector is not new. It grew rapidly in the 1980s as international (Western-led) development agencies such as the World Bank and the IMF levied intense structural adjustment programs. Global South economists like Muhammad Yunus in Chittagong, Bangladesh, carried out microbanking experiments to enhance the livelihoods of marginalized people (2010). Through this microfinance "revolution," civil society organizations turned conventional banking norms upside down and decolonized the business structures to fit with the world's poor. Microcredit, as it was then called, was to provide inclusive financial services that focused on providing economic and social support for marginalized people (of colour).

These southern-based practitioners were fighting the Western model and introducing collective and solidarity economics into the banking world.

For at least three decades, microfinance was the most celebrated poverty-fighting intervention. The Yunus-founded Grameen Bank was awarded the Nobel Prize for Peace in 2006 for making financing available to millions of poor women. But an increasing body of critical literature has emerged against the $70 billion dollar microfinance industry in the past ten years, and that industry is more polarized than ever before.[3] The divide lies between commercial lenders interested in profits, scale, and investments and not-for-profits that focus on using economic resources as tools to alleviate poverty and help the marginalized. The social economy literature still counts microfinance as part of the third sector; however, mission drift is occurring among many retailers microlending to the poor. Quarter, Mook, and Armstrong (2009) make it abundantly clear that organizations that prioritize profits are not part of the social economy. Still, donors and social investors are using public resources to create incentives for commercial banks to scale up operations because of the perceived good they can do. A better path might be to build a movement that tackles structural inequalities through politicized action focused on poverty and social exclusion.

My work is based on empirical methods carried out in three main cases: Jamaica, Guyana, and Haiti. I also refer to the secondary cases of Trinidad and Tobago (the wealthiest country in the study) and Grenada (the smallest country in the study) to broaden the regional perspective. My goal is to examine the microfinance industry and the claims that it is too commercialized. I find that these critiques levelled at the microfinance industry are far more complex than they first appear, and certainly any critique is not as simple as the question of whether it works or does not work.

This study focuses on micro- and small-business people trying to access economic resources in the Black Americas. I draw on diasporic Black feminist theory and a framework of intersectionality to ground my analysis of financial development programs that target marginalized people in the five Caribbean countries. I argue that politics is a chief aspect of decision-making in microlending programs and that paid employees in charge of financial resources within these programs can either conform to cultural bias or react against it. I use Black feminist theory to rethink how Black people engage in the social economy. In three of the cases (Jamaica, Guyana, and Trinidad), microfinance practitioners (privileged people) were not interested in decolonizing the development process, as to do so would mean altering local power dynamics. In other words, these bankers have conformed to alienating politics to further contain and control the masses; they are not in microfinance to help people, but rather to further their own personal goals. In contrast, microbanking in the Haitian and Grenadian cases is a tool used to fight exclusion through collective finance; the bankers in these cases resist the political conformity that oppresses the masses.

In chapter 2, I explore the political and social history of Jamaica, Guyana, and Haiti (the main cases) to show how cultural context and history has affected microfinance development. In telling the history of each place, I reveal how deeply embedded racial and class biases are in the mindset of those working within the microfinance sector in Jamaica, Guyana, and Trinidad. This serves as background for the discussion of the impact of cultural bias in chapter 3. Class-conscious elites (many having light-skinned complexions) manage economic development in slum communities to suit their own purposes. This kind of manipulation hinders certain people's access to microbanking and amounts to a deviation from the tenets of microfinance.

Chapter 4 shows that while the microfinance sector assumes that politics is a bad thing for business, this is not always the case. In Jamaica, informal leaders and politicians interfere in microfinance, capitalizing organizations so that they can refer poor people who adhere to their partisan politics, whereas in Haiti, cooperative lenders use politics and indigenous traditions of the masses subversively, contesting economic and social apartheid. In doing this they take personal risks. Retaliation can be violent against those in charge of microbanking, and Haitian lenders can find their lives threatened when they work to upset the status quo to help economically oppressed people.

Chapter 5 demonstrates that microfinance can be effective when it follows indigenous systems. While this research is about microfinance and its role in helping people in need, it also focuses on the experience of marginalized Afro-Caribbean people in the social economy across the Caribbean region – the Black Americas and Black Atlantic. By acknowledging the indigenous banking systems brought over by African slaves to the New World, I correct the story of cooperative development told in the West. These informal, community-based microbanks – largely absent in the literature of social economy and microfinance – are prevalent throughout the Caribbean region and are clearly the most inclusive of oppressed people.[4] In Haiti (and to some extent in Grenada), cooperative lenders, many of the African diaspora, are heavily influenced by indigenous African traditions of collectivity and not by the projects of white colonizers. This is what makes the microbanking experience more inclusive in those two countries. As the Haitians make abundantly clear, indigenous collective banks, both formal and informal, are an alternative way to do business (Hossein 2012, 2014b). The microfinance sector, however, has privileged Western-influenced commercial models. Perhaps the positive activism that has developed within collective microfinance will push the microfinance industry to start to include these collectives, informal and formal, as legitimate sectors of microbanking.

Acknowledgments

Writing a book of this sort is never a one-person job. My husband, Dr Shayan Sen, supported me throughout the research and writing process. My daughter, Amba Lailah, brought joy to me as I wrote this book. I thank those who came before me from lands as far away as India and Africa, who then settled in the Caribbean and later migrated to North America. My family is made up of entrepreneurs from various parts of the Caribbean – Guyana, Grenada, Trinidad, and St Vincent. My parents, Jacqueline Pearline (an Afro-Trinidadian-Vincentian-Grenadian) and Isaac (an Indo-Guyanese), have given me much love. Thank you to my sister, Annie, who takes care of Amba on her weekly Sunday visits so I can write. Other members of my family kind enough to listen to me over the years were Jolanta and Chris, and the Sengupta clan in both Ireland and India, especially Ma and Baba.

My dear friend from the National Conference of Black Political Scientists, Russell Benjamin of the University of Northeastern Illinois, gave me many useful ideas, especially pertaining to Black Americans. Njoki Wane of the University of Toronto taught me Black feminist thought and pushed me to rewrite the social economy of African peoples. Roberta Rice of the University of Calgary mentored me throughout the book-writing process, reading various drafts of my manuscript and always encouraging me to "go big or go home." My friends also enrich my life: Amina Ally, Chello Rogers, Star Thurston, Agnes Mochama, Khaled Ahmed, Celine Cooper, Rebecca Sanders, and Suzette Strong.

Politicized Microfinance draws on years of doctoral research (as well as more recent research in 2013) and greatly benefited from the ideas of Judith Teichman and Louis Pauly of the Department of Political Science at the University of Toronto. Laura Macdonald of Carleton University,

Richard Sandbrook of the University of Toronto (who offered careful editing of the first draft), and Joseph Wong of the University of Toronto all brought insights to this work at one time or another. York University's Linda Peake gave detailed comments on an early version of a paper on my Guyana case. Yasmine Shamsie at Wilfrid Laurier University gave me useful suggestions on Haiti, which I incorporated into chapters 4 and 5. My new colleagues at York University – including Mark Peacock, Amanda Glasbeek (my mentor), Joseph Mensah, Jan Kainer, Jennifer Hyndman, Tokunbo Ojo (my rock), Kabita Chakraborthy, Kamala Kempadoo, Kimberley White, Richard Wellen, Honor Forde-Smith, Amar Wahab, Sandra Whitworth, Anita Lam, Miriam Smith, Lisa Drummond, Judith Hellman, Susan Dimock, Allan Greenbaum, Teresa Abbruzzese, Eduardo Canel, Alina Marquez, and Simone Bohn – all gave me wonderful support to make this book happen. I want to give special thank yous to Michele Johnson, Annie Bunting, Abubacar Fofana Leon, and Paul Lovejoy at the Harriet Tubman Institute for Research on Africa and Its Diasporas for giving me the first space to present my work. Alison Crosby at the Centre for Feminist Research made me feel at home at York. Deborah Britzman and "the collective" (you know who you are) have been remarkable mentors when I needed the support most.

Hundreds of business people in the Caribbean made this project possible, often taking risks to speak to me. Nobody thinks interviewing business people is dangerous, but it can be. I have many generous souls to thank for keeping me safe and informed. Let me start off thanking my assistants in Jamaica: Althea, Ackney, Wayne, Brian, Betty, and Mary; in Grenada, Belvine; in Trinidad, Clayton and Panther; and in Guyana, Shebeca. In Jamaica, my friends opened up their hearts and homes and made my stay enjoyable: Maxine Henry-Wilson, Sharene McKenzie, Richard Troupe, Brenda Cuthbert, Rhea Alert, and Henley Morgan. Much gratitude goes to the Beharry family in Tiger Bay for hosting me. Thanks to Sankar, Danny, and Michael for teaching me about life in Guyana. In Haiti, my good friends Raoul Jean-Louis and Marie-Marcelle St Gilles always gave me sound advice. I am most grateful for the lovely family dinners at Magali and Sinior Raymond's home in Bel Air, where we talked politics and microfinance. Eric Calpas and his grassroots organization helped me meet small business people. In Grenada, Graeme Fletcher, my good friend from university, was kind with assisting me when I was in the country. There are many people to thank in Trinidad for all their help over the months and years: Carmen Gomez-Triggs, Terry Ines, Hazel Brown of the Network of NGOs, Sherma Wilson, Gary Edwards of UWI–St Augustine, and Ashtine Thomason. Stuart Black, with his great regional expertise, supported my projects in Grenada and Jamaica.

During my Fulbright tenure in Jamaica, I studied under John Rapley, then-president of the Caribbean Policy and Research Institute (CAPRI) (now at Cambridge), who guided me and assisted me in refining my interview tools. At the University of the West Indies (UWI), I grew as a researcher under Anthony Harriott, then-chair of the Government Department, who advised me as I moved in and out of the garrisons. Many thanks to Norma Davis at the SALISES library and the good folks at STATIN and PIOJ, especially Angie Taylor. I miss my goat curry lunches with the late Barry Chevannes. In Guyana, Kadasi Ceres, then-chair of the Government Department, motivated me in a difficult research environment. Scholars at the University of Guyana (UG), such as Michael Scott, O'Neil Greaves, C.Y. Thomas, and Freddie Kissoon, were generous with their time. I also thank Niebert Paul for her friendship while I was a visiting researcher in the International Development Studies program. Malcolm Williams, UG's librarian, was most helpful in tracking down obscure sources. Many kudos go to the staff at the Statistics Bureau in Guyana and the Cartography Department. I thank all the activists in Guyana, many of whom I cannot name because it might put them at personal risk. In Haiti, Louis Herns Marcelin of the University of Miami and INURED and Suzy Castor of CRESFED coached me well.

None of this work would have been possible without money for my study. I thank US Fulbright and the US State Department for funding my Jamaica fieldwork (2008–9). Cornell's Gerry Levine and Brigit Shipman were kind to support my Fulbright application. Special thanks to then-adviser at IIE Cara Wollinsky; the UWI administration's Camille Bell-Hutchinson; the US Embassy in Jamaica's Bernadette Hutchinson; the late Angella Harvey; and my Fulbright colleagues, Lynn Washington, Chello Rogers, and Reena Goldthree. Much gratitude goes to the Inter-American Development Banks' staff people: Claudia Stevenson, Carina Cockburn, Jempsy Fils-Aimé, Sergio Navagas, and Mark Wenner. At the University of Toronto, Lisa Haley at the School of Graduate Studies awarded me travel funds to Haiti and Guyana in 2010. The Department of Political Science awarded me the Frank Peers Award (2009–11) as well as the 2010 Royal Bank Scholarship. Le Centre d'études de la France et du Monde Francophone (Toronto) supported fieldwork in post-earthquake Haiti. Many thanks to the Centre of International Studies, Munk Centre, for the Val Duncan Award to support my field work in Guyana. Funding support from York University's Social Science Humanities Research Council (SSHRC) small project grant and the Faculty of Liberal Arts and Professional Studies' minor research grant helped me carry out fieldwork in Grenada and Trinidad and Tobago in the summer of 2013.

Finding the right editor can be a trying process. I am grateful to Jennifer DiDomenico, my editor at the University of Toronto Press, who created the best place for me to share my stories. Nancy Wills did a superb job indexing my work. Leah Connor at the press was most helpful throughout the production process, and Matthew Kudelka carried out excellent copy edits. Three anonymous reviewers in feminist economics, area studies, and cooperative economics greatly improved this study. And my trusted copy editor over the years, Colette Stoeber, deserves much credit for making my work readable and its format consistent in sharing these important stories.

Nomenclature

Out of respect for the ordinary people I met, and in the tradition of Jamaican, Guyanese, Haitian, Grenadian, and Trinidadian scholars, I choose to use the local dialect as much as possible. In the Jamaican, Guyanese, Grenadian, and Trinidadian cases, I use the patois (or local Caribbean English dialect) for quoting interviewees. For my interviews, I wrote down the responses in patois. Only in a few instances do I translate Creole English to Standard English, as I assume that the language and words are so similar to Standard English that the reader will understand the meaning. Kreyol (Creole French), the national language of Haiti and the mother tongue of most Haitians, is derived from French. Where possible, I use Kreyol words and make translations, usually in English or French, if the meaning is not apparent.

Abbreviations

ACCESS	Access Financial Services
ACLAM	Action Contre la Misère
ACME	Association pour la Coopération avec la Microenterprise
AIC	alternative insurance company
AIR	Agency for Inner City Renewal
AFD	Agence française de développement
ANIMH	Association Nationale des Institutions de Microfinance d'Haïti
APB	Association des Professionnels de Banques
ASCAs	annual savings clubs and associations
BCA	Banque Crédit Agricole
BGB	British Guiana Bank
BPH	Banque Populaire Haïtienne
BRH	Banque République d'Haïti (central bank)
CAFRA	Caribbean Association for Feminist Research and Action
CAPRI	Caribbean Policy and Research Institute
Carib Cap	Caribbean Capacity Project
Carib-Cap I	Caribbean Capacity Project I
CCCUL	Churches Cooperative and Credit Union Limited
CDB	Caribbean Development Bank
CDC	Community Development Council (Guyana)
CDFs	Community Development Funds (MIDA, Jamaica)
CDFs	Constituency Development Funds (in Jamaica and Guyana)

CGAP	Consultative Group to Assist the Poor
CIDA	Canadian International Development Agency
CMN	Caribbean Microfinance Network
CNC	Conseil National des Coopératives
COPE	Credit Organization for Pre-Micro Enterprises
COKCU	City of Kingston Credit Union
CRESFED	Centre de Recherche et de Formation Éonomique et Sociale pour le Développement
DAI	Development Alternatives Inc.
DBJ	Development Bank of Jamaica
DDL	Demerara Distillery Limited
DFLSA	Development Financing Limited South America
DID	Développement international Desjardins
DOL	Development Options Limited
ESSJ	Economic Social Survey of Jamaica
FDI	Fonds de Développement Industriel
FHAF	Fonds Haïtien d'Aide à la Femme
FINCA	Foundation for International Community Assistance
FL	Fanmi Lavalas (Aristide)
Fonkoze	Fondasyon Kole Zepol
GAIBANK	Guyana Cooperative Agricultural and Industrial Bank
GBTI	Guyana Bank for Trade and Industry
GRAIFSI	Groupe d'Appui pour l'Intégration de la Femme du Secteur Informel
GSBA	Guyana Small Business Association
GUYMIDA	Guyana Manufacturing and Industrial Agency
GYD	Guyana dollar
HCDC	Hope for Children Development Corporation
ICIs	informal commercial importers
ID	Initiative du Développement
IDB	Inter-American Development Bank
IFC	International Finance Corporation
IMF	International Monetary Fund
INURED	Interuniversity Institute for Research and Development
IPED	Institute for Private Enterprise Development
ISI	import substitution industrialization
JACCUL	Jamaica Association of Cooperative and Credit Union League

JAMFA	Jamaica Microfinancing Association
JaMicro	Microcredit Limited
JCC	Jamaican Chamber of Commerce
JLP	Jamaica Labour Party
JNBS	Jamaica National Building Society
JNSBLL	Jamaica National Small Business Loans Limited
JPS	Jamaica Public Service
JBDC	Jamaican Business Development Agency
JMD	Jamaican dollar
JSIF	Jamaica Social Investment Fund
JSLC	Jamaica Survey of Living Conditions
KNFP	Konsey Nasyonal Finansman Popilè (rural and/or productive network)
LAC	Latin America and the Caribbean
MARNDR	Ministère de l'agriculture des ressources naturelles et du développement rural
MCL	Micro Credit Limited
MCN	Micro Crédit National
MED	Microenterprise Development
MEF	Ministère d'Economie et de la Finance
MEFL	Micro Enterprise Financing Limited
MFIs	microfinance institutions
MIDA	Micro-Investment Development Agency
MIF	Multilateral Investment Fund (of the IDB)
MINUSTAH	Mission des Nation Unies pour la Stabilisation en Haïti (UN military)
MPC	Ministère du Planification et de la Coordination
Nation Growth	Nation Growth Microfinance Bank
NCB	National Commercial Bank
NDC	neighbourhood democratic council
NDFJ	National Development Foundation of Jamaica
NDM	New Democratic Movement
NEDCO	National Entreprise Development Company
NGO	non-governmental organization
NJM	New Jewel Movement
OPL	Organisation du Peuple en Lutte (Préval)
OPL	Organisation Politiques Lavalas (Aristide)
PADF	Pan-American Development Foundation
PIOJ	Planning Institute of Jamaica
PNC	People's National Congress

PNM	People's National Movement (Trinidad and Tobago)
PNP	People's National Party (Jamaica)
PP	People's Partnership
PPP	People's Progressive Party (Guyana)
PSOJ	Private Sector Organization of Jamaica
QiFD	Quisqueya for International Development
RBTT	Republic Bank of Trinidad and Tobago
ROSCAs	rotating savings and credit associations
SALISES	Sir Arthur Lewis Institute of Social and Economic Studies
SAP	structural adjustment program
SBCI	Small Bank Credit Initiative
SBAJ	Small Business Association of Jamaica
SBDT	Small Business Development Trust
SDC	Social Development Commission
SEBA	Small Enterprise Business Association (Trinidad)
SOFIHDES	Société Financière Haïtienne de Développement
Sogesol	Société Générale de Dolidarité
Sogebank	Société Générale Haïtienne de Banque
SPM	social performance management
SSF	Self-Start Fund (Jamaica)
STATIN	Statistical Institute of Jamaica
UG	University of Guyana
UN	United Nations
UNC	United National Coalition
UNCDF	UN Capital Development Fund
UNDP	United Nations Development Program
UQAM	Université de Québec à Montréal
USAID	US Agency for International Development
UWI	University of the West Indies
UWI/Mona	University of the West Indies at Mona
WOCCU	World Organization of Cooperatives and Credit Unions
WPA	Working People's Alliance

POLITICIZED MICROFINANCE

Money, Power, and Violence in the Black Americas

Chapter 1

Microfinance and Black People

The $70 billion microfinance industry, which claims to create "access to finance" and make banking inclusive, is a highly sought-after intervention in developing and developed countries.[1] When, at the first meeting of the Microcredit Summit Campaign in 1997, it was declared that microfinance would reach 100 million poor families (Midgley 2008, 474; Elahi and Danopoulos 2004, 644), the UN immediately endorsed it as a tool to help meet the Millennium Development Goal of halving poverty in poor countries by 2015.[2] Since that time, the world has been taken up with the microfinance movement. The UN marked 2005 as the International Year of Microcredit for its role in the "First Decade for the Eradication of Poverty from 1997–2006" (Khan 2009; Dichter and Harper 2007; UN 2003).[3]

At the above-mentioned 1997 meeting of the Microcredit Summit Campaign, Bangladeshi economist Muhammad Yunus – the industry's famous champion, 2006 Nobel Laureate, and founder of the Grameen Bank – stated his belief that social exclusion can be overcome through inclusive banking:

> We believe that poverty does not belong to a civilized human society. It belongs to museums. This [microcredit] summit is about creating a process, which will send poverty to the museum. Only sixty-five years after the 12-second flight of the Wright brothers, man went to the moon. Fifty-five years after this summit, we'll also go to our moon. We'll create a poverty-free world. (cited in Elahi and Danopoulos 2004)[4]

That Yunus was awarded the 2006 Nobel Prize for Peace confirmed that low-income women of colour are committed business people (i.e., they repay their bank loans) and that microbanking can contribute to business inclusion and peaceful societies (Yunus 2007a, 155; 2007b; Gatehouse 2006). This profound idea of solidarity banking emanated from Yunus, who had grown up in the global South and who had seen poverty and social exclusion first-hand. In carrying out a study about the Black diaspora and their experience in microbanking, I have found it useful to reflect on the fact that Yunus's lived experience gave him the drive to revive microbanking for excluded peoples.

Indeed, I found the idea of microbanking – providing access to loans for the economically active poor – to be so inspirational that it spurred me to work in business and financial development for a decade. The attraction was very much rooted in my own lineage – my family included low-income business people whose livelihoods depended on access to capital. The revival of microfinance and the fact that it was piloted by people of the global South also inspired me as a woman of colour. Microbanking is important for people of the South. Socially conscious activists from the South, like Yunus, were tired of banks' exclusivity. Early microfinance was a "reinvention," focusing on solidarity circles and collective group banking to uplift marginalized people. In fact, the 1970s reinvention of microfinance drew on powerful ancient money pool systems, also known as rotating savings and credit associations (ROSCAs). Microbanking was a way to reorganize money and thereby challenge conventional banking systems. Black people around the world are familiar with these collective self-help and localized money systems. For persons of African descent, especially those who live in the diaspora or where enslavement and colonization are part of the historical experience, microfinance is lacking. For the African diaspora, especially for low-income Black people, banking can be harrowing. This book attempts to locate the Black diaspora experience in the microfinance industry.

Situating Black Lives in the Global Microfinance Movement

According to the website of the International Year for People of African Descent (UN 2011), about 200 million people of African descent live in the Americas. Knowing that there are millions of Black people in the diaspora, I find it most unsettling that the critics who claim that microfinance does not help people fail to mention that African people and the African diaspora have been deliberately excluded from making decisions and writing on the topic (Bateman and Chang 2012; Karim 2011; Bateman 2011; Roy 2010; Midgley 2008). It is important to take issue with the broader business environment that is forcing many microfinance institutions (MFIs) to commercialize; but in addition to that, there seems to be an effort to downplay or ignore the contributions of the African diaspora to the field. As feminist J.K. Gibson-Graham (2006, 169) makes abundantly clear, diverse microlevel experiments are being conducted and it is important not to depreciate them. The same can be said for the Black diaspora, which engages in microbanking in ways that need to be appreciated. Having worked for the better part of a decade in international development, I do not believe that the lack of research material or investments in the African diaspora is accidental. This book fills the gap and recognizes the engagement of Black people in microbanking. In this UN International Decade for People of African Descent (2015–2024), it seems highly fitting to examine one of the world's most heralded interventions, microfinance, and its impact on some of the world's most excluded people, the African diaspora.

People who have devised alternative forms of banking – including Africans and the African diaspora – have had to do so because of their political and economic contexts. Developing alternative banking techniques can be called a political act, in that these groups come together to challenge conventional and inividualized forms of banking. In *Take Back the Economy: An Ethical Guide for Transforming our Communities* (2013), J.K. Gibson-Graham, Jenny Cameron, and Stephen Healy contend that community economies point to the existence of diverse economies and rethink people's engagement with markets. Wanda Wuttunee in *Living Rhythms: Lessons in Aboriginal Economic Resilience and Vision* (2004) recognizes the diverse ways in which Canada's Aboriginal people organize their livelihoods under extreme forms of white settler colonization.

The microbanking story is about diverse economies and how people come together to pool financial resources. In the 1970s, many bankers-to-the-poor in the global South were not formally trained as commercial bankers and had come to the financial arena with a different set of values. These non-bankers were trying to create a more humane economy, and in doing so they took issue with the elitist approach to appraising marginalized groups for bank loans. Microfinance was novel in that it emphasized a different system – a peer-based one founded on people's willingness to repay – to ensure more inclusionary financing and social relationships. Thus came the term "social financing." But this idea of collective and group economics was not entirely new: it has a long history among African peoples (Gordon Nembhard 2014; Mintz 2010; Du Bois 1907; 2007[1903]).

Having attended a number of annual microfinance conferences over the years, I have observed that even though they are international events, no persons of Black descent take the main stage. At the 2002 Microcredit Summit +5 in New York City, former US First Lady Hillary Rodham Clinton and then-Mexican president Vicente Fox were honoured speakers, and most of the main panels I attended were given by Western NGOs and banks. The microfinance phenomenon that was reborn in the South has become a "white" affair, with a discourse dominated by people of privileged backgrounds. Expensive microfinance programs – I am an alumnus of one of them – provide a demeaning educational process, during which racialized people with extensive field and lived experience are often schooled by the white "experts," many of them quite inexperienced in microfinance. At the prestigious microfinance schools and the lavish annual conferences, the microfinance industry is divided in its vision for the future. As of 2016, the arena is split between those who see microfinance as social finance and those who see it as a commercial venture.

We find supporters for microfinance on both the right and the left of the political spectrum because of the very possibility that microfinance can create access to finance for excluded people. To quote economist Jonathan Morduch, "advocates who lean left highlight the bottom-up aspects, attention to community, focus on women and, most importantly, the aim to help the underserved. Those who lean right highlight the prospect of alleviating poverty while providing incentives to work, the nongovernmental leadership, the use of mechanisms disciplined by market forces on-going subsidization" (1999, 1570). Supporters like Klobuchar and Cornell Wilkes write that "if a social evangelist had a choice of picking one tool, one movement with the goal of emancipating the poorest women on earth, the microcredit phenomenon wins without serious competition" (2003, 26).

According to its advocates, microcredit can do no wrong. Champions of commercialized microfinance, such as Rhyne and Otero (2006) and Drake and Rhyne (2002), argue that along with its scale, microcredit's potential to make financial services inclusive is what has earned it its many supporters (McLeod Arnopoulos 2010; Rhyne and Otero 2006; Woller and Woodworth 2001; Morduch 1999; Smith and Thurman 2007). But the commercialization of microlending has raised questions within the industry regarding whether its players are experiencing "mission drift" owing to the move toward profit-making approaches over poverty-lending approaches (Karim 2008; Christen 2001).

As microfinance strives to commercialize, the universal endorsement of it as a tool for creating "access to finance" requires further scrutiny. The truth is that while access to finance is beneficial for marginalized groups, many people are still being excluded – sometimes by the very same bankers who aim to serve them. Malcolm Harper (1998) was one of the first critics to see the shift in microbanking from a development model focused on poverty alleviation to a commercial model he calls the "new wave" of microfinance. This trend has pushed microcredit toward the goal of profitability. Other early critics of microfinance (Dichter and Harper 2007; Rankin 2001; Mosley and Hulme 1998; Johnson and Rogaly 1997; Rogaly 1996; Dichter 1996) claim that its advocates (such as Brody, Greenley, and Wright-Revolledo 2005; Klobuchar and Cornell Wilkes 2003; Robinson 2001) are blindly committed to "money with a mission," that is, a cure for poverty notwithstanding the pressure faced by these institutions to turn a profit.

The trend toward commercial microfinance organizations such as Grameen Bank was launched by aid agencies in the 1990s. This resulted in an entire sector committing itself to raising interest above market rates, in most cases to ensure that bankers to the poor made a profit and achieved full recovery rates (*Credit Where Credit Is Due* 2000; Rahman 1999; Wahid 1994). This commercialization of microfinance is strongest in the Spanish-speaking Americas and South Asia. MFIs that adhere to profit-driven goals – such as Bolivia's Banco Sol, Peru's Mibanco, Mexico's Banco Compartamos, and India's SKS Microfinance Bank – all have received significant investment capital despite controversies over their excessive profits and questionable collection practices (Bateman and Chang 2012; Sengupta and Aubuchon 2008; Malkin 2008; Navagas et al. 2000; Morduch 1999, 2000).

Ananya Roy in *Poverty Capital* (2010) reviewed the World Bank Group and the US Agency for International Development (USAID), the largest donor agency in micro-enterprise development since 1978. Kamat (2002), in her work on NGOs in India, found that the American development model was built on laissez-faire economics. American aid has contributed to uneven support for enterprise development around the world. Spanish America has benefited from capital for microfinance development to assist poor entrepreneurs; the Caribbean region has not fared as well. The Consultative Group to Assist the Poor (CGAP) – a World Bank agency – conducts extensive research, training, and technical assistance, besides investing in innovation in the microfinance sector. But CGAP has focused mainly on Latin America and South

Asia, and more recently on the Middle East and China. As of 2015 the Microcredit Summit Campaign – a leading advocate for microfinance, headed by an American, Larry Reed – had a staff of ten, none of whom were of African descent. One of the few events on microfinance to take place in the Caribbean was the 2009 Fifth Summit of the Americas in Trinidad and Tobago, which was themed "Securing Our Citizens" and at which US president Barack Obama launched a $100 million Microfinance Growth Fund for Caribbean countries.[5] This pledge reiterated the US commitment to invest in countries that were vulnerable to transnational crime. It seems, then, that the major donors and events do not seem to prioritize the African diaspora's engagement in microfinance development.

The billions of dollars invested in microfinance seldom reach excluded entrepreneurs, and funds are definitely not reaching the African diaspora. Yet no one mentions this glaring reality, not even critics of microfinance. Rich white Americans have, through their family foundations, invested mainly in commercialized microfinance banks (Bruck 2006).[6] At the start of the 2000s, 89 per cent of the capital came from bilateral and multilateral agencies; since then, it has been private investors like the ones just mentioned who are funding commercialized MFIs (CGAP Focus Note No. 25, in Chowdri and Silva 2004). As of 2015, Kiva, the world's first online microlending platform, had not a single person of African descent on its executive team, and neither the Caribbean nor Brazil (a very large country with an African diaspora) is listed as one of the regions it serves. Haiti is featured, albeit with minor representation. This indicates that the flow of money from middle-class individuals, many of whom are white Americans, goes to entrepreneurs almost everywhere in the world *except* the countries of the African diaspora.

Private investments from Blue Orchard, MicroVest Capital Funds, and Sarona, and from corporate foundations such as the MasterCard Foundation in Toronto, direct millions of dollars to commercial microfinance, yet banks for the African diaspora are largely missing from these endeavours. Again, many of the individuals who control these funds are white and privileged. Cultural diversity can be seen in the Inter-American Development Bank (IDB), the Caribbean Development Bank (CDB), and the International Finance Corporation (IFC), but these institutions have made significant microcredit investments in Spanish-speaking Latin America, not as much in the Caribbean. In 2012, the IDB relaunched the Caribbean Capacity project (also referred to as Carib Cap) to increase the technical capacity of microfinance retailers in the

Caribbean region.[7] But a persistent focus on technical capacity does not adequately address why access to finance is not reaching the very people for which it is intended.

As unfair as it seems, monies are not being directed to the African diaspora, a historically oppressed group of people. It seems that the largely white investors and bankers do not tap into public subsidies, instead using their own funds as they see fit, rightly or wrongly. However, a moral dilemma arises when banks, financial organizations, and MFIs access subsidies and concessional loans, and claim to be supporting inclusive finance when they are clearly ignoring the people of an entire region. I say this because, as revealed above, the people of the African diaspora in Brazil, Haiti, and the Caribbean have not had the kind of investment that other regions have enjoyed. Indeed, few investments earmarked for the leading commercial microfinance banks go to African people, either on the continent or within the diaspora. With this book, then, I am pushing to the foreground this story of microfinance's exclusion of the African diaspora. Only fairly recently has the industry paid attention to Africa as a place worthy of investments in microbanking. I know this because I worked for an African American organization in the early 2000s that focused on acquiring funds to support business development in Africa – and this was a difficult and frustrating process.

Microbanking and Inclusive Finance

Microfinance is one of the world's most celebrated institutions, with around $70 billion in investments and at least 205 million people accessing loans through approximately 10,000 MFIs (Reed 2012; Roodman 2012b; Roy 2010; Wahid 1994). For the past 40 years, microlending has been heralded as a poverty-fighting tool in many developing countries – a tool through which significant community improvement can be realized (Bennett 2009; Khan 2009; Yunus 2007a; Gulli and Berger 1999; Smith and Thurman 2007; Robinson 2001). Yet microfinance's project of inclusive financing has faltered, and it does not appear to be as inclusive as it purports itself to be. In 2011 a *Microfinance Banana Skins* report funded by Citigroup examined the global microfinance sector and concluded that microfinance is "losing its fairy dust" – that is, tarnishing its reputation because actors within the industry are abusing their power over the poor (see also CSFI 2008). Microfinance advocates like Rhyne and Otero (2006) have focused their attention on politicians as external actors who infuse microfinance with their own political agendas; but lenders have yet to see that the greatest risk to microfinance comes from *within* the sector. By 2012, the attitudes of industry experts and public sentiment towards microlenders had shifted, as it became increasingly clear that these people were in a position to take advantage of poor clients. The climate is ripe for discussing political bias within MFIs – bias that works against the bedrock principles of inclusive banking.

For all the excitement over the microfinance sector, few scholars have examined the power and privilege held by the educated managers and staffs who control these loans, even though that control does much to determine whether a microcredit program is inclusive or not (Hossein 2015, 2014b; Karim 2011; Rankin 2002). It is the managers and staffs who enable these programs to flourish, or fail (Hossein 2015; Matin et al. 2002). Yunus (1998, 53) argues that credit plays a vital social role and that it has the potential to create social power, yet most advocates do not recognize that the personal politics and attitudes of managers and their staffs can affect – for good or ill – the allocation of credit. Given that managers and staffs are directly and indirectly influencing the lives of ever greater numbers of poor people, a thorough understanding of the politics of microfinance has become salient.

The truth is that political elites shape policies, and they can either encourage or stunt economic development (Collier 2007). After Haiti's 2010 earthquake and fire in the Croix des Bossales market, some of the *ti machanns* (market vendors) refused to make loan repayments. Then-president Rene Préval, with little communication to the MFIs and under political pressure, wrote off these loans, telling the *ti machanns* not to repay them. Haitian microfinance leaders, dismayed by this perceived political interference, lobbied for the state to cover these losses (interviews, August to October 2011). The MFI leaders noted that if the political elites interfered once, they could do so again. In the end, the president reimbursed the MFIs for their losses (interview with senior microfinance manager, 14 October 2010; interview with microfinance network executive director, 6 October 2010; interview with a credit union director, 7 October 2010). Clearly, the autonomy of microfinance leaders who stand up to political and business elites is important to ordinary people who need access to credit.

By 2010, consumer protection policies in the interests of poor clients vulnerable to the unscrupulous tactics of certain lenders had emerged in microbanking (CGAP 2010; CSFI 2008). The coalition "Convergence 2015" lobbies for micro and small entrepreneurs to be protected from the manipulations of elites. Kah, Olds, and Kah (2005) first raised the issue, with regard to political interference in village banks in Senegal, where politicized bankers were giving microcredit based on members' political affiliations. Notwithstanding these and similar findings, political and personal bias among bankers in microfinance has not been a major topic of conversation. The literature does not address politics specifically, but tends to discuss it in a general way (CSFI 2011). Note also that the microfinance industry does not scrutinize the people working in the sector. The 2013 *Microfinance Handbook* (Ledgerwood 2013) declares that microfinance is inclusive, yet it makes absolutely no mention of the personal biases affecting microloan decision-making. One exception can be seen in the acknowledgment in 2015 by the Center for Financial Inclusion, a group in Washington, DC, affiliated with ACCION (an organization that supports commercialized microbanking), that racial bias exists within MFIs (Goldstein 2015).

The literature on microfinance usually views politics as a problem *external* to the microfinance industry. It assumes that political interference occurs when government or political leaders manipulate policies and programs for their own political objectives (CSFI 2008, 2011). In contrast to this, I will be arguing that politicized microfinance profoundly affects the microbanking that Black people encounter in the Americas. I base this finding on interviews with 583 Black people (2008–13), many of whom are micro- and small-business people. That is why it is important to examine the people who manage these financial programs for the urban poor. Political manipulation can take place *within* the sector and often involves the class-based elite biases of the managers who run the MFIs. Lenders' willingness to agitate for the best interests of marginalized clients is a function of politics. Politics can inject itself into microfinance because the local managers and staffs running these programs are often different from their clients in terms of class, race, and gender. It takes a socially conscious mindset, and one that is politically aware and rooted in a lived experience of activism, to contest mainstream commercialized financing for the poor.

The Two Forms of "Politicized Microfinance"

Despite this being an era of market fundamentalism and the commercialization of global finance, there are still many alternative actors that approach banking from a social mission perspective. For example, there are not-for-profits, grassroots community groups, informal banks, and cooperative banks. These alternative lenders do not follow a shareholder model but present a different way of doing business. Jessica Gordon Nembhard (2014) has unearthed centuries of alternative economic practices among African Americans in the United States, and her findings also reveal how other Black people in the Americas – that is, African Caribbean people – have contributed to alternative economics. The social economy of Black people is largely unknown. Black people's struggles in business have led them to devise new ways of doing business. Microbankers, especially those interested in solidarity banking, play a large part in the social economy because they have made it their goal to create inclusive finance. Quarter, Mook, and Armstrong (2009) have suggested that organizations that prioritize profits over social mission are no longer part of the social economy; but this thinking has not yet found its way into development programming – clearly, many managers run commercialized microfinance projects without thinking about the social exclusion perpetuated through this form of banking. The five case studies in this book, by revealing the economic activities of Black people in the social economy, provide a new way of looking at activist work within the social economy and what this means for racialized people in the Americas. In this way, the book shows that certain politicized forms of microbanking can either harm or improve the lives of historically excluded people.

In *Politicized Microfinance,* I argue that commercialized bankers whose personal prejudices are cloaked in neoliberal ideas have fostered a social exclusion that has negatively affected the allocation of microloans. I contend that microfinance as an economic resource can take more than one form; in doing so, I reject the assumption that because microbanking is lumped within the social economy or the third sector, its only intentions are pure and good. I borrow the concept of "smashing up the neoliberal variant of capitalism" from J.K. Gibson-Graham (1996), who sees a need to create space for economic alternatives. The same can be said for the concept of being "politicized": I smash up this term so that it can mean two different things depending on Black people's experiences in microfinance. In my definition, "politicized microfinance" comes in two forms: one that is clientelistic and oppressive (see the Jamaica, Trinidad, and Guyana cases), and another that is activist in orientation and has a social conscience – that is, it is consciously aware (often through lived experience) of the oppressions endured by people of African descent (see the Haiti and Grenada cases). In the negative cases, the concept of "politicized microfinance" refers to the clientelistic politicking and partisanship of the "Big Men," who further oppress the entrepreneurial poor. In the positive cases, politicized microfinance can refer to managers who agitate for social change by making financial resources available to excluded groups. Here, politicized microfinance requires the people in charge of this resource to be politically conscious, activist, and conscientious about the work they do – to the point of taking deadly risks.

To fully understand and engage with the social economy and the Black experience, I take an intersectional approach that will allow us to comprehend the lived reality of oppressed people. By combining feminism as a theory with intersectionality as an interpretative framework, I can examine people's identities, class, race, and gender. I approach politics not only as something external to microfinance, but also as something that is *deeply embedded* in these programs through hierarchies of politics, gender, race, and class. These hierarchies give lenders power over poor individuals, but that same power can also be used to confront biased systems. In this book, I argue from a diasporic Black and feminist standpoint that the latter form of politicized microfinance needs to be activated if microfinance is to truly occupy itself with overturning the social exclusion that has embedded itself so deeply in business and society.

The Polarizing Microfinance Literature

The microfinance literature is full of hubris, with experts on both sides expressing strong feelings about microfinance. This has led to polarization and often detachment from the experience of Black people. In one camp, we find die-hard supporters who cheer on microfinance (Yunus 2007a, 2007b; Drake and Rhyne 2002);[8] in the opposing camp we find the sceptics (Sinclair 2012; Bateman 2011; Maclean 2010; Rankin 2002; Hulme 2000), who flat-out deny that the industry can help the entrepreneurial poor. Critics offer empirical evidence that in certain contexts, microfinance has had a questionable impact on women's empowerment and on poverty reduction (Karim 2011; Ahmed 2008; Rankin 2002; Rahman 1999; Goetz and Sengupta 1996). For example, Roodman in *Due Diligence* (2012a) questions the positive perceptions of microloans with regard to the poor, finding little empirical evidence that microfinance has had a positive impact on entrepreneurs. Rahman (1999) and Goetz and Sengupta (1996) suggest that the concept of empowerment, when incorporated into economic programs such as microfinance, is often used to appease the poor without making positive transformational change in their lives or in society. Sinclair (2012), Bateman and Chang (2012), Karim (2011), Vonderlack-Navarro (2010), Rankin (2002), and Rogaly (1996) all argue convincingly that commercialized microlenders are focused on profits and repayments and that they are failing to create collective action that brings social change. Katherine Rankin's (2001) early work in the Kathmandu Valley in Nepal was a pioneering study that linked the new economic order to microfinance as a means of creating "rational economic women"; she found that the structural violence embedded in microfinance programs binds poor women to their oppressors. Thomas Dichter and Malcolm Harper's *What's Wrong with Microfinance* (2007) was one of the first books to comprehensively question microfinance's impact on the poor. More recently, Milford Bateman's polemical works, including *Why Doesn't Microfinance Work* (2010) and *Confronting Microfinance* (2011), have critiqued commercialized microfinance.

The present book is rooted in empirical data and draws selectively on literature that considers the intersectional bias of the people engaging in the microfinance debates. Local elites can misuse economic resources (Chua 2003) and thereby exert their power over the powerless, with the consequence that these microcredit programs are run in an exclusionary way. Despite this reality, the works that question the impact of microfinance – such as Roodman's *Due Diligence* (2012a) and Bateman's *Confronting Microfinance* (2011) – do not mention personal bias and discriminatory microlending practices cloaked in the guise of neoliberalism by local staffs. Roy's *Poverty Capital* (2010) comes closest to thinking about identities when she questions the way privileged elites in microfinance are preoccupied with their own personal biases. Karim's *Microfinance and Its Discontents* (2011) criticizes the gendered dynamics when educated male microfinance managers dominate poor women clients. But the microfinance industry as a whole has failed to examine the people in positions of power who allocate financial resources to the needy. The unfair allocation of resources through arbitrary politics can have a profound impact on social peace and stability. Microfinance in the form of patronage granted to certain people exacerbates tensions and creates divisions, as people often receive these handouts as politically driven preferential treatment that is (Eisenstadt and Roniger 1984; Stone 1980; Scott 1972). This misuse of power perpetuates poverty and can create anger among the poor masses.

What makes *Politicized Microfinance* timely and relevant is that it takes a critical perspective, using Black women's viewpoints – considering that most of the clients accessing microfinance are women of colour – to examine the cultural politics of microfinance. To this point, no critical work has looked at the lenders themselves, examining how historically rooted prejudices surface to exacerbate local tensions. Microfinance has tended to focus on the character of clients; few empirical studies have scrutinized the people who run these microfinance programs. Microfinance, which was born out of the need to respond to the exclusion of certain groups, can in fact operate in an exclusive manner, picking and choosing among the urban poor with regard to who gets credit. Benson Honig (2000, 106) found in his research that exclusive microbanking was taking place in the Jamaican microcredit sector: "There is too little attention placed on the character of the implementing actors – the employees of these retailers." These employees make judgments about the very poor without considering whether their own norms conflict with those of the people they are supposed to serve. The power of microfinance organizations is seldom questioned. This book thus addresses the need to carry out further research on the role of the employees who are implementing microfinance programs. In light of the growing criticism of microfinance programs, strong-arm tactics in India, and excessive profits in Mexico, we must examine the actors (managers and staffs) who control these economic resources, which are meant to be available to the entrepreneurial poor.

Politicized Microfinance is the first book of its kind to advance the idea that personal politics and a commitment by staff people to do business differently can contribute to a new kind of microfinance. It is also the first study of Black people's experience with microfinance, and the first to distinguish between a form of politics that perpetuates domination and a politics that advances emancipation. Haitians and Grenadians have shown that member-owned institutions can offer an alternative approach to microfinance. These alternative models in the social economy, which are based on collectivity, can organize livelihoods differently (Gordon Nembhard 2014; Bridge, Murtagh, and O'Neil 2009; Quarter, Mook and Armstrong 2009; Rutherford 2000). There has been solid research on the intersections between women and microcredit (Vonderlack-Navarro 2010; Maclean 2010; Armendáriz and Morduch 2007; Rankin 2001, 2002; Kabeer 2001; Mayoux 1999); there has been much less research on microfinance as it relates to race, class, and gender, or on the complexities of partisan and identity politics that may interfere with the allocation of microfinance resources (Hossein 2013b, 2014a). *Politicized Microfinance* is the first scholarly research to present a nuanced picture of the reality of microfinance by looking at the role of managers and staffs in MFIs and their own entanglement in partisan and identity politics in the context of the rigid racialized, gendered, and classed social structure of the African diaspora.

Intersectionality and Black Liberation and Feminist Theory in Microfinance

Once upon a time, criticizing microfinance was risky, precisely because of its stated mission to help the poor (Dichter and Harper 2007). This time has long passed. A kind of hubris exists among its critics – who are often left-oriented and ideological – that speaks more about their own personal politics and less about the people who count on loans to do business. At the same time, evangelical believers in microfinance seem naive in their unshakeable view that microfinance can fix anything. So, given that the current microfinance literature is too ideological and somewhat elitist in its take on microbanking, I opt to theorize my work using Black and feminist literature.

Such a perspective on this issue is virtually non-existent. But in a world where millions of people of African descent engage in microbanking, it is vital to think about the various ways the African diaspora uses microloans. The fact that the UN has declared 2015–2024 the International Decade for People of African Descent makes it doubly important to examine microfinance and its effect on Black people. In this regard, not all places where the people of African diaspora live offer similar experiences. In fact, in culturally diverse environments like the Caribbean region, one cannot assume that identity politics – such as race, class, and gender – even figures into how resources are managed and distributed; nor can one assume that it affects outcomes in similar ways. Feminist literature has done a noble job examining the arenas of conflict and violence for women in microfinance. Gender has been a more palatable topic for discussions about development, and one can locate, with relative ease, solid research on the social, political, and economic intersections between women and credit (Vonderlack-Navarro 2010; Maclean 2010; Rankin 2001, 2002; Mayoux 1999).

Politicized Microfinance brings a more nuanced lens to microfinance research, one that shows that identities operate differently from place to place. Thus, one case may emphasize class and another race, forcing intersectional theorizing to look for answers in local contexts. According to the feminist economists Julie Graham and Katherine Gibson, under the pen-name J.K. Gibson-Graham (1996, 2006), community economies have been taking root in spite of market fundamentalism; it follows that understanding the various ways people live collectively is vital to unravelling the dominant view that there is only one way to organize business and society. In Gibson-Graham's feminist tradition of unravelling the politics of economic possibility, I use intersectionality to consider class-, gender-, and race-based implications as they relate to microfinance by focusing on the managers who make loans and on those who receive them. The allocation of financial goods is a highly political act, and Black people are often on the receiving end of accessing those goods. This is why learning more about those who make lending decisions is important to the study of microcredit. To the best of my knowledge, this book presents the first time this approach has been adopted in the study of microfinance – this, despite the fact that bankers-to-the-poor have significant power over people of colour, and especially women (Hossein 2012, 2013b).

In the Americas, microbusiness ideas have been theorized by Black liberation thinkers; yet those thinkers have often been sidelined within the microfinance and social economy literature. As early as 1903, African American W.E.B. Du Bois, who was of Haitian heritage, was advancing a theory of group economics among African Americans that involved pooling economic activities in order to withstand oppressive power. Group economics would allow Black people to create solidarity businesses and bond together in times of hostility (1907, 2007[1903]). Du Bois's powerful book *The Souls of Black Folk* (2007[1903]) describes communal and collective forms of African business, and this historical grounding is an inspiration for Black people who live outside the African continent. Jamaican-born Marcus Mosiah Garvey, a Pan-Africanist and well-travelled entrepreneur, propounded a philosophy of racial self-reliance in business as a means to counteract mainstream business practices that in many places were connected to the marginalized African diaspora (Ewing 2014; K'adamwe, Bernard, and Dixon 2011; Bandele 2008, 2010; Martin 1983). Note that Garvey was probably influenced early on by community-driven partner banks (collective banks) in St Ann's, Jamaica, where such banks were a mainstay activity in colonial times.

The past theorizing on alternative business systems by persons of African descent is crucial to understanding the present study. In the United States, Booker T. Washington in his seminal work *Up from Slavery* (first printed in 1901) gave meaning to Black business ideas and set out how marginalized people in the Americas could be part of the economic system. As one of America's most important leaders, Washington attracted criticism for his accommodating views on business and industrial trades for Black people. Washington used his power to establish the National Negro Business League as a means to boost Black entrepreneurship during a time in American history when Black people were being lynched. Jessica Gordon Nembhard, one of the few women economists writing on the Black experience in the social economy and cooperatives, has documented in *Collective Courage* (2014) the frightening experiences Black people in United States have had in their efforts to create "intentional communities" as a means to form their own economic livelihoods. In this decade for persons of African descent, it is high time for us to reflect on ideas that speak to the experience of Black people in the Americas; to this end, I turn to Black and feminist theories to provide an understanding of the intersectional oppressions that arise within microfinance.

Many of the ideas developed by Black thinkers and feminists have influenced my own thinking on microfinance development and the social economy. J.K. Gibson-Graham's *A Postcapitalist Politics* (2006) makes it clear that there is a politics of economic possibility in which we find collective and community-based economies. This kind of alternative economic thinking seems to be rooted in actual economic projects through which common people seek to civilize the world's economy. While Caribbean feminists and scholars have not been engaged in the microfinance debates per se, they offer important ideas on enterprise development and culture that are having a direct impact on how microfinance unfolds in the region. Caribbean thinkers also have plenty to say about intersectionality, supplementing my understanding of the local microfinance environment. Caribbean scholar Rosalyn Terborg-Penn (1995) stresses how important it is to use an African lens when examining issues affecting Caribbean societies because of the deep-seated racism directed against Black people. Terborg-Penn's approach opened my eyes to the fact that most microfinance managers and staffs are socially removed from entrepreneurs who are seeking microloans. Haitian American anthropologist Gina Ulysse's *Downtown Ladies* (2007), probably the best text about small business women in the region, also uses an intersectional methodology. In my study, I found that Caribbean female entrepreneurs (208 of the total number, or 71% of the women in this sample) recognized the ingrained biases against them. Some viewed gender as a secondary identity and felt that class or race was more significant in terms of their access to microloans. Feminists, especially those of colour, know that race and class play a role in the allocation of goods and can structure a woman's place in her community (Benería 2003). African Canadian geographer Beverley Mullings (2005), in her pioneering study of Jamaican female bankers, found that internal class divides between middle-class brown and low-income Black (dark-skinned) women make it problematic to assume a united sisterhood. This fact is recognized by Caribbean scholar Lizabeth Paravisini-Gebert (1997), who suggests that we need to understand how multiple identities function and how this plays out in terms of access to opportunities. These regional divisions among Black women with regard to skin "shade," class, and race are thus salient when analysing how microfinance is allocated within the African diaspora.

Understanding the Black community in the Americas and the subtle issues of exclusion is crucial to my research. This is why the present study applies intersectionality when examining the interaction of identities. As Black feminist and legal scholar Kimberlé Crenshaw (1991) argues, intersectionality offers an alternative theory to deconstruct the essentialist frameworks that negate Black people and to provide a road map for combatting underdevelopment. In my work, I link intersectionality with Black feminism of a particular brand: that of the diaspora. Diasporic Black feminist thought is diverse, but I focus on elements that specifically address work, the politics of empowerment, and lived experience. I thus use the framework of intersectionality and diasporic Black feminist thought to contextualize the experience of Black people, especially that of Black women in the Americas (Few 2007; Ulysse 2007; Wane et al. 2002; Hill Collins 2000; Terborg-Penn 1995).

It seems intuitive to link the idea of intersectionality with Black feminism; yet this has never been done when examining how microfinance is allocated along the lines of identities and how these identities interact in relation to opportunities. This is especially important in the Caribbean, where identities are heavily stratified by race, space, class, and gender (Terborg-Penn 1995) and where one identity can trump others. I draw upon specific Black feminist thinkers within the extensive field. One influential text is Patricia Hill Collins's *Black Feminist Thought* (2000), in which she argues that Black women need theorizing that comes from people who know and live their experience. Black women give more credence to individuals who understand the struggle than to those who only read about it. Lived experience is therefore crucial in analysing the impact of microbanking on Black lives. The women in my study are from poor economic backgrounds – like many of the women in my own family – and they have always had to work. Hill Collins (2000) argues that Black women have to find their own voices and have to be able to define their own experience; *Politicized Microfinance* attempts to do exactly this in the field of microbanking. Black women in the United States and elsewhere in the diaspora (e.g., in Canada and the Caribbean) draw on cultural affinity through the shared historical experience of the slavery our ancestors endured. Njoki Wane et al. in *Back to the Drawing Board* (2002) contend that African Canadians need to rewrite the stories of African people. As a student of Wane's teachings, I found her most profound argument to be that lived experience is important in storytelling; looking back to Africa helps explain why the diaspora engages in the kind of work it does. Wane's teachings prompted me to rethink the Black experience in microfinance. As a child of Caribbean parents, I watched my family and community practice business not through the eyes of a white Canadian, but through a different mindset – one in which the lines between family and business are often blurred. But these ways in which Black people engage in the social economy and microbanking are rarely if ever told.

In some ways, my theoretical work with Black and feminist ideas has also become a methodology (Wane et al. 2002). This is similar to Black scholar April Few's (2007) statement in her own work that Black feminism is not just a form of theorizing; it also takes the form of a method. In other words, our own lived experience becomes a technique for analysing the literature and data we collect. Black feminist theory and methods are political tools that confront head-on the bias ingrained in society. By using intersectionality and Black and feminist theory, I take on the role of a kind of "academic detective" who exposes truths that may be difficult for mainstream society and people who work in microfinance to accept. Black feminist writer Audrey Lorde (1984) says something similar when she suggests that Black women have always been the "watchers" as they mimic the attitudes and behaviours of the white dominant culture/oppressors while hiding their own views. I say "academic detective" because what I do is unearth the truth. I raise questions about social economy work that purports to be helping people, and I expose other experiences of affected people of colour in order that they themselves will see what is happening in the name of economic development. To study microfinance, social and economic exclusion, and access to finance as stand-alone issues without looking at the historical role of identities in the Caribbean region is a mistake, as it misses the reasons why certain groups of Black people are purposefully excluded from microfinance (Hossein 2013b).

Caribbean Microbanking Traditions

Among Black people in the Caribbean region, microlending is a long tradition, one that was brought to the Americas by enslaved Africans.[9] In each of the cases in this book – Jamaica, Haiti, Trinidad, Grenada, and Guyana – African slaves and their descendants carried out market activities and engaged in informal savings and lending clubs (Du Bois 2007[1903]; St Pierre 1999; N'Zengou-Tayo 1998; Harrison 1988; Wong 1996; Witter 1989; Mintz 1955). Haitian American anthropologist Gina Ulysse (2007, 83) found that Jamaican women vendors, called *higglers*, were undertaking entrepreneurship as far back as slave times.[10] Female slaves and women under colonization organized informal banks – known variously as *partners*, *box-hands*, and *susus* – to help excluded people meet their livelihood needs (Hossein 2014c; St Pierre 1999; Handa and Kirton 1999; Ardener and Burman 1996). The Penny Bank, a formalized state bank that opened in colonized Dominica in 1949, also made microfinance-type loans (Barriteau and Cobley 2006; Lashley 2006).

When Muhammad Yunus visited the region in 2008, he stayed at the prestigious Pegasus Hotel in uptown Kingston, Jamaica. This visit and venue underscored the importance of microbanking to the region's business elites (Collister 2008). Then in October 2011, Yunus visited Port-au-Prince, Haiti, where he met with clients of Grameen's Creative Lab along with high-ranking officials, business elites, and donors. Yunus's visits to these Caribbean countries and his meetings with whitened and moneyed political and business elites legitimized the work of these two groups, even though the benefits of their poverty alleviation programs were open to question. Despite the billions invested, the English-speaking Caribbean region has not been as successful in microfinance as other regions of the world (Chalmers and Wenner 2001). There is little consensus as to why Caribbean microlending (except in the Dominican Republic) has not fared as well as microlending elsewhere (Tennant 2008; Economist Intelligence Unit, October 2008, 10; MIX 2006, 2007; Westley 2005; Daley-Harris 2004, 2005, 2006; Lashley 2004a, 2004b; Chalmers and Wenner 2001).

Haiti stands out among Caribbean microfinance results: despite political instability and natural disasters, that country's microfinance sector has performed well.[11] Chalmers and Wenner (2001) suggest that a relatively high standard of living and a once highly educated labour force together work to create an aversion to self-employment. One daring explanation is that citizens in the Caribbean lack an entrepreneurial mindset: Bajan-based academic Lashley (2004a) argues that Caribbean people prefer salaried jobs and only turn to enterprise for survival (Lashley interview, 24 April 2009). Ratings expert Damien Von Stauffenberg (2000) argues that failure in Caribbean microbanking is less about culture than about operations: managers do not adhere to best-practice methods and systems. Glenn Westley (2005, 2) points to weak internal management, suggesting that managers, although well-educated, lack the skills, methods, and personal interest to attract borrowers from the shanty towns, which inevitably affects access to microfinance. Middle-class, university-educated loan officers typically have no personal experience in the slums, and this can limit their outreach, as personal fear and cultivated assumptions affect how they work in these communities. While each of these perspectives points to weaknesses that may contribute to limited outreach, these researchers make no mention of how personal or political biases can affect the actions of local managers and staffs.

Case Selection

A comparative study of Caribbean microfinance reveals that microfinance as a development tool has unfolded quite differently in each country. I selected the Caribbean region because it has a sizeable Black population and a distinct group of people managing economic allocations to a marginalized African diaspora. The research in this book shows that politics in socially stratified societies can be either exclusionary or inclusionary: the former in cases of bias (e.g., Jamaica, Guyana, and Trinidad), and the latter in cases of socially conscious politics to fight market fundamentalism through collective institutions (e.g., Haiti and Grenada).

This study of Caribbean microfinance is an important contribution to the emerging critiques of the industry. It reveals that despite millions of dollars being invested in microfinance, the relatively small market for entrepreneurs is being overlooked due to wilful neglect by managers. Microlending in the English-speaking Caribbean reaches less than 15% of those clients who need it, whereas Haiti's lenders, which are mainly cooperatives, reach at least 25% of those who need loans. The Jamaica, Guyana, and Trinidad cases attest to the fact that lenders who are culturally distinct from borrowers often have ingrained prejudices and that this bias affects decisions about who receives microloans. Strong societal perceptions exist within these countries, influencing how economic resources are divided up. A prevailing perception in Guyana is that its people of African descent are lazy and lack the drive to succeed in business. An Indo-Guyanese man, who owns a rum shop in the main floor of his home, quoted a phrase that is commonly heard around the town: "Yuh seem me I tink [points to his own head]. Blackman go no where. Dem want, want, want. Dem want laugh, laugh. We is different [referring to his racial group, Indo-Guyanese]. Not everyting dis eye see, the belly want. We tie di belly not like dem Blackman [in this case, ascribing the virtue of self-sacrifice to Indians]" (interview, Tiger Bay, Guyana, April 2010).

This kind of anti-Black sentiment abounds in the country, affecting societal perceptions of African-Caribbeans as business people. Guyanese scholar Ralph R. Premdas (1995, 24) found that Indo-Guyanese viewed Afro-Guyanese as "economically undisciplined" and, it follows, as culturally inferior. In Haiti and Grenada, socially conscious and gender-aware cooperative lenders – who know their cultural history well and who have been excluded to some extent – have rebelled against this ingrained racialized class politics. The increasing pressure for microlenders to be profitable has forced some to deliberately ignore identity and local politics. The Caribbean region remains deeply affected by its colonial and slaveholding past: every case in this present book is stratified by race, class, and gender. In fact, microfinance managers and staff hold prejudices that contribute to their subconscious control of underprivileged groups.

Given the high rates of inequality in the Caribbean, microbanking is an important recourse for poor people there (CDB 2010, ii) (see Table 1.1 for poverty levels by country).

Table 1.1 Poverty levels in the cases

Country	Poverty Rate
Jamaica	17.6%
Guyana	43%
Grenada	37.7%
Trinidad	21.8%
Haiti	77%

Sources: Jamaica's figure is taken from the annual ESSJ Jamaica Living Conditions Survey in 2010. Guyana's figure is from the Caribbean Development Bank (CDB) Report 2010, 45. Haiti's data (2011) and Trinidad's data (2012) are from the World Bank. Grenada's poverty rate was drawn from the Growth Poverty Reduction Strategy document (2011) by the Ministry of Finance.

Although some of the people who work in the IDB, USAID, and the CDB are concerned about the growing levels of poverty, most view microbanking as a tool for combatting crime and violence in the region rather than inequality. The Caribbean countries in this study show significant levels of poverty and rank relatively low in the UNDP's Human Development Index Report (2009) compared to other Caribbean countries (CDB 2010, 45).[12] In Jamaica, for example, it is reported that one-third of the population occupies property without legal claim (*Jamaica Gleaner* 2009).[13] Jamaica holds the greatest number of poor citizens in the English-speaking Caribbean, and French and Kreyol-speaking Haiti has the greatest absolute number of poor people in the Americas. Guyana and Grenada, the smaller countries in this study, are also challenged by high levels of poverty. And while Trinidad is the wealthiest country of all the cases, it has high poverty levels, especially in urban areas where Afro-Trinidadians reside. In all the cases, African Caribbean people represent the poorest and most vulnerable citizens, and states in the region (with the exception of Guyana) have made microfinance central to poverty reduction programs. For example, the Jamaica Social Investment Fund (JSIF) supports important community projects – including microfinance programs – through the Inner Cities Basic Project (Bowen 2007, 155).

Methods

This study adopted multiple methods in researching the attitudes of lenders and borrowers in fourteen low-income communities across five countries. I interviewed and held several focus groups with 583 people in Jamaica, Guyana, Trinidad, Haiti, and Grenada, and also in Barbados, Panama, Canada, and the United States, from June 2007 to December 2013.[14] As noted in Table 1.2, of the 583 people interviewed, 341 were female (58% of the sample), and most were Black women. The stakeholders[15] interviewed accounted for 37% (218 subjects) of the total sample. The entrepreneurs, or as I call them, business people (also known as *hustlas* in Jamaica, *hucksters* in Guyana, and *ti machanns* in Haiti), are the main subjects of this study and were selected on the criterion of who wanted or who has (or had) a microloan. I draw on the Trinidad and Tobago and Grenada cases as reflections to deepen my regional study.

I spent eleven months in 2009 living in Kingston, Jamaica, which is the country that forms my main case. The slums in Kingston are for

Table 1.2 Interviews of 583 people

Method	Jamaica	Guyana	Haiti	Grenada	Trinidad	Regional experts	Total	Per cent
Number of micro-entrepreneurs interviewed in focus groups	77	6	45	0	0	0	128	
Individual interviews with entrepreneurs, average 45 minutes	156	23	0	17	43	0	239	
Female business people interviewed	146	19	43	8	23	0	231	
Total Entrepreneurs	233	29	43	17	43	0	365	63%
Individual interviews with stakeholders	46	39	35	9	14	10	153	
Individual interviews with bankers and MF experts	28	11	13	5	4	4	65	
Female interviewees	191	35	61	15	35	4	341	58%
Total Sample	307	79	91	31	61	14	583	

Source: Author's data collection from 2007 to 2013.

the most part located in the southwest part of the city, called downtown (south of Cross Roads), and include the neighbourhoods of Trench Town, Bennett's Land, Whitfield Town, Rosetown, Frog City, and the prime minister's constituency of Denham Town and Tivoli Gardens (Howard 2005).[16] In Haiti, I visited the *bidonvilles* (shanties) of Cité Soleil, Carrefour, Martissant, and La Saline, as well as Bel Air in Centre-Ville (Aristide's Lavalas's stronghold) and Jalousie and Flipo in the hills of the chic suburb of Pétionville. My focus groups in Haiti were held in the poor areas of Bon Repos (Port-au-Prince) and in the southern town of Les Cayes. In Guyana, I carried out most of my interviews in 2008 and 2010 in the slum neighbourhoods of Albouystown, in Georgetown, which is ethnically diverse and has a large Afro Guyanese and *dougla* population, as well as East Indian, Portuguese, and Amerindian people.[17] Individual interviews were carried out with entrepreneurs in the poorer sections of the Grand Anse valley, the bus terminal, and the central market in St George, Grenada; and in Laventille, Beetham Gardens, and Sea Lots in east Port of Spain, Trinidad, in the summer of 2013.

Having grounded my study in Black liberation and feminist theory, I had to doubly ensure that I triangulated my data from a diverse range of individuals and settings and methods. So I also interviewed a large number of people across a few countries to make sure I was hearing what I thought I was hearing – that is, that microfinance is limited in what it can do because of partisan and personal politics. In each case, I interviewed at least one staff member in a variety of microfinance lending institutions: commercial banks, cooperatives and credit unions, microfinance organizations and state lending agencies, and moneylenders. These individuals included heads of private finance companies; financial intermediaries making capital for loans available (such as state agencies, private firms, and foreign donors); heads of ROSCAs or informal banking systems; and leaders of NGOs or foundations. Public sector organizations included NGOs, churches, and bodies reliant on donor and public subsidies.

A set of complementary qualitative methods allowed me to uncover politically sensitive issues. Because of the political nature of my findings, and the potential opposition from supporters within the industry, I had to test and retest my methods. Data collection for this project focused on microbusiness people who wanted or who have (or had) a microloan. Business people participated in either individual interviews or focus group sessions and accounted for 63% of the sample (365 business people). In a number of cases, market vendors wanted meetings to take place at their business so that they could work while I interviewed them. Others requested that I come to their homes, which enabled me to observe their home setting and share in their work and life. On several occasions, I remained with a subject for an entire day, sitting beside retailers at home, in a shop, or in a market stall. Many of the subjects had home-based businesses, such as a grocery shop in the front part of the home, and thus I could witness their home and working lives simultaneously. This format allowed me to understand people's contexts and observe them in a typical setting – in other words, to share in their "lived experience" (Marshall and Rossman 2006; Seidman 2006; Maxwell 2005).

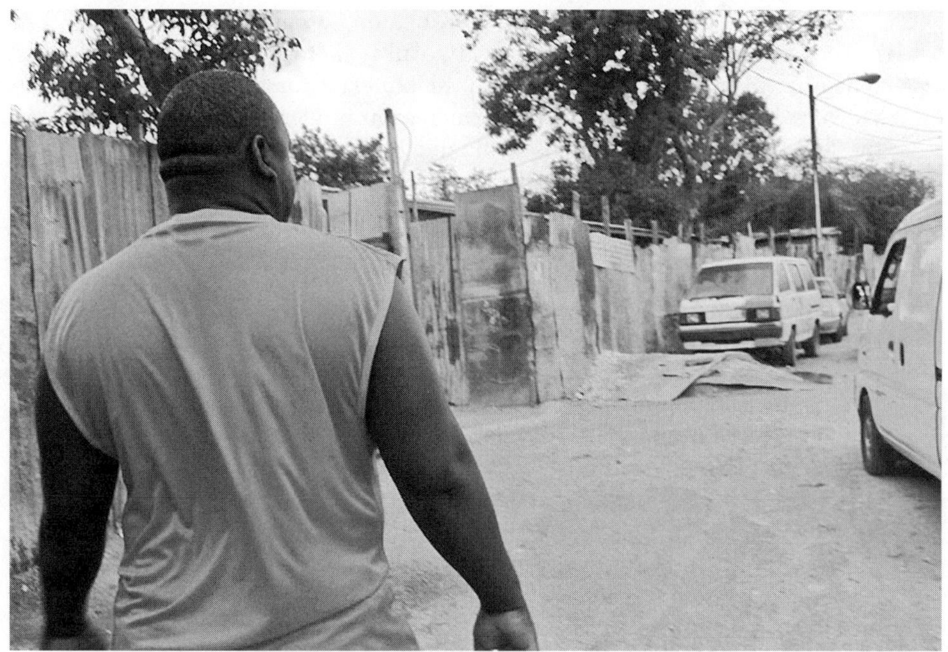

Figure 1.1 Photo of a street in a Kingston slum where interviews took place

My intention was to design interview tools so that people could tell a story and, at times, engage in dialogue. The questions were written so that ordinary people could provide similar information, which could later be quantified and compared; other parts of the tool consisted of open-ended questions so that people could convey a narrative. In-depth structured interview tools focused on four main areas: (1) individual enterprise, (2) politics and microfinance, (3) identities in microfinance, and (4) community development. Interviews with managers and stakeholders were structured and semi-structured. As well, there was a follow-up self-administered survey. Interview tools were standardized as much as possible to enable comparison across the cases, and tools were adapted to fit the local, contextual realities, such as in Haiti to account for the post-earthquake priorities. Ten two-hour focus group meetings (FGs) of six to eleven people were held at neutral locations, such as community centres, churches, or bars, depending on the area.

I conducted the bulk of my FGs in Kingston, Jamaica, arranging five mixed-sex focus group sessions and two all-male focus group sessions, which involved 77 people in total (see Table 1.2 for number of interviewees in FGs). Although the former groups were "mixed-sex," in the Jamaican context women dominated these discussions, with men having only token representation. In fact, women participants often corrected the men, openly disagreeing with their ideas, mocking their use of patois, and indicating that they should "speak propa English" (standard English) and not the Jamaican vernacular.[18] Given that understanding gender dynamics appeared to be important when examining the unique challenges men confront with microfinance, I became concerned about gender balance. For the first time in my career – and I have done many FGs – I arranged all-male focus group sessions (two of them) to ensure that businessmen could offer their interpretations of how microfinance operated.[19]

A large part of this study involved *going local* in order to understand how people live; to this end, I tried to get close to poor citizens to see for myself how they access money for business and consumption needs (Collins et al. 2009; Geertz 1962). The possibility of doing so influenced the selection of communities for this study. After several interviews with local researchers, I realized that to ensure the quality of my research I would need to find research assistants who were community-based and knew the intricacies of the neighbourhoods.

All of my assistants were Black and from low-income backgrounds. Most of them were single mothers with some high school education and were either semi-employed or unemployed (Massiah 1983). Figure 1.1 depicts a typical street with corrugated iron fencing for the tenement yards where my assistants came from. I usually conducted interviews in these places, also known as "yards." I also had a college-educated Jamaican Rastafarian and a Grenadian female college-educated student as assistants; both were useful to this project. All of the research assistants, many of whom were referred to me by non-partisan local notables, had lived experiences in the selected communities, and each brought his or her own instructive lens to the project. It remained unclear to me at times, however, how I could ensure that the people involved in my project were not engaged in partisan and party politics.

Research that requires access to slum areas must be planned carefully in order to safeguard the well-being not only of the researcher but also of the subjects. Borders that are well-known within the community are often invisible to outsiders, and crossing them can be risky and provoke conflict. However, my local assistants knew these boundaries well. It was vital for a trusted person to confirm who I was to the subject, as people were wary of divulging information for fear of reprisals. I also had to abide by rules; in some cases I was allowed to take dictation freely, while in others, such as when I was conducting research in areas of heavy foot traffic, I could not write anything down. As Brazilian Paulo Freire (2010) suggests, knowing how to engage oppressed people is vital to the research process: sometimes knowing when to write and when not to write is important. One of my mentors in Haiti, Professor Louis Marcelin, would listen and discuss topics with subjects in Cité Soleil, and then, once in his car, he would write non-stop to capture as much of what people had said to him as possible. He knew well enough that in certain spaces writing information down intimidated people who were unaccustomed to intellectuals. Taping people made no sense in this region, and I never used a tape recorder during my field research, as this would have limited my access to sensitive information.

Confidentiality is particularly important in Port-au-Prince, Kingston, Georgetown, and Port of Spain, and considering the sensitivity of the politics/bias/money issue, it was best not to tape people or to press them to sign forms. In the region, using "aliases" (nicknames) was common practice, and I did so for all the business people I interviewed in order to protect their identities. In many cases I avoided including details, and modified dates and locations to ensure complete anonymity. Jamaican scholar Imani Tafari-Ama (2006) did the same in her highly sensitive book on drugs and crime in low-income downtown communities. Aliases of subjects included "Fatty," "Brother," and "Big Red." As part of the process, Jamaican research participants gave me the local nickname "Fluffy."[20]

I also collected information from secondary materials, including local newspapers: Jamaica's national papers *The Gleaner* and the *Jamaican Observer*; Haiti's *Le Nouvelliste*; Guyana's private newspapers *Kaieteur News* and *Stabroek News*; and Trinidad's *Guardian* online. I also conducted textual analyses of reports and internal documents, and participant observation of life settings, films, and photographs. In all of the countries I surveyed, especially in post-earthquake Haiti, obtaining recent and microlevel data on the informal sector was a particular challenge.[21] However, Jamaican research institutions have excellent secondary materials and data on the country's social and economic environment. These institutions include the Planning Institute of Jamaica (PIOJ); the Sir Arthur Lewis Institute of Social and Economic

Studies (SALISES); the main library of UWI/Mona; the Statistical Institute of Jamaica (STATIN); and the Social Development Commission (SDC).[22] In Trinidad, the Small Enterprise and Business Association (based in El Dorado) and the NGO Network in Woodbrook hold numerous reports and documents on small business. In Guyana, the Bureau of Statistics and Cartography was helpful when I was accessing general figures by regions, although poverty rates in the slums were unavailable. However, obtaining documents on Guyana's micro- and small-business sector from civil servants is nearly impossible unless you have contacts, for the current regime is antagonistic towards academics of any kind.[23]

Organization of the Book

Politicized Microfinance is organized into six chapters focusing on issues and themes in order to provide comparative analysis between the cases. Chapter 2 maps the political history of the three main cases – Jamaica, Guyana, and Haiti – to explain the unfolding of enterprise development in its cultural context. I also look at two minor cases: Trinidad and Tobago, an oil-rich middle-income country, and Grenada, a small island with a legacy of cooperatives.

Chapter 3 advances new thinking on race, class, and gender dynamics in microfinance and illuminates how the interplay of these intersecting identities leads to exclusion from microfinance. In the Caribbean context, identities affect how economic resources are allocated, and this chapter reveals a deep-seated racial and class bias against African entrepreneurs in Jamaica, Guyana, and Trinidad. In some cases, male exclusion from microfinance contributes to domestic conflicts in poor households (see the Jamaican case); whereas in the Guyana case, the reverse is occurring because Indo-Guyanese males dominate MFIs and lend mainly to men.

Chapter 4 highlights the failure of some microfinance managers to address the powerful impact of partisan politics and its role in the oppression of the urban poor by Big Men. In the electoral democracy of Jamaica, exclusionary microlending is tied to class-based clientelist politics; microbanking is also problematic in the racialized party politics settings in Guyana and Trinidad, where there is a split between educated Indo-Caribbean and poor Afro-Caribbean people. In Jamaica, Guyana, and Trinidad, microfinance operates in an exclusionary manner.

Chapter 5 shows that in spite of market fundamentalism and a trend towards commercialized microbanking, some socially conscious bankers-to-the-poor think about microlending differently. Haiti's oppressive political environment has alienated the *moun andeyo* (excluded masses) for decades, yet in that country there are cooperative lenders who take personal risks to help the masses by democratizing local forms of commerce. This testifies to the idea that microfinance can help redress social injustice when people working in financial cooperatives and *caisses populaires* (credit unions) display political activism in the social economy. Grenadians, too, are attached to credit unions, and they too trust solidarity systems rooted in African traditions of collectivity. In some parts of the Caribbean, collective organizations have influenced the evolution of financial cooperatives and *caisses populaires* from the ground up – quite unlike commercialized microfinance organizations.

Chapter 6 reasserts that in the slums in the Americas and elsewhere, social economy organizations that put people first may actually overcome identity and partisan politics in business development. It is evident that personal bias and exclusionary financing cannot be sustained, and lenders who practice either or both will have to change their ways to stay in business. Marginalized Black people are re-creating business to support the ways they organize their social lives. In the Haitian case, community-driven collective institutions present an alternative way of doing business. These cooperative institutions operate successfully in a profit-driven world and garner the respect of poor entrepreneurs. Indeed, many Haitian lenders resemble the very people they serve and have undertaken political and radical action to fight for social and economic change. As well, the ancestral African banking systems across the region reinforce the point that a quiet form of resistance is at work when people come together collectively to resist commercialized and individualized forms of banking.

Critics of microfinance have debunked the myth of inclusive banking but fall short in their examination of the limits of economic development programs where structural barriers perpetually exclude the African diaspora. *Politicized Microfinance* contributes to the research on microcredit in three main ways. First, it focuses on the Black Atlantic, specifically the Caribbean region where the African diaspora live; heretofore the research has focused mainly on South Asia and Latin America and, more recently, Africa and the Middle East. Second, the work uses Black, feminist, and intersectionality theory to understand how identities (race, class, and gender) affect microfinance allocations. This amounts to a divergence from the plethora of literature examining gender and women, for, as I mention above, race and class are also factors that enable or restrict access to finance for Black people. Third, this study analyses the role of managers and staff people in MFIs and their own political attachments as they create access to or restrict opportunities for some people. The form of politics that individuals engage in as they manage financial services does matter: those who conform to elitist politics reinforce exclusionary practices; those who react against mainstream politics and create alternative banking systems can offer room to fight for social change. That politics takes two forms is a novel idea in this study, one that is rooted in the experience of excluded Black people in the Americas.

Most of the recent critiques have focused on commercial microfinance, and so much has been said that we risk repeating ourselves. While an anti-neoliberal critique has a place, it is not enough to downgrade all microfinance models everywhere. Healy (2009) makes the important point that neoliberalism is in crisis and that now is the time to show off people-focused economies. Given the contextual realities and diverse lenders in the sector, to criticize *all* microfinance is problematic, for such polemic risks withholding help from those who need it. Having carried out extensive field research, I am more convinced than ever that some forms of microfinance do exclude certain groups; I also believe that microfinance is less likely to be effective when the experts are oblivious to the identity and partisan politics within the industry. Critics and advocates alike have ignored that MFI staffs are often made up of privileged individuals, especially at the senior levels, who negatively affect the lending process for their own sake. For microfinance to attain its goal of inclusive banking, the staffs of these institutions must be ready to engage with politics by tackling social exclusion, which means upsetting the structural systems and not simply inserting excluded people into unequal social systems (Galabuzi 2006). Lenders who know first-hand the lived experience of the people they serve are more likely to fight for social change.

For centuries, people of the African diaspora have known that "another world is possible," and they have been carving out practical ways to live and do business. Yet no critique has ever examined how detached microbanking programs are from the lived experiences of communities in need. Lived experience is an important concept in Black feminist thought, as it gives credit to Black people's own knowledge and prioritizes what they have to say about the biases they encounter in life (Wane et al. 2002; Hill Collins 2000). As long as partisan and identity issues plague the microfinance sector and historically rooted prejudices are not taken into account, it is doubtful that microfinancing can be truly inclusive. *Politicized Microfinance* argues not only that economics can perpetually exclude Black people but also that the very politics that interferes with people's access to finance requires an even more committed and engaged form of politics to uplift excluded people and move economies along a conscious path.

Chapter 2

Contextualizing Microfinance in Jamaica, Guyana, and Haiti

"It was slavery – owning other human beings as property, like land, cattle or tools – that led to the birth of the Black Americas, during the lengthy hemispheric oppression of African-Americans."

Sidney Mintz, *Three Ancient Colonies*, 2010, 1

Caribbean people have been colonized for hundreds of years. Mintz points out in *Three Ancient Colonies* (2010) that the Caribbean was where Europeans tested imperial rule and advanced capitalism. Caribbean people share a history rooted in slavery, colonization, and violence and, more recently, dependence on the United States (Mintz 2010; Mann 2008; Fatton 2002, 2007; Paravisini-Gebert 1997; Rodney 1996; Terborg-Penn 1995; Fanon 1967; Smith 1964; Stoby 1931). It is this history steeped in violence, slavery, and the pursuit of wealth that makes it important to highlight the racial segmentation of these Caribbean countries. In *Cultural Power, Resistance, and Pluralism: Colonial Guyana, 1838–1900*, Brian L. Moore (1995) underscores that examining the social history of a people requires listening to its cultural story. Guyana, like other Caribbean countries, has become a highly racialized society as a direct result of its history of slavery. The result of this history is a racialized class structure, with marginalized Black groups forming the base of an economic pyramid (Hallward 2010, 1; Garner 2008, 16; Mars 1995, 172; Burrowes 1984, 26–8; Smith 1964, 100–2).[1] Business elites, often white or lighter-complexioned, have historically been linked to the state for strategic and financial reasons, and these collusions persist today (Horowitz 1985). The cultural bias ingrained in the managers who run financial programs has a powerful impact, reflecting the historically rooted class and race-based oppressions of marginalized groups.

I came to this project assuming that the Jamaican case would provide an example of inclusive microbanking – that because of the country's long-standing stable democracy and legacy of trade unions, its lenders would avoid partisan politics when dealing with the urban poor in Kingston. Given Jamaica's political and economic history, I expected microfinance lenders (mainly women who supported microfinance) to be conscious of the "garrison phenomenon" and to offer loans to remedy the grinding poverty of the downtown communities.[2] Instead, I found a sector riddled with politicized programs that many of the poor avoid. In the case of Haiti, I had assumed that, due to the country's racial and class tensions, dependence on foreign aid, and weak governance, its microcredit programs would be highly politicized. But a reading of Haiti's history makes it increasingly clear that under harsh political regimes, people and civil society cope through community-driven grassroots organizations.

A historical mapping will help us understand the culturally tiered systems in the diverse countries of the Caribbean region, as well as explain why microfinance outcomes differ in each of the cases and how economic resources are allocated. Legacies of enslavement and colonialism are etched in the identities of many Caribbean people; today's racial make-up is a direct result of a history of racial intermingling. As Bakan (1990, 6) states, "the ideology of racism was encouraged and legitimized by colonial powers and those who supported colonial rule." White European slave masters (usually British, Irish, Dutch, Spanish, or French) raped female slaves, and this introduced the new racial category of *mulattos*, persons of lighter-complexioned skin (Mintz 2010). As a rule, the fairer or lighter-skinned a person, the better that person's social position (Hope 2006; Premdas 1995; Bakan 1990). In all of the countries being considered in this chapter, the people in this lighter-skin racial category inherited the wealth and status of their forefathers (Smith 1964, 27).[3]

Cultural identities (race, class, and gender) are very powerful influences when it comes to financial inclusion/exclusion, and one must anchor this understanding in the political and economic history of the cases. The formulators of finance programs to the poor in this region seldom consider cultural identity, even though doing so is vital in the historical and political context of the global South. As mentioned earlier, Guyanese academic Moore (1995) has made the forceful point that to truly know the region one has to unpack its cultural history. In this chapter I map the political and economic history of Jamaica, Guyana, and Haiti (the primary cases for this study) and introduce facts on the secondary cases of Trinidad and Guyana. I examine only those parts of history relevant to understanding microfinance in the region; this will help frame the internal politics that affect the processes of microlending and underline that context is key to the operation of economic and financial development in these countries. My intention is not to present a comprehensive historical review of these regions, but rather to anchor the social divisions in these societies and explain how they play out.

I begin by reviewing the emergence of clientelist politics in Jamaica among different classes and shades of Black (skin colour) as it relates to business development. Then I examine Haiti's activist orientation in economic development in terms of the fight for social justice for the masses. Despite Haiti's predatory political past – the country is steeped in class and racial conflicts as a result of which violent regimes have alienated the *moun andeyo* (outsiders, poor masses) – a strong mutual aid and self-help spirit has emerged. After this, I examine Guyana's pluralistic history and the political elites' (mis)use of race-based politics to control the opposing racial group. I also note that decades-long racialized class politics has affected Trinidad's economic history as well. Jamaica, Trinidad, Grenada, and Guyana – all former British colonies – arrived at independence much later than French-speaking Haiti, but all have experienced despicable horrors through the plantation economy. Except for Grenada, all of the anglophone countries have had relatively stable electoral democracies, with no coups or US occupations. This historical review helps sort out why the development of microfinance in the three anglophone cases has unfolded differently than in Haiti (and Grenada).

Imperialism and Slavery

Caribbean peoples experienced horrific slavery and enslavement for a very long period and were beaten into submission to ensure that they worked the plantations to create profits for the white masters (Mintz 2010). W.E.B. Du Bois in *The Souls of Black Folk* (1903) recognized that the brutality of enslavement against African peoples had an affect both on the continent and in the Americas as it destroyed cultures and kinship. In *Capitalism and Slavery* (2004[1944]), Trinidad and Tobago's Williams argues that the white empires became rich by extracting resources, using the forced labour of Africans. Guyanese scholar Walter Rodney (1982) suggests that it was not that Africa and the colonies could not modernize, but that these places were subject to exploitation by racist colonizers – a part of the story that is often conveniently overlooked. Under colonization, commercial banks financed the activities of the white racist planters, who often grew extremely wealthy by holding Black people in bondage (Moore 1987, 1995). Eventually, the offspring of the white planters inherited the land and wealth (Girard 2010; Gardner 1971; Black 1965).

Saint-Domingue (Haiti) was first colonized by the Spanish, who eliminated the indigenous population on arrival. France eventually took control of Saint-Domingue, which became the most profitable sugar-producing colony in the Americas (Heinl and Heinl 2005). The Treaty of Utrecht (1703–38) granted the British empire the *Asiento* contract, according to which England became the authorized slave distributor for the region (Black 1965; Young 1958). In Jamaica, the white indentured servants (such as the Portuguese and Irish) who had been brought to work the fields then moved into plantation management, as Negro slaves increased in numbers to 200,000 (Black 1965; Smith 1964). Britain gained control of Guyana from the Dutch in 1814 and applied a plantation system similar to Jamaica's in the early years (Mansru 2005; Smith 1964; Bennett 1875). Because the plantation system was not sustainable without forced labour, after slavery ended the British resorted to an expansive indenture system in Guyana and Trinidad, and to a lesser extent in Jamaica (St Pierre 1999; Rodney 1981).

Millions of Africans lost their lives during centuries of struggle against the violent slavers. Meanwhile, anti-slavery movements in Europe stirred resistance in the colonies. Haiti's successful revolution spurred Jamaican slaves to fight their colonizers for freedom in the revolt led by the Trelawney maroons, and in the early nineteenth century, slaves in Jamaica and Guyana launched their own uprisings against the masters (Black 1965), making several attempts before achieving success. Jamaica's maroons, originally referred to as "Coromantes" (runaway African slaves), launched guerilla-style warfare against the European slave system.[4] The maroons fought British slave masters and escaped to the mountains, where they continued to stage attacks on the planters (Black 1965).[5] These slave uprisings in the British colonies forced the passage of the Abolition Bill in 1833; but at that time it remained merely a law on paper. The practice of slavery continued until 1838 (Brathwaite 1971), when freedom finally came to more than 300,000 Jamaican slaves.

The Dutch ruled Guyana, originally Guiana, for two hundred years, and during the eighteenth century the colony changed hands several times between the Dutch and British (Singh 1996; Burrowes 1984; Schomburgk 1970; Despres 1967; Clementi 1939; Bennett 1875). In the Berbice Slave Uprising of 1763, Guyana's slaves, led by Coffey, attempted resistance but were unsuccessful (Hope 1985). In 1814, Guiana was renamed British Guiana (later known as Guyana), and the British remained heavily invested in maintaining their lucrative sugar estates (Hope 1985; Despres 1967). Similar to the Jamaican experience, Guyana's slaves were aware of the abolition movement in England, and in 1823, thousands of slaves revolted in the Demerara Rebellion, which was defeated by the British.[6] Like Jamaicans, the Guyanese people had to wait for freedom until 1838 (Burrowes 1984; Schomburghk 1970). Mintz (2010, 27–9) notes that freed slaves remained in apprenticeship positions for five years, during which time they were kept in slave-like work conditions. Rodney (1996) makes the compelling point that slavery did not in fact end in Guyana until the early twentieth century due to the slave-like indenture system of Indo-Guyanese. The plantocracy economy, controlled by whites, continued for years after the emancipation period, as the British imported cheap labour from India to work on the plantations in order to undercut the demands for market-led wages by the freed slaves (Rodney 1996; Moore 1995). In 1836, foreign banks, such as England's Barclays Bank and Canada's Scotiabank, emerged in the region to further assist the white planters as well as whitened merchants with concessional loans.

The region's cultural politics have often determined who can access its economic resources (Moore 1987, 1995). Guyanese economist C.Y. Thomas's (1988) typology of race and class politics is relevant to the Caribbean context: the moneyed elite, composed of colonialists (whites) or traditionalists (whitened or creole/mixed race), and the political elite (coloured/Black/East Indian), dominate the disenfranchised Black masses.[7] The British first referred to this mixed racial group as "mulattos," and later, Jamaicans called Black people of light-skinned complexion "brownings" (mixed race) (Brathwaite 1971).[8] Within the creole-Jamaican society, a class structure tied to race emerged in which mulattos or brownings had the right to vote and dark-skinned Blacks did not (Rodney 1996, 61–2).[9] I found that the term "Afro-Jamaican" was and continues to be complex, and can include (or exclude) many shades of colour. Mixed-race Jamaicans are able to apply the label "Afro-Jamaican" when it suits their purposes. Today, the island's richest families are white Jamaicans (like the Issas, Stewarts, and Matalons). Over the years, intermarriages have become increasingly complex, with brownings intermarrying with the island's minority whites, Chinese, Lebanese, and Syrians.

Jamaica's Case

Jamaicans, though freed from slavery in 1833, remained colonized by the British. The year 1865 was a turning point in Jamaica's struggle for independence when, at Morant Bay, Paul Bogle, Jamaica's national hero, led a revolt against British rule (Bakan 1990; Black 1965). This marked the beginning of the Jamaican people's resistance to British control. England's response to this rebellion was to appoint a new governor, Graham Grant, to introduce development policies in education and economics and to modernize Jamaica – investments that were welcomed by the Jamaicans. After slavery ended, the colonization project was vested in capitalist projects that focused on economic development in terms of the British Crown's needs.

In the early 1900s, the focus was on economic development. Jamaican farmers felt they were being exploited by the United Fruit Company and in 1929 formed their own association: the Jamaican Banana Producers Association (Black 1965). This and other banana associations spread throughout the productive industries, as workers recognized the need to mobilize into associations and cooperatives in order to improve wages. This movement led to the rise of political groups in 1938, and from these political groups, which were tied to trade unions, emerged political parties focused on the struggle for liberation.[10] In towns and villages across Jamaica, people remained unhappy living under colonial rule. Jamaican migrants working in the Panama Canal Zone realized that the white managers and owners were using their labour unjustly. Among these migrants was Marcus Mosiah Garvey, a leading Black nationalist, who promoted Black pride in the poor urban areas of Kingston, where he lived for a number of years (Sives 2010).[11]

Garvey advanced his Pan-African political agenda through the Universal Negro Improvement Association, which was a movement to free Black people from unjust colonial rule (Ewing 2014; Sives 2010; Bandele 2010; Martin 1983; Black 1965). In the 1930s, Garvey's Black nationalism and entrepreneurial teachings resonated in marginalized areas with the Rastafari movement, another oppressed social group, as well as with the African diaspora in the United States (K'adamwe, Bernard, and Dixon 2011; Grant 2009; Bakan 1990; Martin 1983).[12] British colonizers, local whites, and browning elites in Jamaica found Garvey's

Afrocentrist discourse – which distinguished between local whites and the Black masses – to be divisive. Cousins Norman Manley and Alexander "Busta" Bustamante (later to be named the founders of independence), creole whites who led the country to self-government in 1936, found themselves threatened by Garvey's ideas for poor Blacks to take power (Martin 1983). By the late 1940s, nationalism was on the rise.

In 1955 the People's National Party (PNP) became the first sitting local party and the cabinet was authorized to seek independence. British colonizers granted permission to Jamaican leaders to work with Trinidad, Guyana, and Barbados to set up a federation of the British West Indies. But in 1962, as Jamaicans agitated for independence, the federation broke down. Throughout the 1960s, Bustamante and Manley enticed poor Blacks with promises of jobs, money, and houses to carry out thuggish politicking against other poor Blacks (Gunst 2003; Ledgister 1998; Payne 1994; Stone 1994; Keith and Keith 1992; Bakan 1990; *Harder They Come* 1973). Stone (1986, 1994) argues that since the 1967 election, armed political gang leaders from Kingston's downtown slums have been organizing party activists. At election times, Kingston's low-income communities in the downtown core have become sites of conflict over scarce resources, as people know that having their party in power means money for them. Election violence was so intense in the 1970s that musician Rasta Robert "Bob" Nestor Marley held a peace concert, reflecting on the political wars in his reggae music (White 2000).

Patronage, Gangsters, and Big Man Politics[13]

Jamaica has a population of 2.7 million (World Bank 2009a, 2009b, 2011). The island's long-standing democracy has been shaped by its political history. Today many descendant beneficiaries of the planter class live in hilltop mansions in the wealthy Beverly Hills area, while descendants of slaves live in the impoverished shanty towns below and continue to work in informal markets (Rapley 2003). Socio-economic factors compounded by differences in skin colour have produced a class-based apartheid that divides Jamaicans. Most residents in the downtown ghettos are very dark-skinned; those who control resources are usually educated and fair-complexioned. This colour and class dynamic has changed little since colonial times. For most of the country's history, then, party leaders have been educated, light-skinned browning elites and their followers have been poor Blacks.

There were two main actors in Jamaica's post-independence period: the PNP's Michael Manley (1972–80; 1989–92), and the leader of the Jamaica Labour Party (JLP), Edward Seaga (1980–89). Both men left an indelible mark on the country's politics. Patronage politics were prevalent during the political eras of both Seaga and Manley; in particular, both leaders were associated with the clientelist politics that continue to grip the country (Bronfman 2007, 69). Since independence, the JLP governments under Bustamante, Sangster, and later Shearer (1962–72) have succeeded in institutionalizing political hand-outs to lock up the electoral vote. Once in office, the JLP governments moved the country towards import substitution industrialization (ISI) policies to attract foreign investment and to develop local industries (Jamaican Information Service website, 26 May 2011; Payne 1994).

In most developing countries, the political elite make micro and small loans available through state-owned banks to people who have been excluded from traditional financing (Matin, Hulme, and Rutherford 2002, 274).[14] However, politically motivated financial aid in Jamaica (and the Caribbean more generally) comes with consequences. Kingston, Jamaica's main urban centre, is marred at election time by racialized violence. Whitened political elites promise money, shelter, and jobs to very poor political activists, who will lose these political hand-outs if they fail to deliver the vote for their candidate. Academics have written extensively on this entrenched mechanism, in which elites use uneducated Black masses in the ghettos to carry out heinous crimes to ensure votes and political victory (Sives 2010; Bronfman 2007; Tafari-Ama 2006; Ledgister 1998; Stone 1980, 1986, 1994; Nettleford 1989).[15] Panton (1993) rightly contends that this division between the classes, which is tied to racial markings, laid the foundations for a patron/client framework in Jamaican politics.

Michael Manley – the son of Norman Manley, PNP leader in earlier times – emerged in 1972 as an important leader in the Third World non-aligned movement, where leaders from the global South remained neutral during the ideological war between the capitalists of the West and communist/socialist Soviet Union. Manley developed his own version of "democratic socialism," under which welfare services were provided to the poor and supporters were rewarded with housing, as well as literacy and employment programs, such as the self-employment program. In 1977 the government acquired local branches of foreign banks, such as England's Barclays Bank, and merged them into the fully Jamaican-owned National Commercial Bank (NCB), which began lending to

Black small and medium firms (Thomas 2004, 79). Manley's nationalist policy limited trade between local businesses and America; his government also developed an increasingly close relationship with Cuba. American leaders, antagonized by these moves, restricted imports from Jamaica.

Manley's political rival, Edward Seaga, was an American-born, Harvard-educated son of white Jamaican parents. He had returned to Jamaica as a graduate student to study African spirituality and religions in the countryside and in Tivoli Gardens (West Kingston). Welfare portfolios gave Seaga the power to reward party followers, and he started building housing complexes in Tivoli Gardens (Gray 2004, 179).[16] These buildings are still standing in "Belgium," "Haiti," and "Bumbs" (West Kingston). In the 1980s, Seaga's pro-market politics enticed brownings and near-white Jamaican elites to return home to invest (Sandbrook et al. 2007, 17). These American investors, Seaga's close allies, were given export-free-zone contracts, with the result that President Ronald Reagan wanted to "showcase Jamaica as a free enterprise experiment in the Caribbean" (Panton 1993, 68–84).

As part of market reforms, Seaga implemented licensing requirements on higglers (informal market vendors) so that they became "informal commercial importers" (ICIs) (a policy he dubbed "formalizing higglering"). This enabled the government to collect taxes and to restrict these merchants' importation of goods (Ulysse 2007, 50).[17] Yet no social benefits accrued to this group as a consequence, nor was there any state policy to help the vendors access credit and business training. Ulysse (2007, 277) argues that higglers were negatively targeted by the Seaga government through taxation, the seizing of goods by customs officers, and harassment by police when they sold on the streets or in the open markets. This led to the formation of the Jamaican Higglers and Sidewalk Vendors Association in 1986. Seaga's control of informal traders was rewarded with a constant stream of American aid, and this enabled him to create the Self-Start Fund (SSF) in 1985, a program to support new micro-enterprises in slum communities (Richfield and Pace Investment Limited, 1994). The SSF was managed by Seaga's wife, Carla Seaga, and the main recipients of the microloans were party activists of the JLP.

Like previous elections, those of 1989 were violent. Politicians doled out benefits and money to gangs and activists to bring in the vote. In his second term as prime minister, Manley developed a new political platform – "Better Must Come" and "Power for the People" – which continued the move towards a free market ideology (Sandbrook et al. 2007, 17; Bernal 1994; Best and Forrant 1994; Panton 1993). As part of his shift to the right, Manley launched the Micro Investment Development Agency (MIDA) in 1991 with US$800,000, whose small loans were based on political patronage and clientelism for members of the PNP (anonymous interview; Ffrench 2008; McFarlane 1997; Richfield and Pace Investments Limited 1994; MIDA, n.d.).

For 30 years (from 1962 to 1992), then, Jamaican politics was dominated by white/near-white elites and financed by wealthy families (Thomas 2004; Thomas 1988; Keith and Keith 1992).[18] But all the while, a Black, educated class was emerging in the post-independence period, and when Manley retired from politics, the country's first dark-skinned prime minister, Percival James (P.J.) Patterson, took office in 2006, followed by the first female leader (also dark-skinned), Portia Simpson-Miller (Robotham 2000, 1).[19] In 2007, Bruce Golding (2007–11), a browning from the JLP, took over Seaga's old West Kingston constituency. In July 2010, Golding's constituency rioted when citizens, women in particular, opposed the Americans' request that local Don Christopher "Dudus" Coke of Tivoli Gardens be extradited to face drug and weapons trafficking charges. Politicians routinely deny that such alliances exist; the press routinely exposes their existence (Harriott 2008; Rapley 2006; Hope 2006).[20] The controversy once again implicated politicians, including Golding, in nefarious dealings with known drug dealers. This led to Golding's sudden resignation in October 2011.[21] Portia Simpson-Miller was re-elected prime minister on 29 December 2011.

Despite class inequalities and clientelism to control votes, Jamaica's state since independence has been stable, and its democracy seems secure (Stone 1986). Clientelist tendencies in Jamaican politics make it difficult to imagine that such manipulation is absent in economic programs (such as microfinance) in the garrisons. Big Men (political elites) continue to control the slums, as do the "Dons" (gangsters), who emerged as important actors in providing welfare during the 1980s, when structural adjustment programs and reforms made it harder for politicians to disburse benefits to their followers. Dons are informal community leaders who run lucrative illegal activities (e.g., drug and weapons trafficking networks) and provide security and welfare services for slum residents in exchange for complete control of the community. With the rise of the narcotics trade in the Caribbean since the 1980s, Jamaicans have become highly aware of their politicians' alliances with Dons. Indeed, the collusion between politicians and Dons is a common theme in popular film, theatre, music, and media.[22] Political gifts, kickbacks, and hand-outs from both politicians and Dons are deeply entrenched in downtown Kingston (Keith and Keith 1992).

Slums in Kingston are broken down into areas affiliated with the two political parties: PNP and JLP. These slums, also called "garrisons," take on a "political tribe" persona: residents are either "PNP" or "JLP" depending on which political party controls the area. An entire community votes one particular way, and there is no tolerance for opposition. Some garrison communities have an established structure, referred to as an "order," in which a Don informally controls all of the community's affairs (Rapley 2006, 95–7; Figueroa and Sives 2003, 66).[23] In songs and movies, the concept of "politricks" (politics characterized by dishonesty) is widely discussed among poor Jamaicans, showing that they are aware not only of how politicians use them for votes, but also of the high costs of any benefits that come through partisan politics when Dons are involved (Bonitto 2008). Dons are tied to the political elites and must ensure that residents vote for the correct party. They guarantee votes in exchange for government contracts.

In the 1980s, structural adjustment programs (SAPs) imposed by the IMF scaled back welfare functions. This left informal leaders to fill the gaps and provide basic welfare services and policing in certain marginalized areas. Because of increasing profits from the extortion of business elites and the drug and weapons trade, Dons now often have more financial resources and power than elected leaders. For example, Tivoli Gardens' former Don, Christopher "Dudus" Coke, mentioned above, whose informal trade and registered legal businesses are known as "Incomparable Enterprises" and "Presidential Click," received state contracts for millions of dollars in construction projects and for the cleanup of gullies and sewage systems (Robotham 2003, 215; Charles 2002, 32).[24] This is relevant to the Jamaican microfinance arena, for it explains how partisan and identity politics interferes with the social empowerment goals of microfinance. In 2010, the capture of Dudus for extradition to the United States led to widespread disorder and rioting in West Kingston and resulted in the deaths of policemen and residents (Al-Jazeera 2010).

Haiti's Case

Haiti's cultural history is similar to Jamaica's in terms of the intermingling between white and Black people. The French slave masters raped *les Bossales* (African-born slaves, also called Congos), and this created the *mulatre* (mulatto/mixed race) group (Trouillot 1995, 67; Casimir 1993, 74). On independence, the *mulatre* emerged as the dominant class (Heinl and Heinl 2005, 22). Intermingling has resulted in complex racial groupings based on shades of skin colour, but the three dominant groups are *les blancs* (whites), *les mulatres*, and *les noirs* (Blacks).[25] Most of the *moun andeyo* are Kreyol-speaking (Mintz 2010, 120; Hallward 2010, 1; *The Agronomist* 2003; *Voodoo and the Church* 1998).[26] Casimir (1993, 112) found that long before independence, the two competing groups, *mulatres* and *Bossales*, united to fight the French oppressors. The quest for freedom began in April 1792 when France agreed, through the Jacobins' decree, to give freedom to certain creole-Africans (Haitian-born Blacks, often of some white heritage) (Heinl and Heinl 2005; Dubois 2004). After two centuries of slavery, Haitians, inspired by the 1789 French Revolution, carried out a violent revolution to overthrow the French (Girard 2010; Robinson 2007; Paquin and Brax 2006; Heinl and Heinl 2005; James 1989).[27] Once the slaves had been freed, Jean-Jacques Dessalines and Toussaint L'Ouverture, both creole-Africans, led the Bossales to claim independence from France (Smartt-Bell 2007; Heinl and Heinl 2005; Dubois 2004; Trouillot 1995; Farmer 1994; Maguire 2006). Dessalines and L'Ouverture needed to appeal to the *mulatres*, the freed slaves, and the Bossales in order to usurp power from the French (James 1989). In this bloody revolt, Dessalines and his troops defeated Napoleon's army and forced all French settlers to leave.

On 1 January 1804, Haiti became the first Black republic, but it remained isolated and an outcast from the international community for a long time (Mintz 2010; Acacia 2006; Dubois 2004; Stotzky 1997; Trouillot 1995; Farmer 1994). After the French left, the whitened elites – referred to as "bourgeoisie" or "*mulatres*," but more specifically, the French-speaking Catholic whitened minority – dominated the very dark-skinned, uneducated, Voodoo-worshipping Haitians (descendants of the Bossales), both economically and politically. According to many Haitians, the Black elite first manifested itself through Dessalines and L'Ouverture, although a pro-Black politics, referred to as Noirism (Black nationalism), had been visible in Haiti in the early 1800s (Robinson 2007, 15; Heinl and Heinl 2005, 21).[28] Historically, Haitian descendants of the Bossales have resorted to education to move up the social and economic ladder. Today, some Black cooperative lenders have used education to bring financial services to underprivileged women; other politicians of a similar class background have sought political power (e.g., Aristide).

For 21 years following its independence in 1804, Haiti's identity as the first free Black republic remained an international secret to the masters, yet a dream to slaves all over the Americas (Dubois 2004, 304). Slavery was not abolished in Britain until 1838 and in America until 1865, and as a consequence, Western powers were anxious to contain the truth about Haiti's independence so as not to inspire slave rebellions on plantations elsewhere and jeopardize the lucrative slave trade (Mintz 2010). The great Haitian scholar Michel Trouillot (1995, 89) has argued that a Black state was largely unthinkable at that time, because it challenged the global order of commerce, slavery, and colonialism. During its period of diplomatic isolation, Haiti was the target of aggression from Germany and others (Fatton 2007, 138–9). Internally, freedom from a colonial power did not mean peace for Haiti's citizens: Haitian leaders since Jean-Jacques Dessalines (1804–06) have adhered to *politiques du ventre* (politics of the belly) dictatorships, leaving the masses in abject suffering (Szeftel 2000).[29] The policy of isolation ended in 1825, when France forced Haitian officials to take out a loan (equal to US$21 billion today) from French banks to compensate the French for property losses, including loss of slaves.

Haiti is one of the world's poorest countries, with its people trapped in extreme poverty (GOH 2010; Fatton 2006, 17; McCoy 1997, 1–5). At least 77% of its 10.12 million people live on less than US$2 a day (World Bank 2011; GOH 2010, 2; CDB 2010, 45; Dupuy 2010; FAO 2008). Hallward (2010, 1) emphasizes that a mere 1% of the people own the country's wealth. The country's political unfolding – from revolution and independence in 1804, to American occupation from 1915 to 1934, to the post-Duvalier era since 1986 – reflects the unstable and predatory nature of Haitian politics (Fatton 2007, 2–6; 2002, 137; Maguire 1997, 156). The country has had at least 45 heads of state and about 20 constitutions since independence, and power in the country has swung between educated *noirs* and whitened elites (Paquin and Brax 2006, 143; Heinl and Heinl 2005, 119–301). In the early 1900s, US president Woodrow Wilson, who had imperial designs on the country, invoked the Monroe Doctrine and deployed American marines to Haiti, where they remained for 20 years (1915–1934) (Girard 2010; Paquin and Brax 2006, 176; Farmer 1994, 18).[30] During the US occupation, Haiti was governed by *mulatres* hand-picked by the Americans – Phillippe Sudré Dartiguenave, Louis Borno, and Sténio Vincent (Fatton 2007, 147–149), which again left the Haitians descended from the Bossales subject to racialized class politics. In the years following the American occupation, coups d'états, military dictatorships, and terror under the violent regimes of supposed Noiriste (pro-Black) leaders like François "Papa Doc" (1957–71) and Jean-Claude "Baby Doc" Duvalier (1971–86), and Jean-Bertrand Aristide (second presidency 2001–4) have continued to undermine Haiti's economic development, as I will elaborate below.[31]

Scholarship on Haiti (e.g., Maguire 2006; Fatton 2002, 2006, 2007; Rotberg 1997; Farmer 1994; James 1989) has compared the country's socio-economic situation to apartheid, under which the Kreyol-speaking *moun andeyo* have been marginalized by the bourgeoisie. Port-au-Prince comprises two extreme worlds: one rich, the other very poor (N'Zengou-Tayo 1998, 118; Rotberg 1997, 137; Stotzky 1997, 20–2). Yet these two social groups are very much intertwined. The country is divided by class and race: a tiny minority – mostly *blancs* and *mulatres* but also elite *noirs* – controls the country's wealth from their secluded villas in Pétionville, Montagne Noire, Bel Vil, and Peguy Ville. Dupuy (2007, 25–6) argues that the Haitian bourgeoisie (elites) have been split into two dominant groups: Blancs and *mulatres* control the private sector, and the elite *noirs* dominate the state. From the city below, the *moun andeyo* look up at the wealthy mansions of the elites; from their hilltops, the *blancs* and *mulatres* can see the *bidonvilles* (shanty towns or slums) of "Jalousie" and "Flipo," constant reminders of the grinding poverty of the excluded *moun andeyo*. In January 2010, a magnitude 7.0 earthquake struck the southern part of Haiti, killing about 300,000 people and leaving 1.5 million displaced and living in "tent cities" in Place St-Pierre and Place Boyer, further reinforcing the country's social and economic divides (Castor et al. 2010, 22; Chauvet 2010, 5–10).

Yet whatever the conditions, the Haitian people have always been resilient. Haitians are descendants of Beninese (then Dahomey) slaves, who brought West African informal banking concepts to the Americas and relied on these systems during times of austerity (Fatton 2007). These *gwoupmans* (community groups) tapped into an African heritage of working together, referred to as *kombit* in Kreyol (Fatton 2002, 52). Fatton (2007, 221) has found that the heritage of *gwoupmans* organized by the poor under repressive political regimes has persisted in Haiti. For example, the first official cooperative was organized in the difficult financial times immediately following the American withdrawal in 1934 (Montasse 1983). As there was no state structure in place to meet people's needs, the poor organized themselves into cooperative groups, fashioning them after the *sol*, a local savings program brought over from Africa (Heinl and Heinl 2005; Reinert and Voss 1997).[32] A decade later, in Jacmel in 1946, under the pro-Black (Noiriste) Dumarsais Estimé government (1946–50), the first formalized financial cooperative – *caisses populaire* – was started in the country (Montasse 1983, 18).

Haiti's early, inspiring revolution had been followed by a vicious downward spiral of cruel dictatorships. Elite *noirs* like Faustin Soulouque, François Duvalier, Jean-Claude Duvalier, and Jean-Bertrand Aristide all used an adapted version of Noiriste (Black nationalist) politics to justify their power, claiming that they had the right to rule because they were dark-skinned Blacks and promising they would rule in favour of Blacks. But all of these regimes were brutal in different ways, with informal armies directing violence against the poor (Rotberg 1997), and with elites using the state's resources to enrich themselves. As a result, Black liberation discourses have had little resonance with the masses (Castor 2006).

After the US occupation, a succession of Noiriste leaders – such as Dumarsais Estimé (1946–50) and Paul Magloire (1950–56) – were elected. Although they ran on a Noiriste platform as critics of American imperialism, they did little to improve the economic situation for Haitians (Girard 2010, 8). The successive Duvalier regimes of father and son – from 1957 to 1986 – continued to rule Haiti with extreme violence (Girard 2010, 110; Heinl and Heinl 2005, 539–624; Saint-Gérard 2004).[33] In 1957, François "Papa Doc" Duvalier outlawed civil society groups and associations; used his personal armed gangs, the Tontons Macoutes, to brutalize the opposition; and controlled foreign aid for his own personal use (Marquis 2007, 157).[34] His son, Jean-Claude "Baby Doc" Duvalier, continued his father's policies until his overthrow in 1986 (Farmer 1994, 19–21). The collapse in food production and increasing dependency on American imports resulted in the exodus of the rural poor to sprawling *bidonvilles* such as La Salines, Carrefour, and Cité Soleil (Port-au-Prince), which currently holds about three million people (Dupuy 2010, 196).

In the early 1950s, Jean-Bertrand Aristide – a Catholic priest inspired by liberation theology who came originally from the outskirts of Port Salut (in the southern part of the country) – relocated to the slums with his mother (a micro-entrepreneur, *ti machanns*). He was thus very much aware of the economic injustice against the *moun andeyo* (Girard 2010, 117; Robinson 2007, 28). According to Fatton (2007, 197), Aristide preached *tout moun se moun* (all human beings are human beings). At his St-Jean Bosco church in Bel Air, he started the *Ti legliz* (Kreyol for "Little Church") movement, where he rallied Blacks against the dictatorships of Jean-Claude Duvalier (1971–86) and later General Henri Namphy (1986–88) (Girard 2010, 117–22; Hallward 2010, 139; Robinson 2007, 29; *The Agronomist* [film] 2003). Namphy (1986–88) was aware that Aristide's supporters were mounting a formidable opposition against his corrupt and elitist regime, and in 1988 his soldiers led the St-Jean Bosco massacre against them, killing at least thirteen parishioners (Girard 2010, 117). Aristide's brand of Noirism grew among the marginalized, as well as among activists, such as the journalist Jean Dominique, who would be assassinated in 2000.[35] Aristide's *Ti legliz* developed into a political movement in the *bidonvilles*. In the 1990 election, his Front National pour le Changement et la Démocratie (later to become the Organisation Politiques Lavalas [OPL]) was the first democratically elected party to take power in Haiti (Fatton 2006, 19; Robinson 2007, 31).

In the early years of his presidency, Aristide embraced social and economic justice as a mean to rebuild civil society; this seemed to be a progressive form of Noiriste politics (Dupuy 2007, 1; Heinl and Heinl 2005; Rotberg 1997). On assuming power in 1991, Aristide's civilian government brought charges against the Tontons Macoutes and investigated the bank accounts of certain members of the elite. Aristide's reforms were met with opposition from the military and business elites in Port-au-Prince. After only eight months in office, Raoul Cédras, a light-skinned commander, overthrew Aristide and forced him into exile in the United States. US president Bill Clinton assisted Aristide's return to power in 1994, offering foreign aid in exchange for neoliberal economic reforms (Heinl and Heinl 2005, 719). Aristide lifted the interest rate ceiling on loans (which was 22% per annum) and was awarded with a generous foreign aid package from USAID (UNCDF 2003, 151).[36] At this time of liberalized markets and increased interest rates, commercial banks launched microfinance programs. However, these reforms were resisted by the local business elite and their families, who had benefited from high interest rates and felt threatened by these new pro-poor policies. They saw Aristide's reforms as a move towards redistributive taxes (Dupuy 2007, 113–120; Farmer 1994, 25).

Aristide was prohibited by the constitution from three consecutive terms as president; however, his comrade and OPL ally René Préval was elected in 1996. But once Préval was in office, their relationship deteriorated over Aristide's opposition to a number of proposed market reforms (Dupuy 2007, 200). Aristide broke away from the OPL and founded his own political party, Fanmi Lavalas (Family of the Flash Flood), to compete against the OPL. Immediately after he won the 2000 election, Aristide disbanded the army and police, which were controlled by business elites (who had worked to prevent his election). It is alleged that he set up in their place a secret paramilitary force called the *Chimères* (gangs),[37] made up of unemployed youth from the *bidonvilles* of Bel Air and Cité Soleil (Girard 2010, 192; Fatton 2007, 212; 2006, 21; Dupuy 2007, 21; *Les Chimères de Cité Soleil* 2007; *Human Rights Watch* 2004).[38]

Widespread kidnappings, extra-judicial killings, and corruption characterized governance under the second Aristide government (2000–4) (Fatton 2007, 210–12; *Human Rights Watch* 2004; *The Agronomist* 2003), as well as the Préval administration (2006–11). In 2004, US president George W. Bush's administration set out to force Aristide's resignation and paved the way for his controversial exile to South Africa (Fatton 2007, 206; Robinson 2007, 215). This external interference led by the Americans to oust Aristide remains controversial.[39] After the term of the US-appointed interim leader, Miami-based Gérard Latortue, ended, Préval was again re-elected in 2006. This period of political instability lit a fire under warring gangs, many of which splintered off into "cells" that fought one another other for turf and power (Girard 2010, 213).[40] Haiti is a dangerous place to live and work, and many people go missing and/or are assassinated for reporting malpractices of the state and its international partners or for trying to jolt the status quo (anonymous interviews, October 2010 and August to October 2011).

Haitian class conflicts are highly racialized, and this gravely affects ordinary people. In April 2008, rising food prices (many of the poor resorted to eating mud pies) led to protests and food riots in Pétionville and Centre-Ville (Pierre 2011). In 2010, fraudulent elections, riots, and tire burning were commonplace, and the slow rebuilding process following the 2010 earthquake led to frustrations being unleashed against the UN and other international organizations. Haitians were also angry over crimes allegedly perpetrated by the Mission des Nations Unis pour la Stabilisation en Haiti (MINUSTAH, the UN military force), whose troops were accused of raping women and children and causing the cholera epidemic (Amnesty Haiti Annual Report: 2012; Harvard School of Public Health 2011; Midy 2010). If these issues were not enough, in January 2011, ousted dictator "Baby Doc" Duvalier returned to the country for nebulous reasons; he was arrested on arrival and then released (Amnesty Annual Report 2012). Several months later, former president Jean-Bertrand Aristide returned to his luxurious Tabarre residence near the US Embassy (ibid.; Hossein 2012). In April 2011, Michel

"Sweet Micky" Martelly (a former *kompa* musician) was elected president in a run-off vote, and after much delay Laurent Lamothe was confirmed as prime minister on 16 May 2012.

Haiti's motto, *l'union fait la force* (unity is strength), reflects Haitians' awareness that they can achieve change through collaboration. Despite their neglect by the state, marginalized groups have followed democratic traditions by organizing in their own communities. In these limited political spaces, *moun andeyo* have resisted, forming social support groups, such as cooperatives, where the poor come together and pool resources and lend support to one another. Since 1937, long before the concept of microfinance existed, Haitians, inspired by African concepts of *kombit*, have been organizing local monies, creating vibrant cooperatives to meet their collective interests. By the time donor-funded microloan projects came to Haiti in the 1990s, Haitians were already familiar with microlending. It is Haiti's long experience with grassroots-style microbanking among socially conscious Blacks that makes its small business sector inclusive.

Guyana's Case

Guyana is the only anglophone country in South America, and it identifies itself culturally as Caribbean. It is one of the poorest countries in the English-speaking Caribbean region. This relatively small country has great diversity among its population of 756,000 (World Bank 2011), being composed of six recognized races (East Indians, Africans, Europeans, Amerindians [indigenous peoples], Chinese, and mixed race), as well as three main religions (Christianity, Hinduism, and Islam) (Hope 1985, 13; Smith 1964, 117). The 2002 National Census (2002, 2) found that the largest ethnic groups were East Indians at 43.5% and Africans at 30.2%, with mixed-race (*dougla* [African/Indian] and others) at 16.7%, Amerindians at 9.2%, and whites and Chinese less than 1% each.[41] This cultural diversity is rooted in the colonial and imperial experience. Guyana was first ruled by the Dutch (1580–1803) and later by the British (1803–1966) (Dalton 1885). These slave masters raped African female slaves and introduced a mixed-race group of white and Black. African male slaves were feared, belittled, and defined as lazy by white masters (Rodney 1981); female slaves were viewed as submissive and sexual.

The British planters relied on free labour and subsidies to make a profit from their rice and sugar estates. Many of the planters were wealthy upper-class people who hired overseers, often Irish and Scottish men from lower classes, to manage the slaves (Moore 1995). After slavery ended, between 1838 to 1917, the British continued operating the plantations by resorting to large-scale indentured labourer programs (Premdas 1995, 19). The colonial leaders and the planters thwarted African entrepreneurialism by importing cheap foreign labour to undermine markets. The British East India Trading Company imported Indians (called *coolies*) as workers, and they were the largest group of indentured servants, who worked the plantations for very little pay. In this way, white planters could avoid giving in to Africans' wage demands (Greenidge 2001). Mansru (2005, 68) argues that this importation of cheap migrant labour limited African emancipation, for the low wages accepted by the East Indian workers on sugar and rice plantations undercut the bargaining power of the freed Africans (Mansru 2005; St Pierre 1999; Singh 1996; Burrowes 1984; Rodney 1981; Nath 1950).

The freed slaves responded negatively to the Indian immigrants, not only because they undermined their bargaining power with the planters, but also because they regarded these foreign-born Indians as inferior due to their language and religions – Hinduism and Islam – which they saw as cultural attributes far from the Western ideal (Rodney 1981, 180). Leo Despres (1967, 66–75) makes the important point that East Indians held on to their culture and did not acculturate like Afro-Guyanese. This suited the planters, who were able to control the East Indians. The indentured servant program thus resulted in strong tensions between Africans and Indians.[42] But at the same time, the intermingling of these two dominant groups introduced another mixed-race category unique to Guyana (and Trinidad) – the *dougla* (offspring of Africans and Indians).

As migrants were imported into the labour force – following the end of slavery in 1833 and subsequent apprenticeships – the freed slaves began to pool their earnings from agricultural sales and wages to form cooperatives. It was through these informal banking groups that the Negro "village movement" grew (1838 to 1852). Guyanese historian Maurice St Pierre (1999, 69–70) reports that cooperatives became the only alternative for Blacks, who were denied financial services under colonial rule. According to Mathews and Danns (1980, 52–3), cooperatives helped the African slaves cope with the harsh environment. In 1914, freed slaves formed "task gangs," which organized into cooperatives – such as "Up and On Clubs," "Buying Clubs," and "Saving Unions" – to meet their livelihood needs. Buxton is an example of Africans coming together to buy title for land to establish a home for emancipated slaves (Greenidge 2001, 17; Daly 1974, 141; Smith 1964, 40).

Guyana's political history is a complicated one steeped in class interests and racial divisions. The dominant groups were largely excluded from participating in the formal economy (Young 1958; Stoby 1931; Dalton 1885). In colonial times, commercial banks like the Colonial Bank (later changed to Barclays, UK) and the British Guiana Bank (BGB) catered only to white planters and later to the "whitened" indentured laborers, such as the Portuguese and Chinese, who later became peddlers, shopkeepers, and merchants (Moore 1987; Young 1958).[43] By the 1880s, the Portuguese were the retail giants and could secure credit from European banks in ways that Afro-Guyanese could not (Premdas 1995, 21; Duncan 1990, 17–39; Rodney 1981, 33; Daly 1974, 166; Despres 1967, 63; Smith 1964, 78).

When the first bank to assist slaves, the Post Office Savings Bank, was founded in 1828 (Daly 1974, 166), it could not meet the demand. By the time of independence, banking had become a contentious issue: the whitened business elites had access to finance, while the majority of citizens – both East Indian and African Guyanese – did not (Smith 1964). The current system is thus rooted in a racialized colonial context that played the races against one another (especially Indians against Africans) (Garner 2008). The Portuguese and Chinese, who had originally been imported as indentured servants, transitioned into the merchant class once the British started importing cheap labour from India (St Pierre 1999; Moore 1995; 1987; Despres 1967; Smith 1964). And after the English left with the coming of independence in 1966, those whitened elites who stayed – again, the Portuguese and Chinese – inherited political and economic power.

Modern-day politics are firmly rooted in the racially polarized politics of Guyana's past. In 1966, two leaders had emerged: the Afro-Guyanese Linden Forbes Sampson Burnham and the Indo-Guyanese Cheddi Jagan had forged an alliance to end British colonial control. Jagan, Guyana's father of independence and a person from a humble social background, saw an opportunity to use the country's racial demographics for his own agenda. He called on the Indo-Guyanese to "*apanjaht*" – Hindi for "vote for your own kind" (Nettles 2007, 63; St Pierre 1999, 138; Despres 1967, 228). Despres (1967) explains that for the Indo-Guyanese, *apanjaht* also refers to the cultural habits formed through racial identity, religion, and cultural norms. Moore (1995) further points out that culture gave groups an identity and consciousness that allowed them to define themselves in relation to other groups.

This sort of cultural awareness created deep divisions between racial groups (ibid.). Jagan and Burnham together created the People's

Progressive Party (PPP); but by 1955, this arrangement had broken down, and Burnham broke away from the PPP to create the People's National Congress (PNC) for Afro-Guyanese (Gibson 2006; Trotz 2004; Singh 1996; Despres 1967; Smith 1964). By the 1960s, race riots were shaping the country's politics. On "Black Friday" in 1962, people rioted against new taxes brought in by the PPP (Singh 1996, 77; Hope 1985, 50), and by 1963–4, racial violence between Jagan's Indian base and Burnham's Afro-Guyanese constituency was growing worse (Premdas 1995; Hope 1985; Despres 1967) – between 1962 and 1964, at least 175 people were killed and thousands more injured, and hundreds of women were raped (Trotz 2004; Burrowes 1984). In the 1960s, Guyanese of Portuguese and Chinese descent emigrated elsewhere, and this gave the Indo-Guyanese an opportunity to rise as the dominant racial group in business.

Forbes Burnham's 21-year authoritarian regime (1964–85) was characterized by socialist rhetoric and clientelist practices (Burrowes 1984). By the late 1960s, Guyana had become a single-party government led by the minority ethnic group, the Afro-Guyanese, to the exclusion of the large Indian population. Burnham embraced nationalist development in order to confront the foreign-owned enterprises that dominated the economy in the 1970s, such as Bookers Stores Limited, Geddes Grant Limited, and JP Santos and Company Limited (Burrowes 1984, 295; Davis 1979; Smith 1964, 60). Bookers, the largest of these British firms, and referred to as "Bookers Guyana" since the colonial period, finally left in 1976 under Burnham (Sookdeo 1997; Burrowes 1984; Smith 1964). Burnham's government also nationalized sugar and bauxite companies, such as the American company Reynolds and Canada's Alcan (Burrowes 1984, 280–4). The domination by state-owned enterprises discouraged local Indian businessmen from investing in the country, which led to mass emigration (Greenidge 1981).

Burnham's nationalization projects fit with his socialist political agenda. He also drew on the African legacy of cooperative development as part of his agenda. He viewed cooperatives as the mechanism needed "to make the small man a real man" (Burrowes 1984, 246). In his 1970 law, the "Declaration of Sophia," he declared that Guyana was a "cooperative republic" and that cooperatives were the vehicle for economic empowerment (Barrow-Giles 2002, 210). It was his intention to draw on cooperative economics to appeal to Guyanese people of African descent. But his avowed goal – "to make the small man a real man" – never came to pass, for his regime was guided by an educated elite who were detached from the common-day issues of poor Guyanese (Barrow-Giles 2002; Burrowes 1984). Despres (1967, 158–60) has made the important point that the colonial government had founded the cooperative movement in 1945, but this involvement by the state did not make it free and voluntary. Lear K. Mathews and George Danns argue in *Communities and Development in Guyana* (1980) that cooperatives in the country were managed by either colonial administrators or local politicians; they never emerged from the people themselves. In Haiti, cooperatives were people-driven (see below); in Guyana, cooperative development was top-down and elite-driven. That movement may have assisted some poor Blacks, but overall, it was not grassroots in its orientation (Raghunandan and Kistow 1998; Develtere 1993; Lear and Danns 1980; Despres 1967).

Burnham's socialist plans included nationalizing banks and forming them into cooperative banks. In the 1970s, he established a member-owned bank, the Guyana Cooperative Agricultural Bank (later the Guyana Cooperative Agricultural and Industrial Development Bank [GAIBANK]) in order to reach Afro-Guyanese engaged in small-scale agricultural production and trade. In the 1980s and 1990s, GAIBANK (renamed the Guyana National Cooperative Bank under Jagan in 1992) was a pioneer microlender for excluded Afro and Indo business people (Sookdeo 1997). Some view these cooperative banks as the country's first microlenders.

Cooperatives have played a seemingly prominent role in Guyana's history; yet Mathews and Danns (1980, 53) have found that cooperatives have never been an effective strategy – either under colonization or after independence – to assist in the economic development of the people. Raghunandan and Kistow (1998) argue that the Burnham government's subsidies to cooperative banks allowed him to misuse funds for his own personal gain, resulting in financially unsustainable cooperatives. Guyanese scholars seem to agree that there was top-down elite control of economic resources; this is why many Guyanese people I interviewed were reluctant to participate in cooperatives. GAIBANK loans were never repaid by borrowers, and the institution folded. Because it was the government that founded and oversaw the cooperatives, they have not had a good reputation. In 2011, rural cooperatives such as the Thrift and Credit Cooperative in the Essequibo Islands became popular because of their low costs for obtaining credit. Urban-based credit unions – such as National Cooperative Credit Union Limited, Guyana Defence Force Credit Union, Transport Amalgamated

Credit Union, and the City of Georgetown Credit Union – do not offer microloans and have low memberships. Indeed, the stigma attached to cooperative banks persists to this day.

The Black urban masses, who had been duped into believing that the Burnham government would help them, eventually resisted his paternalistic power and corrupt regime (Burrowes 1984). Guyanese scholar Greenidge (1981) argues that the reach of state power had led to rampant fear. The state controlled the private sector and community development. Burnham banned the importation of staples important to the East Indian diet (as well as the wider population), such as flour, split peas, and potatoes (Mars 1995). The harm caused by this political interference expanded beyond the Indian-owned import businesses, and eventually affecting Burnham's Afro-Guyanese supporters (*Kaeiteur News*, 11 December 2011). His corruption deepened an economic crisis in the early 1980s, and poor Afro-Guyanese turned to huckstering (trading) as a means to survive as well as to resist the political handouts of an oppressive regime.

Educated Blacks who questioned Burnham's undemocratic regime became political targets. One of the best-known critics was Walter Rodney, an Afro-Guyanese intellectual who had formed the leftist Working People's Alliance (WPA) (Rodney 1996, 60). Rodney claimed that the Burnham regime's "divide and conquer strategy" was the same that had been used by white colonizers to control African slaves and East Indian indentured servants. He argued that Jagan and Burnham had abused the poor for their own political ends: Jagan was using anti-Black messages to frighten the rural landowning (but poor) Indians into voting for him, while Burnham rallied the Afro-Guyanese to support him. To counter these race politics, Rodney called for an inclusive nationalism, one that would include the two largest racial groups (Dupuy 1996; Premdas 1995; *In the Sky's Wild Noise* [film] 1983). His proposed alliance between the races threatened the political elites, who knew that they would lose their power, which was based on race, if voters united along class lines. It is widely believed that Burnham's fear of Rodney's political opposition resulted in the latter's murder in 1980.

Rodney's death frustrated the citizenry, and state-sanctioned violence escalated against them. Rampant murders, kidnappings, corruption, and serious financial problems led to Guyana's ostracism by Western nations. Clientelism and extra-judicial killings alienated American support: for example, in 1982, USAID cancelled a $15 million loan and the US ambassador was recalled (Majeed 2005, 25). Years of mismanagement and an atrocious human rights record also resulted in the massive emigration of skilled human resources (Singh 1996, 129). Finally, in 1985, change came, in the form of a new government led by Desmond Hoyte (1985–92). Part of the new president's mandate was to formulate policies for micro and small businesses and adopt structural adjustment programs (SAPs), thus moving the country towards market liberalization (Mars 1995, 175). Several microlending programs emerged under Hoyte's government: the Small Business Credit Initiative; Commonwealth Youth Credit; Mothers Development Window; and the Women's Affairs Bureau Revolving Loan Fund (Long 1990).[44] All of these programs had a special focus on poor women and had the goal of reducing poverty. Within a few years, however, these organizations fell apart as a result of mismanagement. Jagan's PPP took power again in 1992, and his policies shifted their focus back to large businesses. With the regime change in 1992, the Indo-led PPP under Jagan licensed East Indian-run banks such as the Guyana Bank for Trade and Industry (GBTI) and the Demerara Bank. By the 1990s, the local banking sector was increasingly comprised of Indian bankers who catered to the Indian merchant class. The Initiative for Private Enterprise Development (IPED) and its founder Yesu Persaud received significant funding during this time, including a $2.8 million grant from USAID and the Pan American Development Foundation (PADF) to launch microfinance activities (Sookdeo 1997; Duncan 1990, 27–8; Long 1990).

For 23 years, PPP administrations (Cheddi Jagan [1992–7], Janet Jagan [1997–9], Bharrat Jagdeo [1999–2011], and Donald Ramotar [2011–15]) have been allocating resources in a racially biased way to the Indo-Guyanese. In May 2015, Guyana's multiracial opposition, the Partnership for National Unity and Alliance for Change coalition, led by David Granger, won the national election, breaking the ruling Indo-Guyanese PPP's 23-year grip on power (*The Guardian* 2015). This new government is a change from the communal politics that has controlled the country for decades.

Guyanese scholar Michael Scott (2007, 69) argues that Guyana's democracy is based on racial interests – on what he calls "communal democracy" – where people are organized along ethno-political lines.[45] As mentioned above, under Cheddi Jagan, the government in 1992 diverted resources to rural East Indian communities by shifting benefits such as housing, loans, and employment from the Afro-Guyanese to the Indo-Guyanese (Scott 2007, 40). Jagan continued this race-based patronage and indeed increased Indian political extremism (Greenidge 2001). In 1997, Jagan's American-born wife, Janet Jagan, took office after

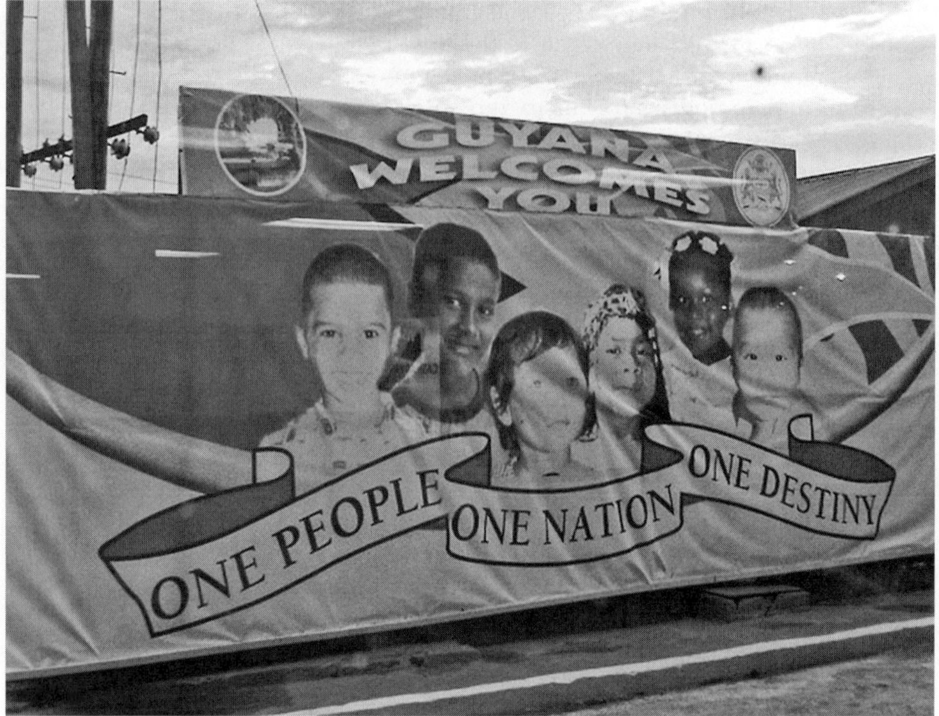

Figure 2.1 A state banner (Guyana) depicting the motto "One People, One Nation, One Destiny" shows children from each of the country's six races.

her husband's death and intensified the racialized system. Caribbean scholar Percy Hintzen (1989, 105) found that "clientelism is expected to play a significant role in elite support particularly under conditions where regime politics and programs have had a negative consequence for major segments of the population." In this way, the Jagans continued to practise patronage to secure their power.

From 1999 to 2011, the Jagdeo-led government turned down development projects when funds did not go to the Indians or to the Amerindians.[46] Like Burnham's politics of the past, PPP politics are very much rooted in the distribution of rewards based on race, with Indian political elites reportedly benefiting from kickbacks through contracts (Gibson 2006, 374). Wilson, Cummings, and Marshall (2007, 101, 110) have also reported that the state allocates development projects to areas according to racial category, and that Black people, *dougla*, and mixed-raced people continue to live in slums in intolerable conditions, with only shared sanitary facilities and no indoor plumbing. In this racialized context, no sense of a shared national identity truly exists. Moore (1995, 11) has argued that Guyana is not a harmonious melting pot; rather, tensions between racial groups run high. Moore (1987, 109) argues that there is a structural pluralism in place that subjects certain racial groups such as Afro-Guyanese to indignities. Thus, the country's motto – "One people, one nation, one destiny" (Figure 2.1) – is a hoax.

Microlenders today make resources available to their allies to further their own political aspirations, excluding outsiders who do not belong to the ruling racial group. An Indo-Guyanese–led regime has no interest in working in slums filled with supporters of the opposition party. This biased allocation of state resources has left one of the nation's poorest groups, the Afro-Guyanese, unable to access vital economic resources. Local dissenters are few, and those critics who dare publish stories against the state and the president are subject to violence and humiliation (University of Guyana, interviews April and May 2010; anonymous interview, date withheld on purpose).[47] Jagdeo's regime (1999–2011) allegedly had links to the narcotics trade, extra-judicial killings, and grave human rights abuses, such as death squads that murdered Afro-Guyanese (Amnesty Report 2010; Gibson 2006, 375; Gibson 2005, 41; Majeed 2005, 97), and citizens are aware of the potential consequences of criticizing the state (Kissoon 2010a, 2010b). In this context, microfinance programs, controlled mainly by Indo-Guyanese, are unlikely to be regarded as empowerment tools by Afro-Guyanese users.

Conclusion

Caribbean political history reveals that slavery and colonization produced a colour-coded hierarchy based on race and class. Mixed-race or brown- (usually light)-skinned people have sometimes inherited power and status from their forefathers and colonial masters. Certainly some of the educated Blacks in these societies have tested the system, but many have conformed to it. Many microfinance managers in Jamaica, Guyana, and Trinidad have chosen to ignore the powerful impact of historically rooted class and race based oppressions within Caribbean society, and this has perpetuated marginalization.

Exclusionary lending in the electoral democracy of Jamaica is tied to class-based clientelist politics, and Guyana's and Trinidad's political parties are class-based racialized entities that divide black and brown people. In Haiti, lenders acknowledge a political past and present steeped in both class and racial conflicts, one in which violent regimes have alienated the *moun andeyo*, and these lenders have become activists who are fighting to democratize financing at the community level. In some ways, the brutal and repressive cultural politics witnessed in Haiti, as well as in Grenada, have forced people to develop their own coping systems in the form of informal cooperatives (Fatton 2007; Montasse 1983).

Each country's response to the politics of disparity has contributed to the different ways in which financial resources for the poor are (mis) used and (mis)managed. Jamaica's democratic tradition, relatively strong trade unions, private property laws, and cooperative practices would seem to be conducive to economic development. Moreover, Jamaica's motto, "Out of many, one people," signals a strong sense of national identity (Thomas 2004, 90). Yet Jamaican society is deeply divided along class lines and to some extent also by colour. Years of Big Men, usually brownings, using power to control Blacks in the ghettos have resulted in the breakdown of trust, and *hustlas* view the privileged brownings running micro-economic development programs in the slums with suspicion.

In Guyana, creole elites replicated the system of the British colonizers and organized ethnic political parties. An Indo-Guyanese–dominated banking environment has left microlenders in a questionable position of power, and understandably, Afro-Guyanese, who have come to expect race discrimination, do not trust these Indo-Guyanese microbankers. In Trinidad's shanty towns, there is a strong sense of racial and political bias. "Boss Lady," who runs her family-owned business in scrap metal in Beetham Gardens (east Port of Spain) explained to me:

> Me, I neva went to NEDCO [the state-run microfinance program]. It's a racial ting and hard to get [a loan], they just bring you down. People der [staff persons are] stigmatizing and [they] let de coolie [Indo-Trinidadians] to get through. Dey only pretending to help us. This government in power is the worse kind [in terms of racial politics]." (interview, 24 June 2013)

As "Boss Lady" suggests in the above quote, microfinance lending in her country is a class-based politicized institution working to help

Indo-Trinidadian voters, not African Trinidadians. In Trinidad, "knife and fork" Indo-Trinidadians are the wealthy and educated ones who wield the decision-making authority in microfinance and who exclude Afro-Trinidadians, like "Boss Lady," in the east Port of Spain shanty towns.

Haiti's race and class politics operate within a weak, undemocratic state, with interference from American aid and political leaders, especially since the post-earthquake reconstruction process began in 2010. Since Haiti's revolution in 1804, the state has continually engaged in violence against its population. Predatory elites and external forces have colluded and acted brutally against the *moun andeyo*, with the result being persistent underdevelopment. Haiti's organizing from below within a complex political environment is what makes its story unique. Grenada is the "spice isle," an English-speaking island of 100,000 people infamous for its military coup in 1979, when Maurice Bishop and the New Jewel Movement took over the government. Similar to Haiti in this regard, it is the only English-speaking Caribbean country to have experienced a coup d'état and state of emergency, as well as a US invasion and occupation. Grenada's intense political history can explain why the Grenadian people are heavily engaged in credit unions, much like in Haiti. After a long series of oppressive regimes, the *moun andeyo* in Haiti have had to turn inwards and develop their own self-help groups. An authoritarian political history would not seem to augur well for a vibrant microfinance sector; yet Haitians have managed to sustain cooperative movements under harsh political environments. The Haitian microfinance leaders I met acknowledged that the corrupt political and business environment had pushed them towards more activist-oriented lending.

The political histories of each of the main cases – Jamaica, Guyana, and Haiti – suggest that educated elites have had both political and personal control of the urban poor's access to money, and this is certainly true in the shadow cases of Trinidad and Grenada as well. In these different cultural contexts, scepticism about the empowering potential of today's microlending is understandable. Of all the countries I consider in this book, Haiti is the most inspiring; there, excluded people living in conditions of authoritarianism and economic apartheid have organized on their own. So, too, in Grenada, entrepreneurs have grounded themselves in cooperative systems beyond the reach of the elites. As a result of the inner strength to organize into groups without any support, lenders view microfinance as a political tool for the poor to counteract economic and political exclusion. Meanwhile, citizens of African descent who live in the slums of Jamaica, Trinidad, and Guyana distrust microbanking institutions and staff. In the next chapter, I further explore these three cases, examining the cultural biases (gender, racial, and class) that have led to people's distrust as well as the malfunctioning of microfinance programs.

Chapter 3

Cultural Politics, Bias, and Microfinance

The common perception is that microfinance can do no wrong. This is because it promises to achieve a double bottom line: first, the financial sustainability of the lending institution, and second, the social benefit of providing loans to excluded business people. The 2013 version of *The New Microfinance Handbook*, published by the World Bank's Consultative Group to Assist the Poor(est), continues to argue that microfinance is inclusive finance. Despite recent crises within the industry, the handbook fails to acknowledge that microfinance can be used as a tool to marginalize and alienate entrepreneurs who do not conform to market politics. In 2012, *Confessions of a Microfinance Heretic*, a tell-all book by industry insider Hugh Sinclair, questioned the integrity of the professionals within the microfinance industry. Although Hugh Sinclair (2012), an insider to MFIs, does not go as far as to criticize the privilege of elite power over the poor, his arguments do suggest there is a class bias active within the microfinance industry.

To date, no one has examined the intersection of identities (race, class, and gender) in microfinance, nor the fact that staff people arbitrarily choose the people with whom they will bank and that these processes are influenced by their own cultural biases – a situation that does not necessarily effect sound business practice. Microfinance literature has not analysed cultural bias in the industry, nor has it considered the motivations of the very people in charge of this worldwide phenomenon (Hossein 2015). This chapter advances new thinking on the cultural politics of race, class, and gender dynamics and illuminates how the interplay of these identities leads to the subjugation and exclusion of many entrepreneurs. I argue that a class-based racism in microfinance dominates in the Jamaican, Guyanese, and Trinidadian cases and that persons of African descent are aware of the blatant discrimination against them.

Identity Politics in Microfinance

Historically, banks in the West Indies have catered to business elites and foreign interests and ignored the business and entrepreneurial needs of the poor. The idea of microbanking emerged fairly early on in the Caribbean region because of the exclusion under slavery and colonization. Slaves carried out market activities and engaged in informal banking (Mintz 1955; Witter 1989; Wong 1996; St Pierre 1999). Faye V. Harrison's work (1988), for example, reveals that Jamaican higglers (female traders) have struggled since the time of slavery to carry out livelihood activities. Haitian American anthropologist Gina Ulysse (2007, 83) has found evidence of an abundance of higgler entrepreneurship in modern-day Jamaica, including the organizing of informal banks.

The Caribbean region has millions of people engaged in small business. So when US president Barack Obama invested $100 million in a microfinance fund to support small business development in the Caribbean, despite its lagging results compared to other regions, this was most appreciated and supported by the region's state leaders. While there is little consensus on why Caribbean microlending has generally not fared well, scholarly reviews of microfinance, particularly of the Caribbean region, have failed to explore the role of cultural factors in microfinance (Honig 1998a, 1998b; Chalmers and Wenner 2001; Lashley 2004a, 2004b; Daley-Harris 2004, 2005, 2006; Westley 2005; Economist Intelligence Unit, October 2008, 10). Caribbean people are entrepreneurial and have had to turn to small business; however, financial programs in support of this sector have generally been limited.

As mentioned above, the issue of how identity politics affects microfinance allocations is absent in such works as Sinclair's *Microfinance Heretic*, Roodman's *Due Diligence* (2012a), and Bateman's *Confronting Microfinance* (2011). In fact, the microfinance industry as a whole has failed to examine the people in positions of power who allocate money to the needy. Political elites, for their part, are not overly concerned about access issues, and they remain impressed by the use of microfinance as a tool (Hossein 2009, 2015). Reports often analyse administrative bottlenecks in the system, but these fail to explain the cultural issues that may be affecting people's access to finance (Tennant 2008; UWI 2006; Holden 2005). The Inter-American Development Bank's

(IDB) Caribbean Capacity Project I (Carib Cap I) focuses on increasing the capacity of staff people, yet it makes no mention of internal cultural politics stunting its outreach. While technical know-how can certainly affect performance, these challenges are not the only ones limiting outreach to the slums. The focus on technical aspects seems a convenient distraction from what is really going on; that is, that the class, racial, and gender biases of the people working in the social economy negatively affect inclusive economic development.

It seems unthinkable that social organizations devoted to the betterment of people would unjustly discriminate against borrowers in need of these financial services, but they do. In the Caribbean context, local managers often come from a class (and racial) background that is culturally distinct from the majority of the borrowers, and this affects decision-making when it comes to allocating resources. Business people accept that some degree of screening must be conducted in lending programs, but 88% (268 out of 305) of the business people I interviewed believed they were being excluded by microfinance managers from accessing loans due to their neighbourhood ("area") and social class ("where they come from"). Trinidad's partisan state monopoly uses microfinance to disburse monies to party supporters without any intention of recuperating these loans. People working in microfinance operations often exclude certain people for reasons of personal prejudice, thereby exacerbating local conflicts. Decision-makers in microfinance are usually socially removed from borrowers who are seeking a microloan – that is, they often do not share class origins or know their lived experience. Ananya Roy (2010) posits that there is a powerful group of people in microfinance who determine how these loans are organized. In fact, these managers, who are distinct from the borrowers, often view credit as a form of charity and underestimate the capacity of these business people.

In the 2000s, third-sector organizations in the Caribbean have emerged with the aim of reaching the economically active poor with financial services. Financial institutions within the region require a licence from the Ministry of Finance and are supervised by the Jamaican Central Bank. Institutions that are not classified as "banks" (such as social-economic organizations) are regulated by separate legislation. Microfinance staff people are highly educated managers (usually with university degrees), and in many cases they are better trained than the average banker. But despite investments and staffing, lenders in Jamaica, Guyana, and Trinidad reach, at most, 10% of the demand.

In Jamaica, of 412,600 owner accounts (entrepreneurs in the informal sector), only 40,000 people accessed microfinance (STATIN 2008; Johnson 2008). In Guyana, of 58,327 business people, a mere 5,000 accessed microloans (Navajas and Tejerina 2006).

Caribbean microbanking is stunted by cultural politics. In Jamaica, women dominate as senior managers and staff people in microfinance, and an anti-male bias emerges when men from downtown slums are excluded from economic programs. Men are well aware of the bias against them and perceive male loan officers as more sensitive to their situation. This came out in interviews in Jamaica, with one vendor stating:

> Prefer a man officer who can deal wid mi. Yuh can say: "Bredrin try and do someting fi mi." Men fas a say dey know someone in 'ere. Man [loan officers are] more relax and can talk to yuh. Man talk free patois and nah care, woman [loan officers] inna der don't like patois ... inna di office. (Translation: Men want male loan officers. Male loan officers are more approachable and more likely to make you feel welcome and let you know they know someone from your community. Male officers will talk in Jamaican Patois [broken English] whereas female loan officers will not speak patois in an office environment.) (interview, "Clifton," age 48, saltfish and crackers vendor, Arnett Gardens, Jamaica)

Sexism in microfinance is not obvious at first glance, because microcredit programs focus on poor women. But female borrowers argue that they are actually *more* at risk when men are overlooked for loans, as this can lead to domestic abuse. This abuse, which cannot be justified on any grounds, indicates that microlending models that privilege women make these women vulnerable to abuse at the household level. In Guyana, Indo-Guyanese bankers dominate microfinance organizations and routinely deny loans to Afro-Guyanese, especially women. In Trinidad, microbankers are partisan and adhere to government policies that redirect resources away from Afro-Trinidadians in east Port-of-Spain. All three cases thus demonstrate that cultural bias affects microbanking processes.

In this chapter, I draw on six years (2007–13) of empirical research, during which time I interviewed 461 people in Jamaica, Guyana, and Trinidad, as well as regional experts in Barbados, Panama, Canada, and the United States. As noted in Table 3.1, 62% (sample size of 188) of the entrepreneurs I met with were women. Stakeholders and bankers

Table 3.1 Interview data from research (2007–13)

Method	Jamaica	Guyana	Trinidad	Regional	Total	Per cent
Number of micro-entrepreneurs in focus groups	77	6	0		83	
Individual interviews with entre-preneurs (average 45 min.)	156	23	43		222	
Female business people	146	19	23		188	62%
Total entrepreneurs	233	29	43		305	66%
Individual interviews with stakeholders	46	39	14	10	109	
Individual interviews with bankers and MF experts	28	11	4	4	47	
Female subjects interviewed	191	35	35	4	265	57%
Total sample	307	79	61	14	461	

Source: Author, interviews and focus groups, May 2007–July 2013.

interviewed accounted for 157 of the total sample (author's survey data, August 2009). Lenders accounted for 32 people, and at least 42 stakeholders were interviewed.[1] Most of the interviewees were women – 265 (or 57%). Overall, then, a strong female voice is present in this study.

Jamaica and Microfinance Exclusion

In Kingston, Jamaica, 96% (293) of the small entrepreneurs interviewed were very dark-skinned persons of African heritage who demonstrated distrust towards the highly educated lenders (see Table 3.1 above). A sharp class division makes it hard for residents or managers on either side to feel comfortable in the social and geographic space of the other, regardless of skin colour (Gray 2004, 17). The prevalence of this class divide was illustrated to me by a dark-skinned Afro-Jamaican at the Planning Institute of Jamaica (PIOJ), who admitted to me that she would never work in the garrisons – that is, the slums – because she was "afraid of the place [and people]." Furthermore, she confided, "you are going to places that many Jamaicans never go all their lives." The fact that middle-class Afro-Jamaicans avoid the garrisons was underlined by another microfinance expert (who cannot be named), who claimed she never goes downtown even though she is active in designing loan programs for the poor. Correspondingly, downtown residents who come uptown to the historical landmark Devon House (a restored colonial home) are uneasy in this setting. Both sides appear to have only

Figure 3.1 Jamaican women in the microfinance industry (Author's survey data 2009)

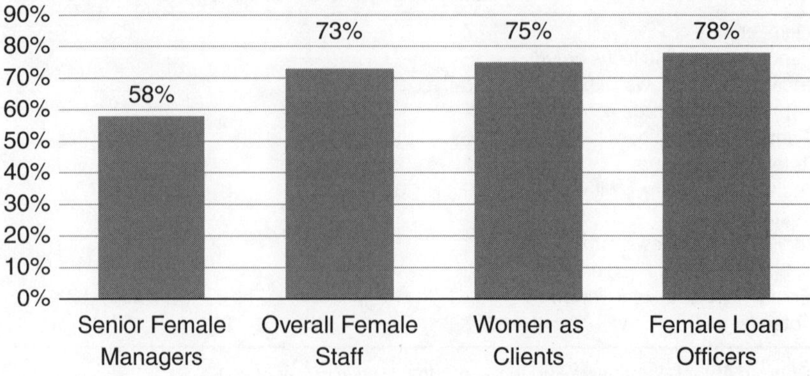

limited knowledge of the other. As shown in Figure 3.1, a significant number of lenders (35%, 11) are located in the exclusive commercial district of New Kingston (near Knutsford Boulevard), far from the residences of the majority of micro and small entrepreneurs.

The uptown/downtown divide in Kingston is a clear geographical separation (see Figure 3.2) that reinforces distrust between the microlenders and business people (Hossein 2015; Gray 2004). One CEO at a microbank justified his (uptown) location by stating that "a New Kingston office is prestige for them [*hustlas*] to come here [uptown] and to sit

Figure 3.2 Location of microlenders (2009)

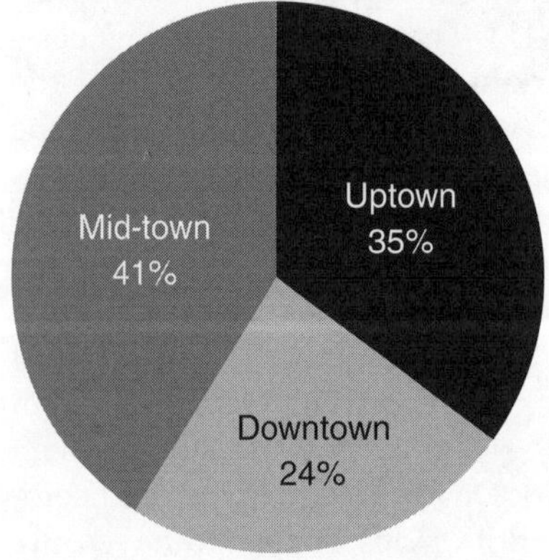

in the AC [air conditioning] and relax at the bank" (interview, 9 March 2009). My own findings suggest that entrepreneurs want convenience and to avoid the cost and time of travelling outside of their area by robo' taxi.

The Jamaican case includes the top 23 microfinance organizations, which cumulatively reached 58,589 clients (as of August 2009).[2] The data reveal that Jamaican women have made inroads into male-dominated banking jobs: at least 75% of the microfinance clients and 73% of the lenders are women, of which 78% are female loan officers who earn between US$9,534 and $20,000 a year, excluding bonuses (interview, manager at Jamaica National Small Business Loans Limited, Jamaica, February 2009). These bankers are educated Afro-Jamaicans (75%, 24) with an average age of 51 years, and nearly all lenders (96%, 30 out of 32) have an upper-class social and economic background – that is, an uptown background/residence – and a tertiary education that, collectively, sets them apart from the poorer classes.

Mullings (2005, 1–5) shows that the employment of middle-class Jamaican women as managers in banks has increased the participation of educated women in the workforce; but at the same time, this feminization of managers has increased the social power of *browning* (light-skinned) women. Increasing the number of female staff has not led to gender inclusiveness in microfinance institutions, and managers in these cases have limited first-hand knowledge of the slums.[3] Gem, a 48-year-old cake seller in Maxfield Park, Kingston, Jamaica, made the following observation:

> Small loan place need to know wi. Wi know to look wi pickney and deal wid money. Dem nah know wi . . . Nuff person inna di bank tink dem betta dan lowa class. (Translation: Microfinance institutions need to know that we can take care of our children and manage our finances. They [microfinance persons] don't know us. Many bankers think they are better than the lower classes.)

Because social class is the predominant source of division, it is not surprising that within the social economy, certain programs are coopted and organized according to class interests (Kamat 2002). In her quote above, Gem, who lives in a downtown slum, captures the frustration that many of the micro and small business people feel toward microfinance organizations that are supposedly meant to assist them. They feel that the condescending and privileged managers who run these programs are biased against them because they are poor and often of darker skin. Even though the majority of individuals running MFIs are Afro-Jamaican and female, poor Jamaicans often (mis)label them as *brownings* because of their middle-class status – again illustrating how class-laden issues affect microlending in downtown Kingston.

In diverse cultural contexts, including the Caribbean, gender must be studied in relation to other identities such as race and class. When microfinance programs focus exclusively on women, men are left out of the programs, which can put women in a precarious position (Rankin 2002, 18; Montgomery 1996, 300). As mentioned above, the fact that there are more female managers in Jamaican microbanking has not made allocation more inclusive. Female privilege in microlending benefits only certain types of women and negatively affects allocation (besides significantly complicating relations between poor women at the local level). Men and certain women remain on the fringes of lending resources because of the inherent biases of the educated middle-class female lenders, who subscribe to a colonial mentality (see Figure 3.3 for the racial breakdown of lenders).

A number of the microbanking agencies have had non-Blacks managing them to assist people who are of African descent. For example, in 2009 the state-owned microfinance programs were led by a Chinese Jamaican, Vivian Chin of Micro Investment Development Agency (MIDA), created under Michael Manley's PNP party in 1991; and an Indo-Jamaican, Carmen Lowers of the Self-Start Fund (SSF), started by Edward Seaga's JLP. In February 2009, the JLP administration awarded US$1.7 million to the Jamaican Business Development Agency (JBDC,

Figure 3.3 Race of Jamaican microlenders in 2009 (32 subjects interviewed).

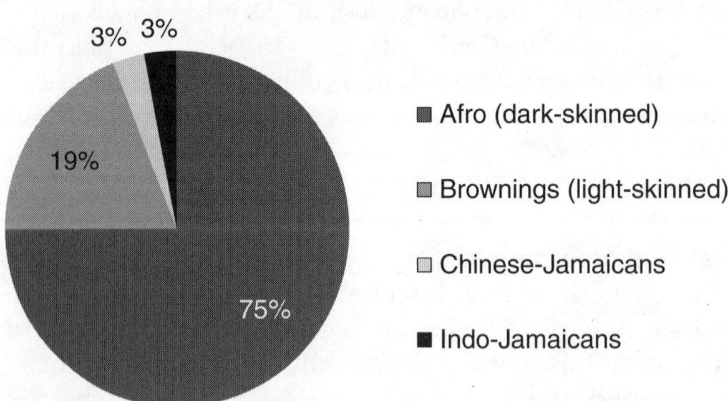

a state agency), headed by a Harvard-educated browning woman, Valerie Veira, to pilot microloans.

Many of the issues residents in the shantytowns encounter because of where they live (such as joblessness) are not issues experienced by the people managing microfinance organizations. One entrepreneur from a political stronghold told me, "Yuh come fram 11, 12, 13, 14, yuh can't get dem money [you will not get a loan]."[4] In Denham Town, Puncy, a 54-year-old business woman, believes that before she even applies for a loan, the workers have already "stereotype that wi won't pay back." Almost all lenders (99%, 73) acknowledged systemic discrimination against slum dwellers, yet even they do not hire people from the downtown areas. Others less overtly set qualifications that are out of reach for most slum dwellers. For example, a leading microlender, JNSBLL, requires loan officers to own a car and possess both a university degree and advanced computer skills (interview, microfinance director, 13 March 2009; interview, credit union manager, 24 February 2009). Most of the poor cannot meet these requirements.

Microfinance managers often simply do not trust or like the people from these marginalized areas. A senior microfinance professional (who is non-Black) justified such exclusion is this way: "Persons from downtown may collude with one another against the program. I just can't work with *them people*" (interview, 15 April 2009). Some lenders assume that residents from the same socio-economic class can collectively thwart the program by failing to make borrowers repay loans or by conspiring against the program. However, one can also see that loan officers who do not come from the slums bring prejudices with them in their professional interactions with these communities that do not bode well for people on the receiving end of the loans. This lack of trust works both ways. A JNSBLL client from Tivoli rightfully asked, "How does a young gyal fram uptown know [about] life 'ere?" (Translation: How does a loans officer who is of middle-class background from the uptown Kingston area know about life in the poor urban areas in downtown Kingston?) While middle-class Jamaicans are hesitant to discuss race, people downtown – that is, those who live in the slums – debate race and class politics continually. Very dark skin colour or kinky hair texture are reasons for discrimination. Comments such as "If I had pretty hair [or] a nice colour (meaning lighter-skin), I would get a loan" were common. Table 3.2 documents discrimination against social class (reflected in neighbourhood of residence, language, and education), race (including hair and skin colour), and gender.

Table 3.2 Types of discrimination reported by Jamaican micro-entrepreneurs

	Maxfield Park	Whitfield Town	Arnett Gardens	Denham Town	Rosetown	Tivoli Gardens	Total
In-depth interviews	22	29	33	15	31	26	156
Class (e.g., location, patois, education)	9	8	13	6	16	14	66
Race (e.g., race, hair, skin colour)	6	12	3	0	2	1	24
Gender	3	4	5	0	1	3	16
Anti-male discrimination %	100%	100%	83%	60%	73%	57%	75%
Discrimination %	82%	83%	64%	40%	61%	69%	68%

Source: Author's data, interviews, 2009

Business people accept that some degree of screening must be conducted in lending programs, but 68% (158 out of 233) of the business people interviewed believe that they are excluded by microfinance managers from accessing loans because of neighbourhood ("area") and social class ("where they come from"). However, the stigma of who is "bad" is far more severe for men (Gray 2004, 103–4). A community leader from West Kingston said that "all men are lumped together as bad and criminal" (interview, 29 September 2009), and indeed, all the male entrepreneurs interviewed in Maxfield Park (100%, 35) and Whitfield Town (100%, 29) felt that an anti-male bias affected their access to credit. So, in an ironic twist, the very target group of the most marginalized (e.g., Black men from the ghettos) feel that microlenders discriminate against them.

Female business people vouched to me that staff people perceive "man fram inna di ghetto as gunman or tief." (Translation: Businessmen from the ghettos are seen as gunmen and thieves.) In the male-only focus groups, male respondents expressed the belief that they were discriminated against because they are viewed as bad people, as bandits. A young male street vendor from Whitfield Town told me, "It is an area ting and where yuh live. See man as a gang and gun ting. Dats how dem [loan places] luk pon it" (Translation: The area where a person lives stereotypes them. Men are seen as gangsters. That is how MFIs see them.) Location and social status, they argued, are regarded by lenders as aspects of character and are used to stigmatize them and exclude them from loans. Yet these managers had been given subsidized funds to provide microcredit to the marginalized.[5]

Community economic development projects are usually introduced to empower marginalized people. In my interviews, though, microfinance managers blamed clients for low education levels: "People downtown cannot navigate MFIs with standard English because they simply lack education and use patois [speak in a creole version of English]."[6] Business people from Arnett Gardens stated in a focus group that males tend to speak in patois (Jamaican English) more frequently than their female counterparts, who "put on" a twang as needed. Stakeholders interviewed argued that the claimed significance of determined language variation or jargon was in fact a ploy to exclude some business people (Gray 2004, 93).

Caribbean scholars like Eudine Barriteau (1998, 189) and Errol Miller (1991, 166) have thoroughly debated the male marginalization thesis with regard to underperforming men in Kingston's garrisons (slums). Miller's point is relevant to this study because he takes a class stand by redefining the concept of patriarchal domination, arguing that wealthy individuals (usually fair-complexioned) oppress not only women but also disadvantaged men from the ghettos (interview, Errol Miller, Kingston, 31 October 2009). One stakeholder, who works extensively in peace-building in the inner cities, remarked, "It is not [just] *any* Jamaican male but poor young men from the marginalized areas who are denied fair participation . . . yeah . . . *not the uptown boys*. Youth from the ghettos are not the ones [clients] accessing loans" (interview, community activist, 29 July 2009). An anti-male bias against inner-city males is prevalent in microfinance due to the negative perspectives of men in the downtown communities.

It is not disputed that people in the low-income areas, including males, are underrepresented in schools and various professional sectors. In Table 3.3, only 32% of the 233 entrepreneurs accessed loans, and only 13% (10) of all loan recipients were male. Women constituted 62% (144) of the sample but received 87% of all loans. While nearly half (45%, 65 out of 144) of all female applicants were successful in obtaining loans, only 11% (10 out of 89) of male applicants were able to obtain a loan. Clearly, vital economic resources are being diverted away from men in the slums.

The reasons Jamaican lenders give for not lending to men is reminiscent of slave and colonial times: lenders, mostly educated women, suggest that inner-city men cannot obtain a loan because "men are lazy" or

Table 3.3 Female–male access to microfinance in Jamaica

Access to microfinance		
Total number/% of business people interviewed	233	
Number/% of women business people interviewed	144	62%
Number/% of men business people interviewed	89	38%
Total business people with microfinance	75	32%
Loans received by gender		
Number/% of females of all female applicants who obtained loans (65/144)	65	45%
Number/% of males of all male applicants who obtained loans (10/89)	10	11%
Number/% women with microfinance loans of total microloans (65/75)	65	87%
Number/% men with microfinance loans of total microloans (10/75)	10	13%

Source: Author's data collection in six slums, February–October 2009.

"men prefer jobs" (salaried jobs) or "men want big money fast." Male entrepreneurs in the slums are aware that there is an operative bias in microfinance against them, one that exposes the hierarchal class legacy from the colonial period that continues to frame social relations in Jamaica. In interviews and in the all-male focus group sessions, 100% (89) of the male business people indicated they had been typecast as *tief* (Patois word for thief) by the staff at these agencies. More than half the lenders interviewed (52%, 17 out of 32) admitted that they "do not treat men and women fairly" and that a clear preference for women does in fact exist. A senior microfinance person stated, "I prefer to give loans to women. It is young men between 16 and 30 years old in high-crime areas who are so violent." In the all-male focus group, men stated that they believed they had to take particular care regarding their physical appearance or they would be automatically rejected for a loan (focus groups in Tivoli Gardens, 25 August 2009, and Arnett Gardens, 22 August 2009.) One interviewee, a car wash owner, stated, "Yuh need fi wear tie, put on nice cologne, and dress up and den dem talk to yuh" (Tivoli Gardens, 22 August 2009).

Lenders apply their own class biases to a definition of "good character." For some lenders, "certain women" – women with several "baby daddies" (women who have had children by different partners) – do not align with their own social mores.[7] Loan officers screen these women out, viewing them as slack and promiscuous and as having "loose morals (focus groups in Arnett Gardens and Maxfield Park, Jamaica, 20 March and 16 May 2009). Loan officers view women who have had children by different men as a potential risk, yet downtown, single mothers are the norm and are not viewed as bad. One interviewee, a 42-year-old single mother with children by different men, owns a sewing business, and she argued that she had been constantly rejected for a microloan because of her lifestyle (interview, Tivoli Gardens, 25 July 2009). According to her, a loan officer "downgraded mi" [insulted me] when he asked, "How many baby fathers do you have?" and "Was the last man any good?" From a business perspective, one might suggest that multiple partners spreads out the risk, because there are more guarantors to help pay back the money. Instead, class-identified staff people judge this woman's unmarried lifestyle to be immoral.

The Jamaica case thus demonstrates that the bankers (most of whom are women), besides showing class bias, privilege only certain women (i.e., the morally acceptable ones) over men when allocating loans. In female-focused microfinance programs, loan officers often select women clients in order to protect their own bonuses, which are tied to performance results (Armendáriz and Morduch 2007, 280). However, when certain women are singled out for loans, these same women become vulnerable to domestic violence, as the men in their lives are angry as a consequence of being rejected by these financial programs (Rahman 1999, 72; Maclean 2010, 513–15).[8] This exclusion of men combined with privileging of women has what Armendáriz and Nigel Roome (2008, 2) refer to as a *disempowering effect* on women, a consequence of the domestic conflicts that ensue.

Imani Tafari-Ama (2006, 189) argues that allocation of subsidies to certain community members contributes to local conflicts. It follows that microfinance also contributes to conflict, for within the same social class, poor men and women perceive themselves as pitted against one another in a scramble for scarce resources (Miller 1991; Mohammed 2000; Tafari-Ama 2006). Barry Chevannes reported situations in downtown Kingston where women who had acquired loans got into physical altercations with one another (interview, 22 October 2009), fighting with daggers, ice picks, and acid as they competed for small loans. As noted above, the discretion over loan access wielded by lenders not only complicates relations among women – with "rich higglers" versus "poor business people (all women)" – but also aggravates relations between the sexes. When managers select "certain female clients" with whom to do business, they exclude men, and this creates a "disempowering effect" for women because it increases the threat of domestic violence (Bedford 2009, 49; Rahman 1999, 72). Many of the female clients I interviewed recognized that they were being favoured over their male counterparts (interviews, "Mrs. Burrell," 18 April 2009, "Miss Paddy," 27 March 2009, Kingston). They also believed that the credit allocated to them complicated their personal lives, claiming that the deep frustration felt by the men they lived with had serious consequences for them (Rahman 1999). Women explained to me that they suffered physical or verbal abuse when their male counterparts were excluded from economic programs, especially in family-owned businesses. Some family enterprises were successful only because the men had agreed to let their female partners navigate the system and apply for the loan. When lenders would rather do business with women, men feel rejected and threatened. This leaves women – who need the loan for the family but want to appease their men – in an ambivalent space.

Increasingly, scholars (Ahmed 2008; Armendáriz and Roome 2008) are criticizing financial programs for their exclusive focus on women because of the resulting domestic conflicts. Numerous interviews in this study underscore that women are vulnerable to domestic abuse by male partners when men are rejected for loans. Men who are chronically unemployed feel societal pressure to make a respectable living and to provide adequately for their families, and when a Jamaican man is unable to carry out these functions, he is perceived as a social failure (Gray 2004). Microfinance focused solely on women may make some men feel emasculated because they are not the "breadwinner." During an all-male focus group, a young man who owns a barber shop in Trench Town recounted that he used to "punch up" his baby's mother (a visiting relationship) because of tension over finances, including a time when she got a loan. Frustrated over his social situation, he explained, "When a mon cyant be a mon, he cyant do nuttin." Bedford (2009, 62) found that in the Caribbean, "wounded masculinities" have a negative impact on women and their families. In no way is it acceptable for men to beat up or "punch up" women over credit, and extending microcredit to men does not mean that some men will not abuse their wives and children. Fauzia Ahmed's work (2008) on the Grameen Bank and masculinity in Bangladesh found that the exclusion of men in microfinance does exacerbate violence in the household; however, there are "high-minded" men who support their wives' business activities, and they should be drawn in as allies.

Women in most places want their men to succeed because it contributes to the well-being of their families. Faye, a 49-year-old vendor from Maxfield Park, argued, "Yuh can't leave mi man down like that. We is all di same inna 'ere." (Translation: You cannot leave our men out. We are all the same in here in the slum; interview, 20 March 2009.) In other words, many women did not feel it was reasonable to exclude men from microfinance programs, because they felt a unity as part of the same class grouping. In assessing how microfinance excludes people through intersectionality, one needs to take note that in this case women felt that their race and class had a greater impact than gender on their exclusion. Programs that rejected men (e.g., their husbands, brothers, and sons) were seen as an affront to them as a family; they believed that their sons and husbands deserved the opportunity for financial success.

Guyana and Intersectional Oppressions

In Guyana, financial development programs operate within a racially polarized political environment under an authoritarian state led by the People's Progressive Party (PPP). The PPP has concentrated resources in its Indo-Guyanese base for the past 23 years, to the detriment of the Afro-Guyanese, and especially Afro-Guyanese women. As in Jamaica, intersectional bias against those who are poor, Black, and female is a problem in Guyana. Wilson, Cummings, and Marshall (2007) have found that persons of African descent are excluded from economic programs and unable meet their basic needs.

Marginalized areas, such as Allbouystown and Tiger Bay, are often labelled as dangerous, filled with "crooks" and "thieves." Many Afro-Guyanese business people live and work in both slums.[9] The business people in these communities have been united in the class-based oppressions they experience. The hucksters I interviewed, including poor Indo-Guyanese residents, were aware that privileges had been set aside for anyone but Afro-Guyanese. Black women, who are often single mothers and their families' breadwinners, have had difficulty accessing microfinance.[10] The government has subsidized economic programs for women, but these programs are tainted. And because the Indo-Guyanese managers in charge of these programs see loans (especially large ones) to Afro-Guyanese as bad risks, Black Guyanese of various class backgrounds have little access to finance, as noted by an Afro-Guyanese male expert at an international agency, who did not feel comfortable sharing his name because talking about financial exclusion is a political issue:

> In this society, certain men [Indo-Guyanese] don't want us [Afro-Guyanese] above them or equal to them in any way. That will not happen – plain and simple. They [Indo-Guyanese] want to keep us out. So we get the royal

runaround when we go to the banks. (interview, senior official, 22 April 2010)

Racial bias is embedded in the analysis of portfolios, which makes it unlikely that Afro-Guyanese will obtain loans, and even when they do, it is for much less than requested. Regardless of their class, Black people find getting a loan from a bank difficult. Class-infused racism is *the* root of the conflict between the two dominant racial groups. Guyanese economist C.Y. Thomas has argued that in an ethnically diverse country, the likelihood of lending being discriminatory against certain identities is high. This challenge is compounded for those who live in the slums. Afro-Guyanese who are poor and female are far less likely to get a loan than Indo-Guyanese (interview, University of Guyana academic, 7 and 13 May 2010).

I found that in Guyana's relatively small microfinance sector, which reaches less than 10% of the demand, Indo-Guyanese dominate as the personnel (see Table 3.4). Two of the main lenders are owned by wealthy Indo-Guyanese men: Initiative for Private Enterprise Development (IPED), and the Small Business Development Trust (SBDT). IPED's founder and chairman is the distillery giant Yesu Persaud, and IPED's CEO is Ramesh Persaud (2010–present). This latter institution is the largest microlender, with a portfolio valued at US$7 million (author's survey data, 6 May 2010); yet only 22% of its portfolio is made up of female borrowers. Thus IPED privileges Indo-Guyanese, and men are more likely to get a loan than women. It is worthwhile to note that their clients eventually graduate to larger loans at the Demerara Bank (also owned by Yesu Persaud).[11] In 1994, SBDT, founded by Sataur Gafoor of Gafsons Industries and Gafoors Stores, was also dominated by Indo-Guyanese personnel (*Kaieteur News*, 11 December 2011; interview, board member, Georgetown, 23 April 2010). In 2010, Indian-born Manjula

Table 3.4 Race of microfinance managers

Race	Number of people	Percentage of total
Afro-Guyanese	2	18%
Mixed-race	2	18%
Chinese	2	18%
Indo-Guyanese	5	45%
Males	8	73%

Source: Author's data collection, 2010

Brijmohan (married to an Indo-Guyanese and vice-president of then-President Bharrat Jagdeo's budget committee) became the director of the organization (interview, senior manager at Small Business Development Trust, 15 April 2010; SBDT Annual Report 2006).

During my field research, it was noticeable that most of the staff I interviewed were Indo-Guyanese. The lenders were well-educated men with an average age of 45 (73%, 8 out of 11). I analysed the race of the bankers in four commercial banks and three microfinance banks. In the interviews with the bankers, their responses differed from the ones given to me by the 39 stakeholders and 29 hucksters. I found a huge gap of understanding the reality of entrepreneurs among the managers of financial programs for the poor. In Table 3.4 (above), only 2 of the 11 managers interviewed were Afro-Guyanese; 5 of the 11 microlenders were Indo-Guyanese, and 9 were non-Blacks (5 Indos, 2 Chinese, 2 mixed-race). Of the stakeholders interviewed (of various racial backgrounds), 60% (30) said that lenders focused solely on profits and favoured Indo-Guyanese as clients (interviews, University of Guyana academic, 13 May 2010; not-for-profit professional, 7 May 2010; civil society activist, 30 April 2010). One senior manager opined that Indo-Guyanese felt a moral pressure to repay loans (though he had no evidence to substantiate this point).

Most of the bankers interviewed (90% [11]) stated that they did not hire loan officers from the marginalized communities, but that they hired people based on credentials. The managers' conviction that race and class should not be criteria for hiring is perplexing, given that these two factors are essential determinants when microloans are being allocated. "Normal" hiring practices – that is, normal by Indo-Guyanese standards – focus entirely on education, and this contradicts the lenders' unique mission of reaching marginalized people. Much as with the Jamaican case, lenders were not interested in working in slums like Allbouystown, Buxton, and Tiger Bay, where many Black microentrepreneurs live. Yet to fulfil the original intention of microfinance, which is to ensure inclusiveness, it is essential to hire individuals who are able to reach people in marginalized areas.

As we've seen in previous cases, the racial composition of the staff in microloan programs influences the types of clients who access microfinance. Afro-Guyanese are less likely to obtain loans because normally these loan officers do not go to the slums. Hiring the most technically qualified staff will not produce a more equitable and inclusive policy. One Indo-Guyanese microfinance manager told me, "A set of people

[Afro-Guyanese] are *not business-oriented* by culture. And these people [Afro-Guyanese] have a 'seize mentality' [to take and never to tell a word, a code of silence] and you can never find them" (emphasis added; interview, Georgetown, June 2010).

Blatant comments like these, which are clearly the result of cultural bias, are degrading to Afro-Guyanese and hucksters. Many lenders exhibit this sort of racial prejudice when allocating credit. Privileged and educated Indo-Guyanese men discriminate against poor Afro-Guyanese, especially women. The small sample from my research confirms that Blacks find it very hard to obtain loans and that being a Black woman is particularly disadvantageous – only 30% of the men and 11% of the women who applied for loans received them, and 25 out of 29 hucksters reported having difficulty accessing loans. The data from this case also suggest that being a Black woman is especially disadvantageous. What is more, the Afro-Guyanese I interviewed recognize this racialized class bias. Afro-Guyanese interviewees branded banks like the Bank of Baroda, the Demerara Bank, and SBDT as "Indian" because most of the lenders had an East Indian background (see Table 3.5).

Women of African descent undoubtedly experience cultural bias, but so do Indo-Guyanese women married to Black men (focus group, Georgetown [Allbouystown], 28 April 2010). One bank manager told me that his bank applies a "married condition" to reduce repayment risks, allocating loans to couples rather than to single women.[12] This requirement (note that this policy did not exist at the Afro-Guyanese–managed Microfin, which no longer existed as of 2012) favours Indo-Guyanese clients, as they are more likely to be married than Afro-Guyanese (focus group, 28 April 2010; Nettles 1995, 428; Despres 1967, 75). However,

Table 3.5 Racial identities of the main banks as reported by Guyana's hucksters

Bank Name	Race
Guyana Bank for Trade and Industry (GBTI)	Indo-Guyanese
Republic Bank	None (neutral)
Scotiabank Guyana	None (neutral)
Demerara Bank	Indo-Guyanese
Citizens Bank	Portuguese
IPED	Indo-Guyanese
DLFSA Microfin	Afro-Guyanese
SBDT	Indo-Guyanese
Bank of Baroda	Indo-Guyanese

Source: Interviews by author, 2010.

my research suggests that the "married condition" also seems to penalize interracial couples: in interviews, "Sita," an Indo-Guyanese vendor married to an Afro-Guyanese man, argued that the married requirement only works for Indian couples (focus group, Allbouystown, 28 April 2010); and Rhea, a Black food seller, explained that being married to an Indo-Guyanese man did not ensure her access to loans (interview at a food stall in Allbouystown, 27 April 2010). While it would require a larger sample to verify this, the "married condition" policy seems to give priority to Indo-Guyanese couples, allowing lenders to reject Black loan applicants regardless of their interracial marital status.

Most hucksters – 83% (25 of 29 interviewed) and 97% (15) of Afro-Guyanese interviewed – could not get a loan (See Table 3.6). "Rushal," an Afro single mother and baker, told me that "microfinance for many is jus' like lotto only rich people win ... betta you na play" (interview, 28 April 2010). Table 3.6 illustrates that only five people had obtained microloans, and three (38%) of those were Indo-Guyanese males; only one (6%) was an Afro-Guyanese woman. As noted above, Afro-Guyanese women appear to have the hardest time getting a loan, and when Black people do receive one, it is likely very small because the staff do not trust them to repay it (focus group, Allbouystown, 28 April 2010; "Nee" interview, 26 April 2010; "Big Mama" interview, 20 April 2010; "Franco" interview, 20 April 2010).

To further reinforce my argument, reports by McGarrell (2010) and Rizavi and Ganga (2006) examining micro and small businesses in Guyana make no mention of class and race discrimination against Afro-Guyanese business people, which again shows that consultants hired to examine the microfinance sector are overlooking the role played by race and class in the allocation of economic resources.[13] I did not analyse the religion of the Indo-Guyanese men in charge of the microbanking

Table 3.6 Microlending by race and gender in Georgetown

	No.	Percentage that received loans	Percentage of total sample
Indo-Guyanese male	3	38	10
Dougla (mixed race) female	1	25	3
Afro-Guyanese female	1	6	3
Total loans accessed	5	17	
No loans	25	83	

Source: Interviews by author, 2010.

programs, but many of the staff, both men and women, were Hindu. Since 1988, the Guyana Small Business Association (GSBA) has been headed by an Afro-Guyanese Muslim; it has a membership of only 215 (interview, Zephyr, April 2010).[14] People in the private sector (who asked not to be named) stated that GSBA is underfunded by the government because of its Black (and perhaps Muslim) leadership. This bias among Indo-Guyanese may possibly be because most Indo-Guyanese are Hindu. Since the indentured period, Hindus have been subjected to exclusionary practices because of the cultural dominance of Christian values (Despres 1967). It seems that race and possibly religion may also be a factor in how microfinance is allocated. After significant delays, in 2010 the state reluctantly created the Small Business Council under the Small Business Act No. 2 of 2004; it was made up of technocrats with no experience in the private sector.

Brian Moore (1987), who has written extensively on Guyana's political history, contended that Afro-Guyanese were "second-class subjects," inferior to whites and to whitened racial groups. Racist comments are seemingly the norm in that country. During my time in Georgetown in 2010, a businessman provided me with a pamphlet by Accabre Nkofi titled *Rebirth of the Blackman* (n.d.), which propounded the racialized class view that Afro-Guyanese are inferior to Indo-Guyanese. In *Cultural Pluralism and Nationalist Politics in British Guiana* (1967), Leo A. Despres argued that each group had negative perceptions of the other because Afro-Guyanese and Indo-Guyanese preferred to live in segregated villages. The 2009 collapse of Globe Trust, owned by wealthy Afro-Guyanese investors, further reinforced the stereotype that people of African heritage are inferior in finance and business.[15] Afro-Guyanese are well aware of the stigma against them at banks and in subsidized economic development programs that are meant to assist them. In Albouystown, one interviewee, a Rastafarian Afro-Guyanese who owns a roadside fruit stand, told me that "IPED is der people, if yuh coolie [Indo-Guyanese] you get bigga loan and easy … Blackmon [Black person] gets pushed round [in the bank]." (Translation: IPED is made up of Indians and it is an Indian-run bank. If you are Indo-Guyanese, you can get bigger loans. An Afro-Guyanese loan applicant gets no help at the bank; interview, 20 April 2010.) He went on to say, "Government is racialized, and we 'ave to ignore it ... They [political elites] only separate the nations [separate different racial groups]" (interview, 20 April 2010).

Another interviewee, a mixed-raced 21-year-old huckster of used clothing, echoed these sentiments: "Most people [Indo-Guyanese] get through without a thrill [have no obstacles in microfinance] ... If [his or her] hair [is] straight [reference to Indo-Guyanese]. It's about race, and straight hair can help you" (interview, 24 April 2010). Most of the stakeholders (82%, 41) interviewed argued that bankers are unable to stay neutral because they cannot "go against the grain" – that is, they must support the government's policies to exclude Afro-Guyanese (Ramharack 2005). Rushal, a pourri (snack) vendor of African descent, argued that "government only luk at big businessman, not wi [Afro-Guyanese]. Government want wi [Afro-Guyanese] t' stay poor" (Translation: As long as Afro-Guyanese remain poor, the state can control the opposition) (focus group, Allbouystown, 28 April 2010).

Black entrepreneurs play a vital role in the slums in selling goods from Indo-Guyanese businesses. Black hucksters also render a variety of services, such as hairdressing, car repair, cleaning, running salt goods shops, and selling cooked meals and snacks like pourri, potato balls, and *poulari*.[16] The nine single mothers I interviewed were traders and the heads of their households (see Table 3.7, below), yet they could not access social services. They did their trading in Stabroek "Big Market" or in Pennington's, where they bought goods from the Indo-Guyanese who run wholesale shops on Regent Street. Based on an appraisal of these businesses, most of the hucksters I interviewed should have easily qualified for a microloan.

Because Afro-Guyanese perceive bankers as adhering to an internal bias to help their own racial group, they do not trust their claims that they are helping empower the poor. Proving cultural bias is usually

Table 3.7 An intersectional analysis of microloans in Albouystown, Georgetown

Applicants for loans	Total number	Percentage of Total
Number of hucksters interviewed who applied for loans	29	100
Women hucksters	19	66
Male hucksters	10	34
Hucksters with a loan	5	17
Recipients of loans		
Female applicants	2 (1 Indo; 1 Black)	11 (of female applicants)
Male applicants	3	30
Women with microfinance	2	40
Men with microfinance	3	60
Black women	1	5 (of female applicants)

Source: Author's data, 2010.

difficult, for there is no hard evidence of any particular discriminatory microlending policy arising from racist views against Afro-Guyanese. Nonetheless, the attitudes of senior managers, most of whom are educated Indo-Guyanese men, reflect entrenched prejudice. In my interviews, 72% (21 out of 29) of the hucksters interviewed, including poor Indo-Guyanese, stated that it was Afro-Guyanese who were most discriminated against. The Blacks I interviewed claimed that the current political environment is dangerous for them because they have been labelled as the opposition (interview, community activist, 3 May 2010; Gibson 2005). Many of the bankers I interviewed (7 out of 11) admitted to me that race is a problem, but a "problem" only in the sense that Black borrowers are less likely to repay. A senior banker justified exclusionary practices:

> I see the people who don't repay [loan defaults] and they were almost always a Blackman [referring to both women and men]. They [Afro-Guyanese] don't have an honest culture … they want money but they don't feel to repay [loans] like wi Indians. I need [Afro-Guyanese to repay] my money but they don't pay me back. (interview, male banker, date withheld)

This stereotypical view of Blacks as bad business people is common in the banking sector. The managing director of one bank told me that

> some people [Indo-Guyanese] are more prone to business … they have a natural talent for business. A large part of it is cultural [being Indo-Guyanese]. Some Blackmon [Afro-Guyanese] don't want to be rich; they are not dissatisfied with how they are. You give them a leg up and they shrug their shoulders – a lot of them don't want to get out of the barrel. (interview, May 2010)

Narratives like these belittle the business acumen of Afro-Guyanese, and the bias in staff hiring makes it hard for other perspectives to counter them. I found that bankers were aware of their own exclusionary tendencies against marginalized groups; however, they denied that their ingrained prejudice was having an impact on Afro-Guyanese people. During my visit to one of these retailers, the seven staff present (out of the nine working there) were all Indo-Guyanese. And when Afro-Guyanese *are* hired as bank staff, a different problem arises: they face physical risk from Indo-Guyanese clients. Racism affects the loan collection process when Indian clients harass Black staff. A female senior manager, for example, reported that she had to transfer out a Black male loan officer after an Indo-Guyanese client told him, "[expletive] We fix your boat [drown/kill you] next time you Blackman cross over" (interview, 10 April 2010). An Afro-Guyanese bank manager recalled being harassed by clients on a site visit: "They cussed me and [the clients] asked 'Why is dis Blackman [Afro-Guyanese] here [in the community]?'" (interview, senior loan officer, 22 April 2010). Managers use situations like these to justify their reluctance to hire Black staff, on top of their treating Afro-Guyanese as if they were void of moral character and inherently incapable of sound business practices.

Clearly, Indo-Guyanese bankers resort to credit language and practices when justifying their biased lending practices. Furthermore, they contend that microfinance policies were not in fact created to assist Afro-Guyanese living in an oppressive environment:

> Race is a problem but microfinance practitioners will not discuss it. In my program, people who do not repay are *always them* [Afro-Guyanese]. This is confidential [information] and I ask that you do not use my name or quote me ... Between you and me [referring to me as a person of (partial) Indo-Guyanese descent], it is true they [Afro-Guyanese] don't repay [microloans]. No one will say this to you as I have. (interview, senior-level bank manager, date withheld)

Programs that target Indo-Guyanese clients are hiring fewer and fewer Afro-Guyanese staff, and this has reduced outreach to Blacks, because the front-line loan officers focus on Indians. During one interview, an Afro-Guyanese huckster described her difficult time getting a microloan: "(East) Indians get through ... When I went down to Brickdam [the SBDT office] and ... I had a hard time there, dey lef' you jus' so" (interview, 20 April 2010). In other words, Indo-Guyanese were served first, and she was left waiting (and ignored) by the staff until she felt obliged to leave. In my fieldwork in Guyana, I found very few Indo-Guyanese bankers who sympathized Blacks because of the culturally biased lending practices they faced.

Trinidad: Party Politics and Racialized Class Bias[17]

Trinidad and Tobago,[18] with a population of 1.3 million, is an economic powerhouse in the English-speaking Caribbean, with skyscrapers and booming oil and gas industries (World Bank 2013). Yet despite the wealth generated by oil, the country remains socially divided. When slavery was abolished in the region, Africans moved to the towns in search of paid labour, while Indian-indentured servants on the plantations remained in the rural areas and peripheral towns such as Princes Town, Chaguanas, Couva, and Talparo after their contracts expired (Bissessar and La Guerre 2013, 107; Williams 1944). This racial divide continues to affect the country.

In Trinidad, party politics is pervasive. According to Figueria (2010), Trinidadian parties win by exploiting race and class-based issues and the notion of a "superior race." In 1956, Dr Eric Williams, an Afro-Trinidadian, became the country's first prime minister (Ferguson 1997). Williams's classic text *Capitalism and Slavery* (first printed in 1944) documented the negative impact of forced African labour and extraction politics on the Trinidadian people. Williams, who founded the People's National Movement (PNM), dominated Trinidad's political arena for 30 years. In downtown Port of Spain is Woodford Square, where Williams brought political debates to the ordinary citizen (*Inward Hunger* [film] 2011). The PNM drew its support from poor Afro-Trinidadians, who were enlightened by Williams' fiery rhetoric, which tapped into the politics of slavery (*Inward Hunger* 2011). The elections of 1956 and 1961 were violent, with *marabuntas* – gangs from east Port of Spain linked to the PNM – terrorizing opposition areas (Bissessar and La Guerre 2013, 55). To this day, the PNM for the most part maintains a stronghold in the shanty towns of east Port of Spain.

The PNM, which held power from 1956 to 1986, was viewed by some as a nationalist Black party. In the 1970s, Williams's leadership and Black power consciousness moulded a positive Black image (*Inward Hunger* 2011). But Bissessar and La Guerre (2013, 59) argue that during this time of Black nationalism, a "collietude" was rising – that is, an Indo-Trinidadian form of cultural pride. In 1995 an Indo-Trinidadian trade unionist, Basdeo Panday, and his party, the United National Congress (UNC), rose to power. Except for a short-lived PNM mandate (1991–95), the UNC and a coalition of parties called the Congress of the People (COP) have held power for the past 18 years. In 2010 the first female prime minister, Kamla Persad-Bissessar, an Indo-Trinidadian Hindu from Siperia (a rural area), assumed leadership of the UNC (Bissessar and La Guerre 2013, 150; Sookraj 2010). Persad-Bissessar had learned from the errors of Panday, who during his term had given high-profile hand-outs to Sea Lots and slums in east Port of Spain – actions that saw a backlash from the Indo-Trinidadian business community, which felt that Panday was pandering to the "other" side (Bissessar and La Guerre 2013, 190). With regard to microfinance resources, the policy of Persad-Bissessar and the current regime has been heavily influenced by these earlier blowbacks against inclusive programming from Indo-Trinidadian party supporters (Hossein 2015).

While party politics in Trinidad and Tobago is clearly race-based, Bissessar and La Guerre (2013, 19) make a compelling argument that it is also class-based. The "knife and fork" (i.e., educated) Indo-Trinidadians control the distribution of economic resources. Under the People's Partnership, Persad-Bissessar has ensured that resources go to the party base and its supporters. Previous PNM administrations had done much the same: under Williams (1956–81) and Manning (1991–95; 2001–10), middle-class Blacks benefited more than poor Blacks (ibid., 45–8). For more than a decade, class-based politics have contributed to the exclusion of business people living in opposition strongholds from access to financial services (Hossein 2015; Storey 2004).

Microfinance, as a means to assist marginalized people in slum communities, is an important development tool in Caribbean states (Microfin 2002). In Trinidad, 283,000 people live in poverty; that is 21.8% of the population (*Trinidad and Tobago Guardian Online*, 23 May 2012).[19] A significant number of those in abject poverty live in the shanty towns of Laventille, on the east side of Port-of-Spain. East Port of Spain sits atop the hills and alongside the Beetham Highway, which links the city to Piarco airport. In this place of social exclusion, unemployment, and crime, the need for business services is great (Ryan 2013a, 2013b). Yet under an administration led by Indo-Trinidadians, class-based racial party politics are interfering with allocations to Afro-Trinidadians in east Port of Spain.

Opposing administrations in Trinidad have used microfinance as a form of appeasement and patronage to their party's racial base. The political elites use the local concept of "pan tap" (a patois term for person in charge) to assert their power (Bissessar and La Guerre 2013, 63). This extends to microfinance: state elites use microloans as a political tool for containing business people in the slums. Hebe Verrest, in her work (2013) in Trinidad, has found that business development programs are being withheld from entrepreneurs due to the bias of educated elites. Whether under the PNM or the PP, the National Enterprise Development Company's (NEDCO) state monopoly of microfinance does not seriously consider the activities of business people from east

Port of Spain, where only clients with political connections seem to get loans.[20] These economic resources are misused by political, educated elites, who treat the inhabitants of Laventille with condescension.

Trinidad's microfinance, then, is a state monopoly that has been infiltrated by party politics. Since the 1995 shift in political power to Indo-Trinidadians, poor Afro-Trinidadians have been left in the slums without access to economic resources. The state-owned microfinance sector is controlled by Indo-Trinidadians, and these political elites misuse financial resources to contain (and to punish) poor business people in low-income opposition areas, most of them of African descent. In 2002, during his second term as prime minister, Patrick Manning, an Afro-Trinidadian, started NEDCO, ostensibly to assist the Black urban poor in Laventille, a PNM stronghold (interview, Ministry of Labour and Micro-Enterprise Development, 20 June 2013). However, a microfinance expert at the International Finance Corporation (who cannot be named) pointed to NEDCO's failing loan portfolio: arrears (non-payments) exceed 75%, largely due to partisan microfinance (Hossein 2015; interview, 25 February 2014). NEDCO was created to reach mini-micro (not defined) and micro (up to TT$250,000 per year) as well as small businesses (up to $5 million per year) (interview, NEDCO, senior manager, 18 June 2013; Cabinet LSMED775–7 minutes, 25 April 2002). To ensure access to finance, NEDCO has a subsidized interest rate of 8% simple and a nominal processing fee of TT$25 (which critics argue is to support its party members). During a visit to NEDCO, I observed that its staff were largely of Indo-Trinidadian origin, a change in staffing that reflected the political environment.

NEDCO is headed by an Indo-Trinidadian, Ramlochan Ragoonanan. As mentioned earlier, borrowers from east Port of Spain perceive that politicians are "pan tap" in microlending and that this benefits Indo-Trinidadians. Interviews revealed that the partisan aspect of NEDCO has alienated credible business people who seek loans, many of whom are African (interview, Third World Network, 2 May 2013; interview, businessman at SEBA, 17 June 2013). It is telling that no microfinance banks are located in the densely populated communities in east Port of Spain, which are predominantly Afro-Trinidadian and strongholds of the PNM opposition.[21] Trinidad's microlending reaches far less than 10% of the 80,000 to 100,000 persons in need of loans (interview, labour ministry official, 20 June 2013). As of May 2013, NEDCO had 5,961 clients (52% of whom were women) (interview, senior manager at NEDCO, 18 June 2013) and was reaching 6% to 7% of the demand – far below expectations.

Table 3.8 presents findings from my research in Trinidad, based on a sample size of 75 interviews in the east Port-of-Spain communities of Beetham Gardens, Laventille, San Juan, and Sea Lots in June and July 2013. These slums are predominantly Afro-Trinidadian; however, there are significant Indo-Trinidadian and *dougla* populations.[22] In Sea Lots, I had to meet with the gang leader to avoid repercussions for the business people interviewed. The micro-entrepreneurs in this study accounted for 57% (43 interviewees) of the total sample. More than half of them were female.

All of the business people interviewed (43) had been denied loans from NEDCO. Activists of the Third World Network of NGOs have found that government-owned microfinance programs are highly subsidized so that interest rates are low for its own supporters (interviews, two community activists, Port of Spain, 2 May 2013). One councilwoman (name withheld on purpose) asked me, "Who is NEDCO helping? Who are the people running its programs?" (interview, 18 June 2013). The political status of NEDCO thus reinforces the perception that it is a racialized class institution existing to help those who support the government. In an interview in Beetham Gardens, the "boss lady" of a family-owned business in scrap metal said:

> Me, I neva went to NEDCO. It's a racial ting and hard to get [a loan], they just bring you down. People der [staff persons] stigmatizing and [they] let de coolie [Indo-Trinidadians] to get through. Dey only pretending to help us. This government in power is the worse kind [in terms of racial politics]. (interview, 24 June 2013)

Table 3.8 Interviews in Trinidad (2013)

Method	Trinidad	International and regional experts	Total	Per cent
Individual interviews with entrepreneurs (average 45 mins.)	43	0	43	
Number of female businesspeople	23	0	23	53
Total entrepreneurs	43	0	43	57
Individual interviews with stakeholders	14	10	24	
Individual interviews with bankers and microfinance experts	4	4	8	
Interviews with females	35	4	39	52
Total sample	61	14	75	

Source: Interviews by author, 2013. This case's findings are published in Hossein 2015b.

The current government will not come into the slums, which are perceived as Black. In another interview, a Beetham Gardens resident with 32 years of business experience explained, "What hambugs [bothers] people is not the government because dem come and go. But dey say they help wi and they don't. They also give de whole place a bad name and cast we all the same. This time is Indian man time" (interview, 24 June 2013).

It is clear that microfinance is affected by "pan tap" politics, which dominates the country's governance. The business people I interviewed were well aware of the race and location-based privileges set aside for non–Afro-Trinidadians. "Rastaman Curtis" of Laventille told me, "Government control money fi wi. As a Blackmon I can't wait of dis or dat crab connection so I use Sou-Sou [an informal bank] to meet my needs" (interview, 18 June 2013). Of the 43 business people I interviewed, 40 (93%) stated that the government had created partisan microfinance that was directing money to its base.

Conclusion

The cultural bias (race, class, and gender) in social economy organizations is rarely outed. Economic development critiques tend to focus on the inner workings or technical aspects of programs and not on the paid employees managing these projects. In the Caribbean, it became apparent to me that staff people were comfortable talking about gender identities but were less eager to talk about a racialized class bias in their programs. In these three cases, it is glaringly obvious that gender is not the only cultural factor influencing loan allocations (Hossein 2013b). Racialized class elites in these countries play out their own cultural preferences when determining who will get to borrow money. Jamaican browning managers (who are mostly female), for example, have interrupted a fair lending process by imposing their own middle-class sensibilities on men and women, because they have the power to do so. The result is a policy to enact female privileging that has in fact put certain women in a precarious position and created gender-based conflicts between men and women, as well as among poor women in the same socio-economic group (Montgomery 1996, 300; Rankin 2002, 18).

In each of the cases, it is clear that business people of African descent remain on the fringes of microfinance programs, even when those programs are intended for them. The cultural politics embedded in these programs has limited their ability to reach legitimate business people in need of financial assistance. It is clear that in all three cases, the educated lenders of class privilege held racialized class biases and allocated microfinance disproportionately, excluding certain people with a moral lifestyle and personal style that violated their own concept of middle-class norms. In none of the cases was it a priority to increase people's capabilities or to use microloans to assist people's economic development. Because of the failure to understand class, race, and gender politics, microcredit programs intended to help the vulnerable have fact exacerbated tensions.

The notion that economic development programs can help the very poor has enormously influenced the global microfinance industry. Yet as we have seen in this chapter, Black Jamaican, Guyanese, and Trinidadian business people cannot access these economic programs because of the biases of colonial-minded lenders. The Afro-Caribbean business people across the region that I interviewed contended that local elites try to interfere in the microfinance process to keep the targeted groups in a position of need. In the next chapter, however, a different scenario unfolds: I show that the cultural bias in lending decisions by unscrupulous political actors can result in violence or the threat of it. Specifically, I examine how Haitian lenders evoke an activist orientation in financial programs to fight for the poor, and that they take grave personal risks in doing so.

Chapter 4

Violence against Borrowers and Lenders in Microfinance

The social economy exists to fill the void when the state and the private sector fail to meet the needs of marginalized people. In its early beginnings, microfinance was a part of the social economy (and many microfinance institutions still are) – that is, it was a social movement of sorts working to confront unfair elitist financial systems. Yet as chapter 3 revealed, cultural bias has infiltrated targeted economic development programs, leaving the urban poor distrustful of programs that are intended to assist them. We can see the reality of political control of the poor reflected in Jamaican movies and reggae songs, which often refer to the consequences of political handouts. Any potential for social empowerment of people through access to money for their businesses is thus inhibited by clientelist practices. But an even more troubling issue here is the violence that can erupt as a result of microfinance programs. Although the concept of violence in microfinance is almost never discussed, it needs to be acknowledged that when these loans are disbursed in the slums, informal actors (gangsters) and clientelist politicians can insert themselves into these programs and threaten the lives of people in need of help.

In *Three Ancient Colonies* (2010, 31), Caribbean scholar Sidney W. Mintz likens the plantation economy in the Caribbean to feudalism, stating that there was "violence of every kind" in the region. Violence was so ingrained in the origins of these countries that structural violence in society has permeated the microbanking arena. Violence and the tiering of certain groups is a profound reflection of the region's recent past. The violence I speak about in Caribbean microfinance programs unfolds in two distinct ways: violence against the borrowers, and violence against the lenders. In Jamaica's extreme case, for example, gangsters or Dons involved in microfinance threaten borrowers' lives, leaving business people in fear of the lenders. This threat of violence becomes tangible when notorious drug lords capitalize financial programs and assist in their processes. In Haiti, on the other hand, it is the lenders and individuals managing economic development programs who can encounter hostility, threats, and possibly death.

The very act of the "Big Man" bestowing money upon the urban poor in specific social contexts, such as slums, is highly political (Hossein 2015). This chapter exposes the clientelist relationship, which, in its extreme form of partisan and gangster involvement in financial services, has dangerous consequences for clients. I discuss two questions in this chapter: First, what happens when the financial resource of microfinance is used to incite violence against borrowers? And second, is it also possible that violence can be directed against the lenders themselves? One form of violence is directed against the borrowers as a way to maintain a corrupt environment, and the other form is against socially conscious lenders who make loans with the intention of upsetting the exclusionary environment and bringing about economic democracy. In Jamaica, the failure to examine the people who get paid to organize microfinance programs can have dangerous consequences. And in Haiti, in the 91 interviews I conducted, mainly in Port-au-Prince but also in Les Cayes in southern Haiti, the violence directed against lenders (not borrowers) was a response to the activist manner in which microfinance was taking place. This distinction between the two forms of violence deserves some attention, because those progressive lenders who challenge unfair financial systems represent a form of politicized microfinance that confronts head on the biases and structural inequalities that may be affecting people's access to economic goods.

While the perception is that professionals working in economic development try to create business opportunities for excluded groups, the extent to which this is actually happening is not clear. Ananya Roy (2010) argues in *Poverty Capital* that the elites who manage microfinance programs need to be better scrutinized. In the Caribbean setting, social politics figure heavily in how informal and formal actors (with power) are able to insert themselves into these programs, increasing the possibility of financial exclusion of the urban poor. Intimidating political elites impose themselves on small business people and limit their access to these services. In an era of scarce resources, gangsters have become increasingly important, as they supply resources, enforcers, and advisers for local economic development projects.

Clientelism, in which a Big Man rewards the urban poor, is part of the business environment in Jamaica; these rewards can include microloans that provide important welfare assistance (Tafari-Ama 2006, 189). In this type of informal politics, political support/loyalty is expected in exchange for a loan. Loans made by the Big Men – especially Dons – come with severe consequences for non-payment. Business people discover that when they participate in microbanking they become beholden – or, to use their expression, "binded" – to a Big Man, a situation that can be life-threatening. Don involvement in lending is seen by business people as a dangerous collusion, and this is why they often exclude themselves from such politicized microfinance programs.

The Jamaican Case: Partisan Microfinance

The legacy of clientelism that Jamaican political scientist Carl Stone first wrote about in Jamaica's political history is still relevant in its current politics, and the "garrison politics" phenomenon is still unique to the downtown slums, as politicians seek to control the ballot box through hand-outs. A senior manager in a microfinance program told me that "politics consumes persons in the ghettos and this is all they want to do." There is a prevailing view in Jamaica that citizens who live south of Cross Roads (i.e., in the downtown slums) are all partisan (Figueroa and Sives 2003, 63). What they fail to add is that politicians from uptown are often the patrons, interfering in loan programs. Many slum dwellers are defined by outsiders in terms of their alignment with one of the two political parties, JLP or PNP (their "political tribe"); indeed, a person's political party is assumed because of an address (Duncan-Waite and Woolcock 2008: 4; PIOJ 1997).

Middle-class Jamaicans assume that *all* people from the slums want entitlements (Gray 2004, 96); however, the findings in this case study disputed such assumptions. Of the business people I interviewed, 79% (184) claimed they were not politically active and hotly contested the supposition that they were. The term "politically active" is defined as a person who is engaged in party politics. "Ionie," a 43-year-old single mother of six and a "sweety" (candy) and fruit seller, complained, "Some people inna 'ere get loan and 'aff no plan. Some people jus' get tings and others [who have a business] don't" (interview, February 2009). Ionie was one of the many business people I interviewed who are frustrated that political activists in her community access microfinance on the basis of politics rather than business.

In this context, is hard for entrepreneurs from marginalized communities to access microbanking. Table 4.1 (below) shows that most business people (61%, 142 out of 233) interviewed in six slum communities either do not have, or never had, a loan. Of those who *did* have a microloan, 32% (75), 59% (44) received one because of a (perhaps perceived) referral by a politician. An important finding in this study is that a significant proportion of business people (who are not political) refused to seek loans (41%, 96) from programs they deemed political. When I asked business people (233), "Did you have a hard time accessing a microloan?," I discovered that many hard-working business people had excluded themselves.[1] These entrepreneurs (who wanted a loan) had made a conscious decision to self-exclude because of the internal biases they perceived in the lender. At first, I assumed that "nah bodda with dat" meant that people did not attempt to get a loan; but I learned that these words indicated that these qualified people had made a calculated decision to opt out of programs because they saw them as political projects.

The government's seemingly well-intentioned support for the social economy and economic development is laced with contradictions (Bowen 2005, 2007). On the one hand, political elites claim that

Table 4.1 Perceptions of the political affiliations of select microfinance actors (random ordering)

Microfinance actor	Political party affiliation
Jamaica National Small Business Loans Limited (JNSBLL)	Jamaican Labor Party (JLP)/ Mixed
Access Microfinance (ACCESS)	JLP
Nation Growth Microfinance Bank (Aubyn Hill)	JLP
Credit Organization for Pre-Microenterprises (COPE)	None
Jamaica Business Development Agency (JBDC)	JLP/State
Self-Start Fund (by Seaga)	JLP
Development Options Limited (DOL)	People's National Party (PNP)
Micro Investment Development Agency (by Manley)	PNP
Micro Enterprise Financing Limited (MEFL)	PNP
Churches Cooperative and Credit Union Limited (CCCUL, General Manager Basal Naar)	PNP
First Union Company	None
Kris An Charles Company[2]	None
Pan Caribbean Financial Services (PCFS)	None
City of Kingston Credit Union (COKCU)	PNP/Mixed

Sources: Author's data, 2009; *Jamaica Observer*, *The Gleaner*, *Sunday Herald*

professionalized institutions (those not directly involved in politics) are best suited to make loans; on the other, they provide state agencies with funds for economic development, thus becoming directly involved. Elected officials also allocate constituency development funds (CDF) to lenders. Politicians (and microbankers) assume that business people who reside in slums do not understand what goes on in the Jamaican Parliament. Yet most of the entrepreneurs I interviewed were aware of the CDF portfolio to support certain financial programs for the urban poor. These scenarios contrast sharply with the global image of microfinance as a non-political tool to help the economically active poor.

A manager at a leading retailer recounted how politicians referred potential lenders to it: "People come and say my MP sent me. And once persons were approved for the loans, all loans were written off as not a single person repaid the loan" (interview, 11 July 2009). It is understandable that bankers would not want to highlight these political connections. In effect, lenders tolerate capitalization from politicians as long as they believe that business people are unaware of this relationship. For their part, politicians see the value of allocating financial resources to microloan projects in the communities they represent (Kah, Olds, and Kah 2005, 25). The CDF, valued at US$233,000, was part of former prime minister Bruce Golding's program for helping MPs carry out development projects for the poor.[3] A local academic (who will not be named) who consults at Jamaica House (the prime minister's residence) confirmed that the "CDF is operational in microfinance and it is wired [set up] to channel funds to politicians from the very beginning." This person continued, "I know this for a fact. Anyways, this is no secret." In other words, politicians channel money as cash payments, which they call "microloans," to constituents through the banks.[4] This arrangement allows the politicians, especially those representing garrisons, to demonstrate that they are helping activists through referrals and at the same time to show critics that they are legitimately lending to the urban poor.

Politicians approach bankers they know, and who they assume share the same party interests, to work with them to make microloans available to their constituents. In theory, such a relationship, in which cash-strapped lenders can access more capital for microfinance to help the poor, does not seem problematic. But given Jamaica's history of politicians conferring monies upon the urban poor in return for political favours, it would seem that politicians have simply found a new medium for replicating the old system. The slum communities I worked in are all strongholds controlled by one of the two major parties, and the politicized nature of these constituencies is such that certain loan programs are complicit in perpetuating these clientelist politics. Some bankers take capital from elected officials hoping that the information will not be accessible to the public; politicians are less discreet because they want assurances that their party followers will benefit from the money.

In interviews with citizens of Arnett Gardens, a slum that has had long experience with drug wars and internal conflicts related to partisan politics, it was clear that they were frustrated; 88% (47) reported an anti-partisan attitude. As a way to reject party politics, many residents have turned to self-employment (Social Development Commission [SDC] interviews, 25 September 2009). But business people looking for microfinance are concerned about the links between politicians and bankers, which are common knowledge. In fact, it was citizens – business people in particular – who brought the use of CDF in microfinance to my attention, when they expressed concern that the fund was being used to reward party followers. Key informants (in the slums) advised me to look for a CDF office at Jamaica House, where I found, unbeknownst to the development experts there, an entire program dedicated to CDF. These informants from the downtown communities, who are ordinary men and women, were able to name politicians who endowed lenders (interviews at Office of the Prime Minister [OPM] OPM, 22 July 2009). Table 4.2 summarizes the four elected representatives who channel the CDF to selected micro lenders.

Politicians have the power to blacklist citizens who do not campaign for them. "Rasta Lady," a pudding seller, reported that party activism is a requirement for receiving loans and that the local politician penalizes citizens who are not active (e.g., go to rallies) by not referring them for a loan. In Maxfield Park, party activist and business woman "Peta-Gaye," a 26-year-old grocery shop owner, claimed that her political representative

Table 4.2 Constituency development funds (CDFs) and politicians in Jamaica

Slum community	MP and political party	Microbank
Arnett Gardens	Omar Davies, PNP	JNSBLL
St Andrew Western[5]	George Hylton, PNP	CCCUL
Whitfield Town	Portia Simpson-MillerPNP (now PM)	JBDC
Maxfield Park	Peter Philips, PNP	JNSBLL

Source: Jamaica House, Constituency development office, August 2009; Members of Parliament List, 2007.

referred her to the bank where she now holds a microloan (focus group, 20 March 2009). In Arnett Gardens, "X," a 39-year-old single mother and owner of a haberdashery, is convinced that her party connections helped her receive two microloans (Interview, 16 May 2009). "X" learned about the microfinance program at party meetings, where she was able to ask the MP for a referral (interview, 16 May 2009). In Upper Rosetown, "Colonel" (a former gunman to a politician) said he was able to access microfinance because of his relationship with the political liaison person (interview, 13 May 2009). "Dragon," who owns a small grocery shop, claims that she can access finance through her party leader (interview, 1 May 2009). Aside from these few persons, most business people in this case were not party activists. It seemed, however, that party activists accessed credit more easily than those who were less politically active.

The neutrality of microfinance is compromised when funds are dispensed by politicians (e.g., via CDF), for this corrupts the goal of that sector, which is to ensure fair, inclusive, and equitable development finance programs. Critics of the CDF program suggest that it functions as patronage, or "pork barrel politics" – that it gives politicians the power to allocate state resources (i.e., microcredit) where they see fit. One microlender told me, "At a party fundraiser, the PNP candidate [who has access to CDF] asked us [the retailer cannot be named] to become their bank in the community. This is a great opportunity." This microfinance director grew up in a PNP constituency. Another MP (who cannot be named) said he gave JNSBLL, a major lender, the sum of US$81,395 from the CDF, justifying it as follows: "I am tired of giving people J$5,000 [US$58] and then the same people show up asking for money again the next day." Because politicians provide funding selectively to the microfinance lenders they feel best serve their interests, not all lenders have access to these funds.

Political Referrals in Microfinance

The Jamaican case examines perspectives from six downtown slum communities, known as garrisons: three controlled by the People's National Party (PNP), and three by the Jamaica Labour Party (JLP).[6] According to Amanda Sives (2002), "no significant social, political, economic or cultural development can occur within a garrison without tacit approval of the leadership of the dominant party." Maxfield Park is an exception: with multiple informal leaders competing for control and power over the community, this slum experiences regular violence. Most microlenders work in the PNP part of Arnett Gardens and the JLP stronghold,

Tivoli Gardens. Trench Town, the PNP's Arnett Gardens, and the JLP's Lower Rosetown are politically represented by Omar Davies, a PNP MP (Members of Parilament List, 2007). This area is susceptible to conflicts because competing factions of JLP members live in the stronghold of Rema. Arnett Gardens' Texas area has become a hub for several Christian and evangelical churches and NGOs. Yet Lower Rosetown (a JLP stronghold), which has a vibrant local community led by activist elders such as the late Michael Black, has no microlending offices in the community because it is in a PNP-dominated area. This reflects the politicized nature of microfinance – the PNP provides loans only where it has support.

MPs interfere with the allocation of microfinance resources through the (mis)use of state resources to influence MFIs to lend to constituents based on a political referral. As noted above, business people are aware of the ties between MPs and lenders. Citizens in the downtown slums recognize lenders and see them involved in partisan activism by listening to the radio, attending weekly community meetings, reading newspapers, watching the news on television, and going to community events. At a public microcredit event, for example, an entrepreneur recognized a microfinance lender immediately as a member of the PNP. While some managers do not recognize the negative impact of their partisan politics in microfinance, other lenders do, and these latter managers are opposed to colleagues being active in partisan politics. But it is no secret in the community that certain microlenders are allied with a political party. As of 2014, the IDB continues to endow politically active people in microfinance. These actions replicate the Big Man politics that perpetuate party privilege for a select few. As a result, business people, especially those who are anti-partisan and who recognize this behaviour, continue to exclude themselves from these programs (Hossein 2016).

A significant number (40%, 93) of the stakeholders interviewed, including microlenders, revealed important connections to political figures, and these lenders act in explicitly political ways (binding themselves to specific politicians) by taking referrals of clients from politicians. As stated above, such connections between bankers and politicians make (mostly apolitical) ordinary people suspicious of microcredit and social economy organizations.[7] Lenders around the globe know that for loans programs to succeed, they need to be free of politics (Rhyne and Otero 2006, 19), yet most Jamaican managers (64%, 20 out of 32) believe that party politics has embedded itself in microbanking. Conversations with people in business and newspapers articles in Jamaica, in *The Gleaner* and the *Jamaica Observer*, reveal perceived (and real) political affiliations among microfinance lenders.[8] In fact, peers in the industry were eager to "out" those persons perceived to be political. During one interview, for example, a microcredit expert had a training manual for the PNP on the office desk. A significant number of the staff I interviewed (40%, 13 out of 32) identified themselves with one of the two political parties, a clear indication that partisan politics do have an impact on microlending. When neutral managers want to avoid party politics in a sector, the party loyalty of microbankers can create tensions. Political referrals are common ploy in these environments (see Table 4.3). In a 2009 interview, a program officer at what was then the Canadian International Development Agency (CIDA) told me that "there are political aspects, very much so, in the microfinance industry, and understanding how people [microfinance staff] connect to each other can explain partisanship in the sector" (interview, 10 July 2009). Microlenders themselves recounted to me which politicians referred constituents for loans that resulted in loan defaults. While a mere 21% (49 of 233) of the entrepreneurs I interviewed were politically active, a number of economic development organizations were perceived to be part of one of the two major political parties. Most citizens regard loans given through political referrals not as funds to be repaid with interest but as monetary entitlements. It becomes morally hazardous for retailers when an MP's involvement is known (i.e., when people do not repay these loans); understandably, then, retailers do not openly admit their collaboration with politicians.[9] Once a microfinance organization has accepted political referrals/funds from a politician or is publicly identified with one of the major parties, business people view the

Table 4.3 Political referrals in microfinance by sex of client

Number of business people in study	233	
Number of women interviewed	144	62%
Number of men interviewed	89	38%
All business people with loans	75	32%
Business people with no loan	142	61%
Business people who self-exclude	96	41%
Women with loan	65	45%
Men with loan	10	11%
Political referrals for a microfinance	44	59%
Women with political referral	39	60%
Men with political referral	5	51%

Source: Author's data, Kingston, 2009

organization as politicized. Table 4.3 indicates that a significant number of Jamaican people (59%) access loans through a political referral.

Gangsterism, Microfinance, and Entrepreneurs

In some downtown areas, gangsters have developed a power structure parallel to the state, and they control the community. Although Dons are not officially part of the microlending landscape, they have become informal lenders of considerable importance because they provide low-cost loans and ensure that borrowers repay. Dons are highly aware that business people in the slums struggle to survive financially and that there are limited funds for downtown businesses (Hossein 2016). By making loans available to residents, therefore, the gangsters increase both their power and their popularity. Community economic development experts benefit from this informal power because clients' fear of gangsters ensures that they repay their loans. Unlike local politicians, gangsters often have grown up in these slums, and they know what motivates compliance. Recipients pay back Don-issued loans (which usually require no paperwork and offer flexible terms) because people know the consequences should they default. Several community residents and stakeholders told me that Dons use the loan system to launder money from the illicit drug and weapons trade.

When economic development practitioners ally with the Don-controlled structure in slums in order to ensure excellent portfolio performance, this has a negative impact on social development. Individuals engaged in economic development programs in the social economy enter dangerous territory when they use these unethical practices to advance their own businesses. I found that when small business programs, including credit unions, lend to former/current criminals or gang members, it complicates access for citizens who do not want to be involved with criminals. One microfinance officer enthused that when ordinary people see a "Badman" (gangster) paying back his loan on time, a message is sent to other clients to do the same. In another case, a microcredit project manager working with gangster(s) in the area was doing so in order to ensure their staff had "zero problems." At a field agent training session in a slum community, the director boasted that "a Don's support means that the project would be free from defaulting clients" (training for credit officers, 7 March 2009). However, this link between lenders and the criminal underworld – used to maintain the status quo – indicates that microbanking operates in a negative fashion.

While those at the top of these institutions may or may not agree with Donships, frontline staff quite blatantly use the informal system. One manager confirmed that his program made microloans available to projects owned by gangs, and made no apologies for it. Lenders rooted in the social economy and operating in the slums admit that they work through gangs because they recognize the Dons' power to make borrowers follow their policies. One senior microfinance manager stated: "Our program is fine in Tivoli Gardens because of the Don." A loan officer reported: "Dons can make people repay their loans." One project in a downtown community reported that when its computers were stolen, the Don made sure all the items were returned and offered to have his men break the thieves' legs (Morgan interview, 27 March 2009). This form of justice – "jungle justice" – is a familiar phenomenon in downtown communities (Duncan-Waite and Woolcock 2008, 27; Robotham 2003, 216).

Microfinance lenders are aware of the oppressive social conditions in the garrisons and use the informal power wielded by the Dons to their own ends. As seen above, gangsters in microfinance scare clients into repaying loans, which results in positive ratings for the lender.[10] A young business person in Tivoli Gardens recounted that a loan officer warned her, "I hope that nothing will happen to you if the Don finds out about this [unpaid loan]" (bar owner interview, Kingston, July 2009). Microloan officers use such statements to scare business people because they want to achieve their economic targets and thereby earn their bonuses, and business people are aware of this (Hossein 2016).

Microfinance organizations are compelled to work through these informal bosses, and this further marginalizes business people, besides subjugating them to an undemocratic order (interviews with community leaders and civil society experts, SDC field staff; Robotham 2003, 216). Many Black people, though, resist these oppressive systems and turn to financial systems they trust. People who opt out of economic development programs often turn to informal banks, called partner banks, choosing this alternative source for loans as a means to resist the politicians and gangsters who are attempting to control them. In this way, they assert their financial independence through resources they trust.

The Haiti Case: Activist Microbanking[11]

Haitian commercial banks have historically ignored poor entrepreneurs and catered exclusively to *les blancs* and *mulatres*. In 2012, the two international banks in Haiti, Canada's Scotiabank and America's

Citibank, reached about 100,000 (or 1%) of the country's 10.17 million people (World Bank 2011; Wells 2010). Despite the social and economic inequality, microfinance projects in Haiti appear to be reaching economically active citizens (Zanotti 2010). That lenders there are reaching these people is a striking contrast to other cases of microfinance, especially in the Caribbean region, where the data suggest that the individuals working in microfinance organizations have failed to be activist in their orientation (Sinclair 2012; Roy 2010). Haitian managers reveal that homogenizing the microfinance sector is a big mistake, and that it is important to acknowledge that some lenders are taking on dangerous work when they make loans to the poor.

Unlike in other Caribbean countries, entrepreneurs in Haiti do not resent *caisses populaires*. This is mainly because the *ti machanns* are aware of the violence perpetrated against lenders. Many lenders have their lives threatened when they engage in microbanking, because by financing the *moun andeyo* they are undermining the entrenched racialized class system. The *caisses populaires* in particular serve as an alternative business system, one in which people can work together to generate shared dividends and reinvest profits in communities. This is a real-life example of people thinking about new ways of working together under extreme market politics. In *Civilizing Globalization* (2014), Richard Sandbrook and Ali Burak Güven argue that there are myriad ways for states and people to rethink market fundamentalism from the ground up.

Taking on elites and fighting for a share of financial goods can be risky. Normally one thinks about the violence inflicted on poor people, but there can also be violence that targets the actual lenders in microfinance – indeed, violence against lenders is a real threat in Haitian microfinance. Because so many of these lenders were raised in much the same class circumstances as the *ti machanns*, they are vested in counteracting clientelist practices. The socially conscious bankers I interviewed argued that for the *moun andeyo*, democracy is impossible without economic democracy. Economic democracy for Haitians is more important than political rights; it is about organizing markets and businesses in an inclusive manner. This kind of activist language antagonizes the political and business elites.

Lenders and the Lived Experience of the *Ti Machanns*

In the Haitian case, the concept of lived experience touted by Black feminists points to exactly why lived experience matters in reaching marginalized groups. Big business in Haiti is controlled by a handful of families, whitened Haitians, who have inherited their wealth. For most Blacks, education has been the vehicle for upward social mobility. Hence, many commercial bankers and technical staff are Black (dark-skinned) and have abundant first-hand knowledge and lived experience of the very people for whom they work. These lenders, only two generations removed from their clientele, are aware of Haiti's entrenched biases and hostile environment. Other people who are tied to the idea of helping oppressed people often do not have this same direct experience, and in a harsh political environment where people's lives are at risk, that awareness inspires people to do microbanking. These lenders with lived experience cannot be diverted from their mission to change the system because they themselves have been victimized and have experienced first-hand the economic and social oppression of their clients.

Haitian lenders are relatively young, with an average age of 38 (*Colloque sur la Microfinance*, 28 September 2010). Of the managers I interviewed, 65% (31) were educated Blacks and 12% (6) were *mulatres* (mixed race); the rest were *blancs* and foreign-born expatriates. Joseph Similien, one of the 31 managers I interviewed, is head of Micro Crédit National (MCN) and originally from Carrefour (a poor neighbourhood in Port-au-Prince). Another, Sinior Raymond of the Association pour la Coopération avec la Microentreprise (ACME), was raised in Grand'Anse and often went to school having had only coffee for breakfast. Marie-Marcelle St Gilles-Gérard of Kotelam in Port-au-Prince, who is originally from Artibonite, used education to move to a higher social class, as did Carine Clermont of Groupe d'Appui pour l'Intégration de la Femme du Secteur Informel (GRAIFSI). These microfinance managers, men and women alike, are typical of the professionals engaged in microfinance: they come from modest economic backgrounds and overcame a culturally biased environment through education and self-determination to end up running important financial institutions (interviews, October 2011).

Socially conscious lenders are aware of the deeply embedded cultural bias, and they possess the race- and class-consciousness to counteract exclusionary politics. For them, microfinance is about co-opting economic resources for the masses, which is a radical – even dangerous – notion in Haiti. The activist perspective of these lenders fits with the Black political philosophy of Marcus Garvey, who advocated for entrepreneurship to free marginalized people (Bandele 2010; 2008; Martin

1983). And this mentality is not restricted to lenders who come from this class background; it also frames the thinking of whitened local elites and foreigners in Haiti. For example, some microfinance organizations emphasize the need to hire staff who are fluent in Kreyol, the national language spoken by the *moun andeyo*. At Fonkoze, the largest microfinance organization in Haiti, the staff speak Kreyol in their offices as a political statement of their support for the people they work with, manuals are published in Kreyol, and meetings take place in that language. In 2010, then-American director Anne Hastings (1995–2012) learned Kreyol as an expression of solidarity with her the clients (interview, Hastings, Port-au-Prince, 4 October 2010). Donor-subsidized American NGOs (e.g., Fonkoze, FINCA) tend to hire well-educated expatriates or (certain) diaspora and *mulatre* staff – people who are not connected to the social realities of the *ti machanns*. Once hired, though, these privileged individuals adopt a Black social consciousness sympathetic to the marginalized groups, even if this means betraying their own social group. Black Haitians, who dominate the technical staff (and who come from the masses they serve), are locally grounded and have influenced a new way of thinking. It is inspiring to see how Blacks and *mulatres* work together in the microfinance industry, though this is not the norm in the country.

Microcredit outreach in Haiti has increased over the past two decades as a result of diversified staffing and the entry of commercial lenders; these same developments have driven social change within banking. In the 1990s, under the Aristide administration, USAID became interested in commercial banks. Pierre Marie Boisson, a *mulatre*, on behalf of the Association des Professionnels de Banques (APB, Banking Professionals Association), was hired to introduce microfinance in commercial banks (interview, senior commercial banker, Port-au-Prince, 11 October 2010). *Mulatres* opposed to the racial/class divide lobbied their respective commercial banks to open up banking to the masses and confronted stiff opposition; but they persisted despite ostracism from their social peers. Haiti's microbankers view microfinance as an act of defiance against an oppressive economic system.

Microfinance managers have developed a home-grown microfinance sector that aims to socially and economically empower the poor. In this, the Haitian microfinance sector is unique (Hossein 2014b). Black Haitians in these organizations either grew up in the poor social conditions faced by microfinance borrowers or have family members who share the socio-economic situation of their clients. They in turn hire staff who are familiar with the social groups with whom they work. The fact that NGO and association managers come from the same social class as borrowers influences how they carry out microfinance services to the poor. As mentioned above, commercial bank executives and board members are from the middle-class *mulatre* group (as noted in Table 4.4), and educated Blacks hold senior technical positions in these banks. It is important to note the racial heterogeneity among microfinance managers and the fact that all lenders, regardless of race, share a common perspective as to why they make loans to the *moun andeyo*.

Murders of Microfinance Professionals

The lenders know that microbanking will not end the racialized class warfare in the country, but many argue in Haiti that small loans can be a starting point for expanding opportunities for the *moun andeyo* to improve their economic situation. Haitian lenders (as well as whitened

Table 4.4 Race/colour of the heads and technical staff in Haiti's microfinance sector

Type of lender	Leadership	Technical staff
Member-owned institutions		
Caisses populaires	Black	Black
Credit unions (not regulated)	Black	Black
KOTELAM	Black	Black
Non-governmental and non-bank institutions		
FINCA	Foreign/white	Black
Fonkoze	Foreign/white	Black
GRAIFSI	Black	Black
GTIH	Black	Black
FHAF	Black	Black
ACME	Black	Black
Initiative du Développement (ID)	Foreign/white	Black
Commercial microfinance banks		
Sogesol	Mulatre	Black
Micro Crédit National	Mulatre/Black	Black
Banque Populaire Haïtienne	Black	Black
Informal banks		
Sol	Black	Black
KNFP–community banks	Black	Black

Source: Author's data, 2011. Data also reprinted in Hossein 2014b.

and foreign managers) are politically conscious and espouse an "economic democracy" philosophy for microfinance (Hossein 2014b). It is this radical push for economic democracy that exposes lenders to death threats, which are sometimes carried out. High-profile lenders who fight for economic democracy and social justice have sometimes been murdered.

In carrying out this research, I met spouses of managers who confided to me that they were worried for the safety of their partners, not because of the clients but because of the rich. The economic elites find their power threatened by microfinance services. A number of professionals in economic development have been murdered, perhaps as a result of personal circumstances, or perhaps because they saw microfinance as a tool for transforming society, which would have threatened elite control of commercial financial systems. In 2000, a Fonkoze employee, Amos Jeannott, was kidnapped and murdered. No ransom was issued, only a threat to Fonkoze's director to close down operations (National Coalition for Haitian Rights 2012). In 2003, Danielle Lustin, former director of Fonds Haïtien d'Aide à la Femme (FHAF) and vice-president of the board of Konsey Nasyonal Finansman Popilè (KNFP, a rural microfinance network), was assassinated without any explanation (Le Nouvelliste; e-mail, details withheld on purpose, 3 November and 5 December 2010). In June 2010, the feminist activist Michèle César Jumelle, director general at the Société Financière Haïtienne de Développement SA (SOFIHDES, a microfinance bank), and her husband Yves Clément (who worked in economic development), were gunned down. In July 2011, Guiteau Toussaint, chairman of the board of the Banque Nationale de Crédit (BNC), who was recognized for restructuring the state-owned commercial bank to keep it from bankruptcy, was murdered weeks before he was to launch the first-ever competitive housing mortgage for ordinary people, called *Kay Pam*, or "My House" (Haitian Truth 2011). Taken together, these crimes strongly suggest that microfinance can be a dangerous occupation. The reasons why these professionals were murdered are only speculative, as all of the cases remain unsolved.

Blacks and some *mulatres* are cognizant of the risks involved in trying to change the way things work in Haiti. Yet they persist in taking personal risks, viewing microfinance as a tool for bringing about economic democracy. The murders of microbanking professionals illustrate how risky it is to co-opt financial resources for excluded people, as community development threatens local elites. Economic development programs confront Haiti's structural inequalities and injustices. Clearly, employees in the microfinance sector are not doing this work simply to make a living; they are personally invested in social change. Their passion for their work is driven by the humiliation they and their families have experienced at the hands of the country's elites. For these managers and staff, microfinance is a way to contest racialized class and gender-based oppressions. The *ti machanns* are mindful of the country's exclusionary politics and are grateful for the risks these lenders take to work with them.

Conclusion

Caribbean entrepreneurs in the slums are disadvantaged, and targeted economic programs can be clouded by cultural and partisan biases that exclude these entrepreneurs from the business services they require. Lenders who are aware of the embedded clientelist activities in microfinance can adopt a political stance to undo these unfair practices. Those who remain neutral in microfinance are shirking their activist responsibilities and keeping people down. This is why it is essential that microlenders in these complex societies become "politicized" – in other words, they need to become politically conscious and pro-poor in their activism. If they do not, political elites and gangsters with access to financial resources will use their power to disburse those resources in partisan ways. To counteract their activities and their countries' legacies of colonialism, microfinance has to be activist in nature. Microfinance managers who work within the informal political system of gangsters and politicians are perpetuating the inequality and subjugation of poor people, and it is doubtful such microlending can improve people's livelihoods. Within a Black feminist framework, it is evident that the historical experience of power and control is replicated in modern-day microfinance programs. Just as the planters once decided which resources their slaves received, the politicians and the Dons now implicated in economic development determine who in the slums get access to microloans. Their involvement in a financial resource contains dissent and can lead to threats on people's lives when clients try to weaken the informal rules.

It is nothing new that informal politics in microfinance programs has negative effects on the lives of the poor: it limits their capabilities and can even endanger their lives. As shown in this chapter, the relationship between microfinance lenders and dubious political and informal actors has confounded the social empowerment aspect of microfinance. The links between bankers and informal actors have made business people suspicious of microcredit. The reputation of microfinance as inclusive finance that creates opportunities for the economically active poor has been severely compromised by Big Man politics. The (perceived) collusion between bankers and gangsters or politicians sharply undercuts the role of the social economy, which is supposed to assist people in need on a level playing field so that they can develop themselves, not only economically but also socially. Because of the collusion of gangsters and politicians within the social economy, many ordinary people have avoided engaging in formalized business development programs.

Violence takes two forms: one threatens and weakens people's social development through corrupt politicians and gangsters; the other is directed against those who are striving to upset an unjust social system. Haitian lenders, Black and white, are working from within the industry to combat the social and economic apartheid against the urban poor. Certainly there are limits to what Haitians can do to co-opt microfinance. But clearly, microfinance does not have to be one-dimensional, and in some countries the people hired by these agencies are putting their lives at risk when they opt for a career in microfinance. In chapter 5, I show that efforts to create alternative models, such as the cooperative and collective one in Haiti, are challenging the idea of commercial models. Both this chapter about violence and the next chapter about collective models demonstrate that within the social economy there is a need to take a stand in microbanking. Activism in microfinance involves either embracing confrontational and anti-establishment politics or developing a model that will benefit the people who need assistance. To suggest that cooperatives may be a better business model than commercialized banking can be dangerous, especially in the Haitian case, where cooperatives are viewed as a socialist project to counter elite and commercialized business models.

Chapter 5

Alternative Banking among the African Diaspora

"No one has to tell me what *caisses populaires* are I know them from long time ago … before I was even here [born]."

"Miveline," a *ti machann* from Bon Repos, Port-au-Prince, focus group, 9 October 2010

Money pools, where people collectively lend and save among themselves, existed long before banking to the poor was ever named (Hossein 2013a; Dunford 2009; Ardener and Burman 1996). Feminists J.K. Gibson-Graham (1996, 2006) in their critiques of market fundamentalism have long argued that collectives are a source of camaraderie and way for marginalized people to build a new economic life. In *The Great Transformation: The Political and Economic Origins of Our Time*, Karl Polanyi (1944) in retelling history argued that the economy is embedded in social relationships and that how people made a living was a function of people's social lives and not solely focused on business. People of African descent around the globe engaged in informal self-help collectives long before the arrival of cooperatives in Europe (Gordon Nembhard 2014; Gordon Nembhard and Pang 2003; Ardener and Burman 1996; Geertz 1962). These self-help banks are a form of micro-banking to help socially excluded people access economic goods.

The social economy, with its focus on microfinance, has ignored the important work informal banks do in both developed and developing countries. Ardener and Burman (1996) in their edited collection *Money-Go-Rounds: The Importance of Rotating Savings and Credit Associations for Women* document that self-help banks are grassroots economic programs that evolve within communities to counteract social and financial exclusion. These informal banks resemble the French and French Canadian tradition of the *économie sociale*, which is grounded in activism and civil society (Quarter, Mook, and Armstrong 2009; Shragge and Fontan 2000). Gordon Nembhard and Pang (2003) document how in marginalized ethnic communities in the United States, excluded groups have created inspiring and caring collaboratives. The informal collectives I write about are also very much part of an activist tradition, one in which the managers truly care about their members. Hossein's (2013a) study about banker ladies found that as far back as the 1700s, millions of Afro-Caribbean people under slavery were engaged in group banking. Gordon Nembhard's (2014) work on African Americans traces self-help banking groups among enslaved African-Americans to the sixteenth century, finding evidence that people were creating communities for themselves. What is certain is that collective microbanking is definitely not a new concept for Africans or for the African diaspora in the Americas.

Informal collectives are a deeply embedded African tradition, one that, for a historically oppressed group of people, speaks to the functionality of getting things done. Informal banks are a real-life aspect of the social economy, one that pushes against unthinkable forms of marginalization. The quote of "Miveline" with which this chapter opened reflects a theme I heard over and over again, one that speaks to an institutional memory, a "second nature," or a personal feeling that many excluded Haitian people have when it comes to *caisses populaires* (credit unions). These people were raised by loved ones who belonged to cooperatives. Millions of people in the world just like "Miveline" have long been accustomed to various forms of collective financial organizations being a part of their lives. For generations, marginalized groups have used these informal banks to meet their livelihood needs. In the 1880s in Europe, the German *Raifeissen* model offered small loans to the working poor (Roodman 2012a, 56; Guinnane 2001, 368; Harper 1998, 8). By the 1900s, this model had spread to North America, and a French-Canadian clerk, Alphonse Desjardins, was piloting loans through the *caisses populaires* in Levi, Quebec (Shragge and Fontan 2000).

The microcredit revolution in rural Bangladesh came during a period of economic liberalization and structural adjustment programs, led by the Bretton Woods and leading industrialized nations calling for commercialization. In 1976, Muhammad Yunus, an economics professor at the University of Chittagong, revived the concept of microloans through a group lending model when he made a personal loan of $27 to a group of 42 stool makers in rural Bangladesh (Karim 2008; Counts 1996). The Grameen Bank, an innovation from the global South, began as an alternative model that emphasized solidarity and collectivity in making finance inclusive for poor rural women (Yunus 2007a, 205; 1994; Schreiner 2002, 591). In 1983, Yunus officially launched the Grameen Bank, which aimed to make microcredit a tool for financially empowering people in ways that would have a positive social impact on their lives (Yunus 2007a; Sengupta and Aubuchon 2008; Counts 1996; Wahid 1994).

As quoted in the introduction to this book, at the very first summit on microcredit in Washington, DC, in 1997, Muhammad Yunus, former director of the Grameen Bank, claimed that microloans could help lift entrepreneurs out of poverty. But by the late 1990s, the sector was moving towards commercialization (Sinclair 2012; Rankin 2001). The steady move by commercial lenders away from the social aspect in microfinance has increased criticism of the sector (Roodman 2012a, 2012c; Roy 2010; Karim 2008). During the Convergences 2015 World Forum in Paris, a document titled "Global Appeal for Responsible Microfinance" was tabled that urged the industry to make the industry accountable to its millions of poor borrowers. The Paris appeal calls for collective financial institutions to focus on people. Gordon Nembhard (2011) has argued powerfully that the combination of micro-enterprise development, collective wisdom, and cooperation can strengthen racially marginalized social groups. Despite this, the commercialized microfinance industry has overlooked the contributions of informal banks, cooperatives, and credit unions in microbanking.

In this chapter, I argue that collective lenders, be they formal or informal, recognize their country's social history and do business differently. I focus mainly on the Haiti case, for it is the country from which I have gathered substantial empirical evidence, but for reflection, I also draw on the Grenada case as needed. In general, the microfinance industry has overlooked cooperative lenders and in doing so has missed an important opportunity to learn from cooperative microbanking models. This chapter focuses on formal and informal collective institutions, examining different models for doing microfinancing. In both Haiti and Grenada, credit unions and cooperative banks are influenced by indigenous banking systems such as *susu*, partner, box-hand, and *sol*. These local African traditions of informal banking reveal that Black people have long had systems focused on helping people thrive in commerce, including under slavery and colonization. The cooperative banking story is also important in that it confronts commercialized microfinance. People who choose collective banking, where dividends are shared by members, are practising a quiet form of resistance in that they are ultimately rejecting commercialized microbanking.

Commercialized Microfinance

In the 1990s the microfinance industry (including the Grameen Bank) shifted its focus from poverty reduction to commercialization. Organizations focused on financial viability have significantly raised their interest rates (CGAP 2006; Drake and Rhyne 2002, 4; Wahid 1994, 11). This shift in microfinance has provoked a debate about the original intention of microcredit (Midgley 2008, 477; Wilson 2001, 244; Rahman 1999, 79). The following question has arisen: Are institutions tasked with helping the excluded access financial services able to do so when they are pressured by investors to recover their costs and become financially sustainable? Malcolm Harper (1998, 9) was one of the first people to describe this move from a development model to a commercial model as a "new wave" of microfinance; he found that supporters at both ends of the political spectrum embraced the shift towards profitability. The debate over social financing and commercialization continues in the industry.

The commercial side is dominated by a neoliberal political philosophy (Dichter and Harper 2007; Harper and Arora 2005; Rankin 2002). Commercial microfinance institutions (MFIs) that adhere to the tenets of economic liberalization and commerce – such as Bolivia's Banco Sol, Peru's Mibanco, Mexico's Banco Compartamos, and India's SKS Microfinance Bank – all have received significant investment capital for credit despite controversy over excessive profits and questionable collection practices (Sengupta and Aubuchon 2008, 12–17; Navagas et al. 2000, 338; Morduch 1999, 1576). One of the donors that have provided capital for microfinance to assist poor entrepreneurs is USAID, the largest donor agency in micro-enterprise development since 1978, particularly in the Americas. These US investments have led to the expansion of commercialized microfinance (Midgley 2008).

Private Western investors have inserted at least billions into commercial MFIs, and make returns on those investments (Sinclair 2012). Pierre Omidyar of eBay, the Bill and Melinda Gates Foundation, the Michael and Susan Dell Foundation, and Bob Pattillo of Gray Ghost, among others, have invested billions in microfinance (Bruck 2006).[1] At the start of 2000, 89% of the capital of MFIs came from bilateral and multilateral agencies (CGAP Focus Note No. 25, in Chowdri and Silva 2004). By 2012, private investments from such groups as Blue Orchard,

MicroVest Capital Funds, and Sarona had surpassed foreign aid in microfinance. Corporate foundations, such as the MasterCard Foundation in Toronto, have also made grants in microfinance, and in 2005, Kiva, the world's first online microlending platform, allowed middle-class individuals to invest in micro-entrepreneurs in the South. Throughout all of this focus on and debate over commercialized microfinance, very little research has considered the development of collective institutions engaged in microbanking.

Resistance, Politics, and Cooperative Banking

During Europe's industrialization in the 1800s, ordinary people like the Rochdale weavers protested against market fundamentalism and organized from the ground up, creating collectives as an alternative model for earning a livelihood. Credit unions, which are owned by their members, run counter to the commercialized shareholder model in that they advance the idea of people-owned businesses (Whyte 2001). Caribbean banker ladies who mobilize scarce funds from marginalized people so that they can finance one another's projects serve as an excellent example of resistance to commercial banking systems (Niger-Thomas 1996). In times of adversity, Africans and the African diaspora relied on collective systems they knew and trusted. In *Collective Courage* (2014), Jessica Gordon Nembhard posits that the organizing of African-Americans is an untold story, viewed as subversive mainly because the idea of group ventures runs counter to individualized forms of capitalism. Yet collective institutions have long been part of the region. By incorporating indigenous systems of collectivity, people ensure that financial programs reach marginalized groups. People on their own terms are thus devising more humane banking systems that work for communities (Polanyi 1944). This alternative model counters commercialized banking, and for that reason, it comes with risks.

But taking risks to engage in collective systems is par for the course in the Caribbean region, where freedom has not come easily. The African diaspora in the Caribbean, and in other parts of the world, has been deeply affected by enslavement and colonization (Gordon Nembhard 2014; Benjamin and Hall, 2010). At critical moments in their histories, people of African descent have rethought how to organize their social and business lives. Gordon Nembhard (2014) shows in her work that African-Americans in a hostile, racialized environment were engaging in cooperative economics as a means to include themselves in society.

After Haiti was emancipated in 1804 through the efforts of great leaders like Toussaint L'Ouverture, Jean-Jacques Dessalines, and Henri Christophe, it was kept in isolation for 100 years out of fears that its freedom would undermine the slave trade and monopolistic capitalism (Amin 2013; James 1989).[2] The Grenadian people's independence in 1974 also unfolded through authoritarianism and violence. The extreme hardships experienced by Haitian and Grenadian people under unstable political leaders encouraged many people to revert to African systems of collectivity in order to cope. The demographics of the two countries are similar in that they are primarily made up of descendants of slaves, with social systems that resemble other plantation economies in the Americas. Within this class system, (near) whites are at the top and others are tiered according to skin colour – the lighter-skinned citizens, *mulatre* (the Haitian term for mixed-race/light-skinned) or *red* (the Grenadian term for mixed-race/light-skinned), are better off economically than the majority Africans (very dark-skinned), who remain at the base of the pyramid.

Partisan and identity politics of race, class, and gender complicate access to finance. In this climate, collective lending makes money accessible to millions of Caribbean people in need. Cooperatives have often been introduced to countries by colonizers and local elites in ways that corrupt governance (Develtere 1993). The Haiti and Grenada cases show that formal, member-owned institutions like financial cooperatives and credit unions are firmly embedded traditions within marginalized communities. Moreover, these collective institutions have been strengthened by the earlier work of "banker ladies" in the region, which I will discuss in more detail in a later section. Caribbean women across the region have organized informal banks for excluded groups in order to provide them with banking options.

Veronica, a member of a credit union in St George, Grenada, who owns a small snack shop in the bus terminal in the downtown core, stated in an interview:

> They [banks and microfinance banks] treat us [self-employed people] like dogs. Always asking plenty questions and don't help [us]. As small as my parlour [shop] is I have things going on but they don't see it. They think we are dogs with nuttin' goin' on. So I ask you, who are they really helping? (interview, 13 June 2013)

The alternative banking systems that credit unions and cooperatives provide are known as "poor man's banks." In other words, people who cannot bank elsewhere go to credit unions or to informal banks. Marginalized people trust these alternative systems because they see the individuals managing them as preserving a cultural institution and as having a different mindset than mainstream bankers. What is more, the people in collective institutions are working to bring about economic change from *within* communities, and they do this knowing full well the risks they take. The collective banks in Haiti and Grenada put people first and present an alternative business model for the collective good.

The Haiti and Grenada Cases

Haiti and Grenada stand out from the other cases in this study because they have experienced internal coup(s) d'état and social revolution(s). I believe that as a consequence of various harsh events (e.g., enslavement, colonization, US invasion), social revolutions grounded the people in the collective to fight against unfair systems. The world's first Black liberated republic, Haiti, has experienced successive coups, extreme poverty, and horrific natural disasters since its independence in 1804. Also, the United States invaded and occupied Haiti from 1915 to 1934. Grenada, an English-speaking eastern island with a population of 105,483 (World Bank 2011), was a British colony until 1974. Grenada is the only English-speaking Caribbean country to have experienced a coup d'état, which was led by Maurice Bishop, Bernard Coard, and the New Jewel Movement (NJM) in 1979 (Meeks 2001; Gentle 1989; Sandford and Vigilante 1984). The People's Revolutionary government (1979–1983), run by educated middle-class Grenadians, was a left-wing experiment during the Cold War era. As a result of that experiment, Grenada like Haiti (1915–1934) experienced a US invasion, and was occupied in 1983 under the Reagan administration (Meeks 2001). American leaders had deep concerns about collective enterprises and viewed the group organizing of colonized peoples as subversive, communist, and anti-American. But despite American external colonialism in the region, where the United States has controlled how people of African heritage participate in society (Benjamin and Hall 2010), both Grenada and Haiti have persevered in their cooperative and community-based development.

The analysis in this chapter is based on interviews with 136 people. I have found that the Haiti and Grenada cases stand out from the others in this study because of their collective stand (see Table 5.1). For perspectives on the informal banks, I draw on the views of hundreds of small business people in Jamaica, Trinidad, and Guyana as well as in Haiti and Grenada. My Haiti research was conducted between March 2008 and October 2010, primarily in the capital city of Port-au-Prince and the southern town of Les Cayes. I took two additional month-long trips after the earthquake, in 2011. The bulk of my interviews were in the *bidonvilles* of Cité Soleil, Carrefour, and Martissant, as well as Bel Air in Centre-Ville (Aristide's Lavalas's stronghold) and Jalousie and Flipo in the hills of the chic suburb of Petionville. I interviewed 91 microfinance experts and business people. In Grenada, I met with 31 small business people in the St George bus terminal and central market as well as the Grand Anse valley. I also met with employees in the government, business, and cooperative sectors.

Haiti's African Traditions Build the *Caisses Populaires*

Haiti's cooperative development has been exceptional. In former colonies around the world, cooperatives have been projects of local or foreign political elites, and this has led to top-down control and limited cooperative development (Develtere 1993). Cooperative development in Haiti grew from a long-standing cultural tradition of pooling money, as was carried out by African slaves when they arrived there in the 1500s (Mintz 2010). In French-speaking West Africa, Benin and Togo – countries that

Table 5.1 Interview data about cooperative microlending in Haiti and Grenada

Method	Haiti	Grenada	Regional experts	Total	%
Number of micro-entrepreneurs in focus groups	45	0	0	45	
Individual interviews with entrepreneurs, average 45 minutes	0	17	0	17	
Female business people	43		0	43	72
Total entrepreneurs	43	17	0	60	44
Individual interviews with stakeholders	35	9	10	54	
Individual interviews with bankers and MF experts	13	5	4	22	
Female perspectives	61	15	4	80	59
Total Sample	91	31	14	136	

Source: Data collected from author's fieldwork in Haiti from 2008, 2010, and 2011 and in Grenada in 2013. See Hossein 2012.

Haitians claim as their ancestral lands – have strong traditions of *tontines*. Informal institutions known locally as *sols* (or *tontines* in francophone Africa) reach millions with financial services. The Haitian slaves engaged in *tontines*, which would later influence the creation of the *caisses populaires*, a grassroots movement. The first Haitian cooperative was formalized in 1937 in Port-à-Piment du Nord, near Gonaïves, soon after the US occupation ended (Montasse 1983, 18). Other *caisses populaires* were formalized in La Valée (Jacmel) in 1946 and in Cavaillon (South) and Sainte-Anne in Port-au-Prince in 1951, during a time of repressive politics (*Colloque*; ibid.). People were forbidden to form *gwoupmans* (a local term referring to groups) and cooperatives under the brutal Duvalier dictatorships (1957–86) of François "Papa Doc" and Jean-Claude "Baby Doc" Duvalier (N'Zengou-Tayo 1998, 118). Yet the masses took risks and continued to rely on *sols*, cooperatives, and *caisses populaires* to meet their needs.[3] Even though the Duvalier regimes had made it illegal for citizens to form these associations, people continued to do so (Maguire 1997, 160). Haitian cooperative scholar Emmanuel Montasse (1983) documented the growth of credit unions in the years 1951 to 1983, and suggests that this occurred because during these years people were deprived of basic services. The Conseil National des Cooperatives (CNC) was supervising cooperatives as far back as 1953, with the intention of monitoring activities (Young and Mitten 2000; Montasse 1983).

In 2000, the *caisses populaires* sector experienced a setback in the form of a corruption scandal.[4] Unregistered credit union managers offering high returns on deposits of 10% to 12% per month (thus the "dix douze" crisis) absconded with US$250 million in people's savings (Tucker and Tellis 2005, 118; UNCDF 2003, 154). Despite this experience, the *caisses populaires* have grown and flourished. Haitians, because of their historical and cultural ties, have confidence in these lenders. Indeed, commercial lenders (referred to as *les non-cooperatives*) and NGOs have been influenced by this collective microfinance.[5] This demand for *caisses populaires* systems signalled to the state that it needed to invest in projects to strengthen governance within the cooperatives and the credit union system. Haiti's government invited a CIDA development partner at the time, the Quebec-based credit union Développement International Desjardins, to strengthen the Haitian credit union sector and to create a regulatory framework for it.[6] Within several years of the scandal, the *caisses populaires*, through a DID-supported local network, Le Levier, was providing technical support to more than 340,000 credit union members, 41% of whom were women (Kerlouche and Joseph 2010).[7]

Haiti's financial world is indebted to *caisses populaires* and cooperatives for developing financing that reaches the excluded masses. Despite the setbacks in the cooperative sector, and out of respect for people's demand for collective institutions, the state has elevated the cooperatives by naming them in the constitution (in Preamble 4) – Haiti has declared itself a cooperative republic. Political elites recognize the important role that collective groups and cooperatives have played in the country's history, culture, and development. Indeed, most Haitians I interviewed held the sentimental view that the *caisses populaires* are grounded in African traditions. Haitians also credit the Catholic Church and its network for spreading and developing formalized cooperatives (Fatton 2002). Mintz (2011), in his extensive work *Pratik: Haitian Personal Economic Relationships*, about Madan saras, notes that the informal market economy and the voodoo faith are two important institutions in the country, bringing Haitians together collectively.

Having lived for almost three years in the Mono region of Benin, where many of the African descendants of Haiti came from, it is apparent to me that voodoo and its collective norms have helped Haitians come together and pool resources even under great adversity. The Haitian people I met were adamant that it was *they* who had largely determined which kinds of collectives and cooperatives would suit the nation. Gordon Nembhard (2011) has found that subaltern peoples, and African Americans in particular, who are discriminated against by the dominant society, have had to look inwards to their own communities to work together and create solidarity economics. The decision to enshrine Haiti as a cooperative republic in the constitution thus emerged as a consequence of a people's movement.

Haiti's Microfinance Sector Inspired by a Community Spirit

Haiti's fight for freedom from slavery in 1804 and movement towards a future of independence has involved an internal struggle. Political scientist Robert Fatton (2002, 2007) has documented the numerous authoritarian regimes run by elite *noirs* (Black elites) and *mulatres* (mixed-race) with financial backing from the *blancs* (local whites) against the *moun andeyo* (excluded masses). Yves Saint-Gérard (2004, 84) argues that political elites have misused ideas of Black nationalism to manage and contain dissent from the *moun andeyo*. Bad governance, corrupt politics, and an ingrained cultural bias have contributed to the systematic disenfranchisement of millions of people. Since the 1950s the extreme exclusion of the *moun andeyo* in outlying areas has led to migration southward, so that today, 40% of Haitians live in the *bidonvilles* of Port-au-Prince and the metropolitan region.

Microfinance is an urban phenomenon that has been influenced by the rural migrants moving to the towns and cities, who value informal collective banking systems (*Colloque sur la Microfinance*, 28–29 September 2010; USAID 2008; Shamsie 2006, 45). It has been estimated that two million *ti machanns* (vendors) need access to loans. Unlike the cases previously reviewed in Jamaica, Guyana, and Trinidad, Haiti's lenders reach 25% of the population (500,000) (KNFP 2008; USAID 2008).[8] Gordon Nembhard and Pang (2003) have shown in their work on ethnic Americans that people are crafting caring collectives that prioritize the needs of excluded peoples.

Generations born into the *quartiers précaires* (slums) of Port-au-Prince have had to cope for themselves. The important Kreyol words "kombit" (local organizing) and "gwoupmans" (collective groups) draw on African traditions of regrouping people with very few means (Fatton 2002, 52; 2007, 221). People organized financial resources into *sols* (informal banks) to meet their livelihood needs, and this has inspired the growth of cooperatives. A sense of solidarity and working together inspires an oppressed people to strive for a common goal (Gordon Nembhard 2011). The present study builds on scholarly literature and stories that confirm that Haitians have collective systems that pre-date postcolonial support to the *caisses populaires*. In an oppressive and undemocratic state, *kombit*, *gwoupmans*, and *sols* were ways for excluded peoples to create collective and civil society groups – a testimony to the democratic spirit of the uneducated masses (Fatton 2007, 221; Montasse 1983). Haitians recognize that *caisses populaires* have a vital place in society and that they embody the African traditions that most of them hold dear. The historical development of the *caisses populaires* and the ingenuity of Haitians working in them have created a model that reflects the society. As one Haitian stated in an anonymous interview: "*Caisses populaires* belong to the Haiti people. These *caisses* are accessible, grassroots and embedded into people's hearts, because they focus on people's community, collectivity, and helping each other out which are very important traits for us [Haitians] especially those of us who are poor" (interview, 2 October 2010).

Haiti's microfinance sector takes three broad forms: (1) *caisses populaires* and financial cooperatives, which are regulated by the state, (2) non-cooperatives (commercial banks, NGOs), and (3) informal banks.

The *caisses populaires* and the non-cooperatives are governed by separate laws.[9] Of the non-cooperatives, only commercial banks are regulated by the Central Bank.[10] Cooperative lending and informal banks dominate in terms of outreach to clients: at least 500,000 people are accessing microfinance through these (KNFP 2008). In this study, I highlight that a number of these institutions have adapted to the local culture by introducing group methodologies or informal-type products (such as "Mama Sol") to connect with entrepreneurs. The *caisses populaires* (regulated) and *sols* dominate the microfinance sector (See Table 5.2). Informal banks receive no outside institutional support yet reach millions of poor Haitians.

There are seven commercial banks in Haiti: four private, three state-owned. Of the commercial banks, the German-owned International Projekt Consult firm provided support to Unibank to start Micro Credit National in 1999. Haiti's largest commercial bank, Société Générale Haïtienne de Banque (Sogebank), with assistance from a US-based NGO called ACCION, set up a microfinance bank named Sogesol (Drake and Rhyne 2002). In 2000, Capital Bank created Micro Crédit Capital, and Banque de l'Union Haïtiennes (BUH) started Krédi Popilé (People's Credit) (Chowdri and Silva 2004). The state bank Banque Populaire Haïtienne (BPH) also started microfinance, in 2002 (Tucker and Tellis 2005, 115–16). There are also a number of non-cooperative microfinance lenders: NGOs, commercial banks, and microfinance institutions (MFIs). And there are Association Nationale des Institutions de Microfinance d'Haïti (ANIMH, national microfinance network) and Konsey Nasyonal Finansman Popilè (KNFP, a rural microfinance network for 25 unregistered *caisses populaires*).[11]

Microfinance lending at commercial banks, shown in Table 5.2, arose not only from the socially conscious attitudes of the *mulatres* who lobbied their respective commercial banks to create microfinance products, but also out of the collective spirit of the Haitian people, who know and trust cooperative-type banking systems.When NGO microfinance emerged in the mid-1980s, the Haitian people were already familiar with cooperative models. In 1981, Fonds Haïtien d'Aide a la Femmes (FHAF), with the assistance of America's Women's World Banking, and in 1983, Société Financière Haïtienne de Développement (SOFIHDES), both started group lending to women. In the late 1980s, US-based Catholic Relief Services (CRS) also involved itself in collective banks with USAID funding (interview, Charles, former CRS manager, 6 October 2010; Young and Mitten 2000). In 1989, John Hatch of the Foundation

Table 5.2 *Caisses populaires* and *sol*: Major microlenders (as of November 2010)

Type	Name of microlender and date started	Haitian-run	# of Clients	Active in slums	Donor subsidies	Avg. loan size, USD
Caisses Populaires & Cooperatives	*Caisses Populaires*, 2007 (50–80 members, Le Levier network)	Y	340,000	Y	Y	1200
	Caisses Populaires and Cooperatives (non-regulated)	Y	300,000+	Y	N	
						< 100
Commercial Microfinance Institutions (Down-scaled)	Sogesol (Sogebank), 2000		11,198	Y	Y	
	Micro Credit National (Unibank), 1999	N	10,500	Y	Y	
	Krédi Popilé (BUH), 1997	N	NA	N	NA	
	MicroCredit Capital (Capital Bank), 2000	N	775	NA	Y	
State Banks	Banque Nationale de Credit (BNC)	N	NA	Y	NA	
	Banque Populaire Haïtienne (BPH), 2002	N	444	Y	N	
NGOs and Associations	FHAF, 1981	Y	NA	Y	Y	
	SOFIHDES, 1983	Y	NA	Y	Y	
	FINCA, 1989	Y	8,200	Y	Y	
	GTIH	Y	500	Y	Y	
	Fonds d'Espoir, 1992	N	4,684	Y	Y	
	Fonkoze, 1995	Y	55,000	Y	Y	
	ID, 1998	Y	4,281	Y	Y	
	ACLAM, 1999	Y	5,039	Y	Y	
	ACME, 2003	N	21,000	Y	Y	100 to 500
Informal Banks	Sol	Y	Millions	Y	N	< 25
	Sabotay	Y	> Thousands	Y	N	

Source: Most results taken from ANIMH's report (2008). Results for Le Levier network for the *Caisses Populaires*, ACME, FINCA, MCN, GTIH and Fonkoze results were gathered during Fieldwork in October 2010.

for International Community Assistance (FINCA), an American NGO, also set up group lending in response to the Haitian people's predilection for cooperatives (interview, Vincent, acting director, 14 October 2010). The pioneers in microfinance, whether foreign or Haitian, were entering a small business lending environment that had been influenced by collective financial programs.

In the 1990s, donors like USAID and the IDB became interested in commercializing, or "scaling up," their microfinance operations. This push for commercialization has come to Haiti, but cooperative lenders have pushed back by showing that a credit union model can achieve scale and outreach even more effectively than commercial banks. Haiti's largest NGO, Fonkoze – started by Haitian Catholic priest Father Jean Philippe, inspired by Catholic liberation theology, and directed by an American, Anne Hastings (1995–2012) – is modelled on a group lending system. After taking note of history and the local environment and culture, this NGO allocated its loans to groups of women (interview, Hastings, 4 October 2010; Zanotti 2010; Tucker and Tellis 2005). As mentioned in the previous chapter, Fonkoze's pro-Kreyol policy reflects its mission to reach excluded groups. Fonkoze is not a *caisse populaire*, but the Haitian priests who created it believed that group cooperation was the way to move forward – indeed, this collective action has disturbed the country's capitalists. In Gibson-Graham's *A Postcapitalist Politics* (2006), the authors found that a new economic politics is very much alive – a finding that seems to fit with the Haitian microbanking experience.

One such example is that of a small, French-supported but Haitian-run not-for-profit organization called Initiative du Développement (ID). ID was one of the first lenders to decide that it would be based in and work in the *bidonvilles* (interview, senior microfinance executive, April 2008). In 1999, another not-for-profit, Action Contre la Misère (ACLAM), also began group-focused microfinance with support from the US-based Freedom from Hunger, combining financial services with education. In 2003, Association pour la Coopération avec la Microenterprise (ACME), was founded, supported by George Soros's Open Society and led by Sinior Raymond, a Haitian born in Jérémie in Grand'Anse Department. Raymond comes from a modest social background, and he, like others, was aware of the pull of collective institutions in his society. To me, these people are conscientious microlenders who are ethical in their approach to business. J.K. Gibson-Graham's (2003, 2006) work has centred on this notion of ethical economies and how women and people in different lands engage in community-based economies that put people first. The authors also understand the population's connection to cooperative institutions because of their own personal lived experience and own cultural connections. They see a need to make finance inclusive.

Grenada's Cooperative Experience

In contrast to Haiti, the cooperative experience of Grenada developed under colonization. In the 1930s, nutmeg and cocoa were important cash crops, and the colonial state created boards to manage these exports. In 1947 the Grenada Cooperative Nutmeg Association was formed to help farmers increase their incomes, allowing them to bypass the middlemen. In 1951 the Colonial Welfare and Development fund provided financing to organize production and improve its quality (Steele 2003, 337). In 1954 the Banana Cooperative Society was established to assist in trade with the Canadian Banana Company (ibid., 338).

The 1983 US invasion and occupation following the assassination of Maurice Bishop and members of the NJM occurred the same year that the Grenville Credit Union was created in the second-largest town in the country. In spite of the Cold War, during the Reagan administration (1981–89) people organized collectively as they had done since colonization. Eric Gairy (1967–79) was the first head of state for Grenada, as well as the first figure to come from a modest rural background and to share the African features of the majority of Grenadians (Sandford and Vigilante 1984). In the early years, Gairy was anti-imperialist and committed to increasing the incomes of rural farmers. However, Gairy's anti-local elite and white colonizer rhetoric clouded his governance. In the mid-1970s, opposition grew against Gairy's undemocratic control and the violence of his secret police, the Mongoose Gang (Steele 2003).

Young, educated Grenadians from middle-class backgrounds influenced by the US Black power movement and the Cold War rallied dissenters against the Gairy regime. The 1979 bloodless coup d'état by the NJM installed the left-wing People's Revolutionary Government (1979–83). Its leader, Maurice Bishop of the NJM, was impressed by Tanzania's concept of *ujamaa* (a Swahili word for unity, collectivity, or oneness), which involved moving villagers onto collective farms, and that idea adopted in the NJM's manifesto. Authoritarian politics left the Grenadian people to cope on their own. Given the tumultuous political events, it is clear why cooperative institutions, such as credit unions and *susus*, are widespread and have entrenched themselves in the society.

As of June 2013, Grenada's Cooperative League (GCL) had 10 credit unions and a membership of 42,000, or 40% of the population (interview, Chandra Davis, GCL general manager, St George, 4 June 2013). According to the general manager of the Grenville Credit Union, Devon Charles, "community banks are not concerned about blowing their trumpets but they are there to help people and cooperatives are not going away" (interview, 11 June 2013). Ordinary Grenadians trust credit unions for their banking because of their roots in the community. "Jingle," a business owner of a pizza and food shop at the bus terminal in St George, is sceptical that the government or commercial banks help traffickers (local term used for small vendors):

> Government and them [commercial banks] say dey would 'elp business in market and [bus] terminal. But they only talk, talk and give no help to us. They fear we can't pay. So I don't worry with [their] empty promises and I go to my Communal [refers to Communal credit union]. (interview, 13 June 2013)

Informal Collective Banks in the Caribbean

Rotating savings and credit associations (ROSCAs) are also known as informal banks or money pools, or by the local names given to them in specific communities (Rutherford 2000). In a study about ROSCAs in Indonesia, Clifford Geertz (1962) referred to them as "middle-rung institutions" and argued that they would fade away once formal banks became prevalent and reached into excluded areas. The reverse has happened. One can now argue that informal banks have grown and have even become transnational (Ardener and Burman 1996). Excluded groups of people considered ways to organize commerce in their communities because conventional banks were not reaching most people. Throughout history, Caribbean people have drawn on African collective systems to organize financial programs for themselves and others.

Informal banks or money pools are unregulated financial systems that provide quick access to savings and credit for people, mostly women, who have been excluded from formal banking channels (Ardener and Burman 1996; Geertz 1962; Rogaly 1996; Rutherford 2000). Stuart Rutherford in *The Poor and Their Money* found that informal banks are in high demand among the poor because these banks function efficiently, offering both low defaults and transaction costs. The informality of such banks is what makes them distinctive in their own right and attractive to people. Africans and Caribbean people have embraced the informality of these systems. Informal banks in the Caribbean are a valued African tradition, rooted in the local saving systems of *susus* and *tontines* brought by slaves to the Americas (Hossein 2014a; Wong 1996; Witter 1989; Mintz 1955). Guyanese scholar Maurice St Pierre (1999) notes that informal banks existed in Guyana, with African slaves rotating funds among one another, as they do in the *susu* or box-hand groups. Faye V. Harrison (1988) shows that since the times of slavery, Jamaican higglers have struggled to make a living in precarious economic and political environments and have used partner (discussed below) to meet their financial needs. During slavery and colonization, African slaves maintained rotational credit groups in their markets (Heinl and Heinl 2005; St Pierre 1999).

Informal banks help people to access money from trusted sources and to restore their personal dignity. James Scott's work (1977) in Southeast Asia asserts that quiet forms of resistance exist among villagers. In many ways, money pools are quiet forms of protest against unwelcoming banking systems. African slaves chained and forcibly taken to the Caribbean expressed their defiance of the masters when they pooled their earnings made from the Sunday market day (St Pierre 1999). Under colonization, banks did not lend to the local people, so colonized people turned to what they knew: African indigenous banking systems handed down to them by the generations before them. Women – known as banker ladies – were usually the ones to organize savings from the community; they created revolving funds, where each participant had a turn (Hossein 2013a). After emancipation, freed Africans and indentured servants brought in from India were denied access to formal banks, and they too relied on these local systems for sharing economic resources. In Haiti, slaves participated in *sol* long before independence from the French in 1804. In the documentary *Poto Mitan: Haitian Women, Pillars of the Global Economy* (2008), entrepreneurial women in Cité Soleil are shown rejecting low-paid factory work and turning to *sol* to help them develop businesses. These community-managed banks demonstrate that people have opted out of commercialized financial systems.

Social exclusion from commercial banks has driven up the demand for informal banks (Hossein 2014c). So has the need for individuals to rely less on unscrupulous lenders – such loans would strengthen ties to political elites or informal leaders, as seen in the previous chapter. Tucked away behind her metal cage, Rickie, a 29-year-old bar owner, was thankful for me asking about Jamaican partner banks:

> Pardna. Live for dat ting. Most people here [in his low-income community] don't have go to banks. Dem [the bankers] don't know what's going on here and wi na know what's going on in their banks. Downtown know Pardna ... it is the one ting here for wi. (interview, Kingston, 9 June 2009).

Jamaican political scientist Obika Gray (2003a, 2003b, 2004) similarly points to the widespread urban resistance as "social power" among the urban poor, including among small businesses. Across the Caribbean region, the people of the African diaspora turn to local informal financial groups that they know and trust as a way to harness their own power and to rethink the financial institutions they want in their lives.

Haiti's *Sols* Reach Millions

Haiti has a rich cooperative sector; moreover, informal collectives far outnumber formal ones. The Kreyol word *kombit* encompasses African traditions to regroup people with very few means, and these *gwoupmans* have inspired local economic development programs. Haitians' ideas about collectivity come from their Beninese (then Dahomey) ancestors, who brought early West African banking concepts to the Americas as far back as the 1500s, when slavery was established in Santo Domingo (then Saint-Domingue, now Haiti and the Dominican Republic). In the more than two centuries since independence, the country's politics have been oppressive. Leaders since Jean-Jacques Dessalines (1804–6) have adhered to *politiques du ventre* (politics of the belly) dictatorships, leaving the masses in complete suffering. As mentioned earlier, the first formal financial *caisse populaire* was created in 1937 in Port-à-Piment du Nord, near Gonaïves, and it was no doubt influenced by the informal collectives of the time. Millions of Haitians rely on *sols* to meet their everyday financial needs. *Sols* are not documented, but it is estimated that at least 80% of Haitians participate in the informal sector and rely on them. Given that millions of people want microfinance and that banks reach only about 300,000 people, these informal banks are an important part of people's financial lives in Haiti.

Sols are often created by people well-known in the community. Every month or week, members contribute a fixed amount, such as 100 gourdes (US$2–3), for a cycle that ranges from 6 to 10 months, depending on the number of members. Members agree to contribute regular savings, and when their turn comes, they can use the money for a specified period, as managed by the banker, the "Mama Sol," who is usually uneducated. This system creates a place for the poor to save and borrow money. *Sols* may be completely free with no fixed fees, or they may apply a small flat fee for the duration of the membership (focus groups, Bon Repos, 9 October 2010). *Sols* cost little and are trusted by their users because of their collective, grassroots nature. Poor families have been using these socially embedded banking systems for generations. These organized collectives have helped marginalized people create social capital within their communities. And this capital, mobilized from the grassroots, contributes to local organizing and allows people who are normally ignored to feel a part of their community (focus group, Bon Repos, 9 October 2010).

Jamaica's Partner Banks Help Communities[12]

A partner bank is a locally owned, home-grown institution for people who cannot go to a commercial bank. The cultural context helps explain why partner banks are so relevant in Jamaican society. Politics in Kingston, Jamaica's main urban centre, is marred by violence at election time, during which whitened political elites – usually the ones who have power –promise money, housing, and jobs to very poor (dark-skinned) political activists. If they fail to deliver the vote for their candidate, they will lose the political hand-outs. Academics have written extensively on this entrenched mechanism, wherein elites recruit uneducated Black masses in the ghettos to carry out heinous crimes to ensure political victory in exchange for housing or other financial benefits (Sives 2010; Tafari-Ama 2006). Whitened politicians and gangsters have for many years used slum residents to carry out their dirty work, and this has led people to distrust the political and business elites.

Business people I interviewed told me, "Partna is fi wi, and bank is fi di big man uptown" – that is, the partner bank is for the poor [us] and formal banks are for the rich. "Yuh don't have to be rich or educated to throw partna." Handa and Claremont (1999) surveyed 1,000 people in Kingston and found that 75% of the banker ladies were women between 26 and 35, who organized partner for an average of nine years. These people are aware of the community's needs. For example, "Miss Paddy" has never held a bank account at a commercial bank or credit union (interview, Kingston, Jamaica, 6 May 2009). She is one of the thousands of Jamaicans living in tenement yards downtown who do not have the birth certificate required to open a bank account.

The banker ladies (people in charge of the informal bank), who have not been trained as bankers per se, organize financial programs and create alternative financing devices. They decide who gets access to the lump sum first, and they assess the person's risk of defaulting, as a trained loan officer would do. From their longevity, it is clear that these systems are viable. The members of a partner bank know one another – indeed, sometimes they are related. There are several variants of partner banks; although all are saving plans, many are lending plans as well (Handa and Claremont 1999; Klak and Hey 1992). Each person's contribution to the partner bank is called a "hand," and it is "thrown" (deposited) for a designated period of time; the pooled money is called a "draw." In some partner banks, people draw lots to determine the order for obtaining a loan (interview, three banker ladies, March to July 2009; Rutherford 2000). Peer dynamics ensure that people comply with payment rules, and social sanctions are applied in the case of default.

People want financial systems that enable them to do what they need to do without restricting their freedoms. At least 82% (191 out of 233) of the entrepreneurs I interviewed "throw partna" (participate in a partner bank). Gray (2004, 83) asserts that people in the slums are very close and intent on helping one another. In interviews, the partner bank was the lending model that most people (57%, 133 out of 233) trusted to meet their needs. For them, commercial banks ranked fairly low; that model did not seem to resonate with people. Partner banks are similar to banks in that they offer people a place to save their money and to borrow money. However, entrepreneurs told me they prefer the partner banks because there is "no rigmarole" (paper work), the banker ladies are trustworthy, there are few fees, and access is easy. The banker ladies I interviewed claimed that repayment rates are high (usually 100%) because people trust these systems. Partner banks are deeply rooted in social relationships: they are there when nobody else is and are able to help people develop self-confidence – and their communities.

Susus and Box-Hand: A Regional Phenomenon

In Trinidad and Tobago and Guyana at present, Indo-Caribbean political leaders dominate national politics to the exclusion of Afro-Caribbean people. A pervasive cultural narrative disparages the business acumen of Afro-Caribbeans. Lenders, usually men of East Indian descent, hesitate to make loans to poor Black people in the slums (Hossein 2014a). Meanwhile, the norms that originally developed within the commercial banking sector have been migrating to microfinance programs so as to discriminate against poor clients of African background. In Guyana's microfinance sector, the main specialized microfinance agencies, IPED and SBDT, are managed and staffed by educated middle-class Indo-Guyanese, who lend to Indo-Guyanese clients (ibid.). At least 65% of the small entrepreneurs I interviewed in Allbouystown told me that they borrowed money from box-hand banks and used their savings from penny banks, because they could not access loans.[13]

Class-based racism and partisan politics in Trinidad and Guyana have interfered with Black people's access to finance (even within microfinance programs that are supposedly there to help them). As noted in chapter 3, the largest microfinance bank in Trinidad is the state-run NEDCO. Partisan politics dictates how it conducts its lending, with the result that 75% of its portfolio was in arrears as of July 2013. This suggests that NEDCO is making loans to party supporters, who see such loans as entitlements. Small business people who cannot access loans therefore turn to informal banks (Hossein 2014c).

African slaves brought with them West African traditions of *susus* (group savings plans), through which they mobilized savings on a weekly basis (Mintz 1955; St Pierre 1999). Even under slavery or indentured servitude, Africans and Indians carried out sideline businesses and held market days with the extra provisions they grew. After slavery was abolished, colonized Trinidad and Tobago and Guyana imported indentured workers from India. Africans were now free, but banks and planters made it difficult for them to engage in business. This is why freed Africans pooled resources in saving clubs to buy plots of land and villages.

Susu banks in Grenada are similar to those found in Trinidad, and they too are based on a rotating system. My great-grandmother, Maude Gittens, was a Grenadian-born *susu* banker who lived in Trinidad. She would collect weekly deposits from the *susu* members and give a lump sum of cash to one member. Grenadians participated in maroons (informal collectives) during the authoritarian regimes of Gairy (1967–79), the New Jewel Movement (1979–83), and the US invasion in 1983 (Sandford and Vigilante 1984, 32). *Susus* and box-hand banks are based on daily or weekly plans, with each cycle spanning 6 to 12 weeks. The "boxer" or "box lady" manages the money collected from participants and usually charges a small flat fee (Besson 1996). People trust the *susu* bankers. As "Mummy," an elderly woman with lots of energy who has owned a mango and spice stall in the central market in St George for more than 30 years, explains:

> *Susu* is di ting! [*Susu* is a good thing to have] You [can] get your money when you want it and nobody give you problem [referring to *susu* banker]. You can say to the [*susu*] banker, give me a hand [lump sum of cash] and she will because she know you and what you will do [with the money]. We bind ... no one can change this way. (interview, 14 June 2013)

Susu, partner, and box-hand banks allow excluded people to access large lump sums of cash after saving for a few weeks. This would never be possible at a commercial bank, especially for poor people of African heritage. "Mummy" tried several times to get a loan at the commercialized microfinance bank Microfin, but it was a long drawn-out process that was hard to follow – unlike with the *susu* banks. In interviews, members of *susu*, partner, and box-hand banks were open about the difficulty they had getting loans from banks, indicating that this was why informal banks were so important (Hossein 2014a; 2014c). In Grenada, a rum shop owner in the Grand Anse valley explained this connection to *susu*:

> If you don't 'ave assets to show Mr. Bankman then you get nothing [a loan]. People go to *susu* because it means everybody is growing together and at the same time. What a feeling. *Susu* is what we have and it is straightforward and we will always use it. (interview, 14 June 2013)

In this way, banker ladies give excluded Afro-Caribbean people a safe place to lodge their savings. Not only do informal banks provide alternatives to commercial banks, but they also are a way of restoring people's faith after they have experienced everyday indignities. According to Gibson-Graham and colleagues (2013), everyday people are actively resisting market fundamentalism when they show that they can create economies embedded in the community. In giving money to excluded people, these informal banks provide an alternative to an oppressive system. These banks contribute to strengthening civil society and people's voices.

Conclusion

Millions of African-Caribbean people engage in collective banking systems, and these institutions have strong African traditions. Clientelist banking programs in the Jamaica case have made people rethink where they want to do business. Those who are continually denied access to finance are forced to retreat towards self-financing options like informal banks. Haitians are fortunate that within the microfinance arena, the home-grown *caisses populaires* have a prominent role in society. The most compelling collectives are run by banker ladies, who validate the work of marginalized people in ways that individualistic and capitalist firms do not. Informal banks and *caisses populaires* are real-life double-movements that challenge commercial banks by bringing a sense of community into financial programs.

In communities, people mobilize economic resources from within. Yet these community-based banks often operate under the radar and are not counted as part of the microfinance arena. Some commercial banks, however, are taking note of the affinity people have for collective banks. For example, the Bank of Nova Scotia of Jamaica, the Jamaica National Building Society, and Haiti's Sogebank all realize how popular informal banks are and have offered plans based on these institutions, such as "partner plan" and "Mama sol." But these copycat programs do not offer the same kind of refuge for local poor people. Commercial banks know full well that people have an emotional connection to collective institutions; that is why they try to imitate them. Collective and cooperative institutions, both formal and informal, are concerned with more than just survival or access to finance. These institutions testify to people's perseverance in avoiding being manipulated by economic and political elites to conform to their ideas of mainstream business.

For generations, people have perfected informal banks and cooperative institutions as means to reach excluded people. In doing so, they have demonstrated that marginalized people do not sit idly by and let commercial banks and newer microfinance programs alienate them. The Haiti and Grenada cases show that the alternative banking systems of cooperatives and credit unions focus on savings (not credit or debt) and dividends to build wealth *within* communities. Furthermore, banker ladies across the region have remade financial systems based on ancestral systems of collectivity that put people first. The community-driven banks that are rooted in group action are a stand against individualized modes of banking. This is perhaps why the commercialized microfinance industry has downplayed the influence that cooperative banks have on people's lives. It is worth noting that contesting economic liberalism by organizing alternative banks comes with risks. It takes courage for a socially conscious group to take a stand against the commercial model. The story in Haiti, and to some extent in Grenada, of credit unions and informal banks indicates that people are coming together to create collective banks throughout the region. Yet the microfinance industry has remained silent, not recognizing these contributions of cooperative lenders in microbanking. The most impressive demonstration of this contribution in most visible in the everyday risks Haitians take when they engage in collective institutions and in this way voice that collective institutions are a better alternative for ensuring inclusive finance and economic democracy.

Chapter 6

Banking on Indigenous Systems

Black people in the diaspora have for centuries been creating social economies for themselves in inhospitable environments. Studies by Gordon Nembhard (2014), K'adamwe, Bernard, and Dixon (2011), Mintz (2010), St Pierre (1999), and Du Bois (1907) show that African people in the Americas have been reorganizing business in various ways to uplift their racial group. For the most part, however, the social economy literature has ignored the contributions of Black people, and the microfinance literature tends not to focus on countries where African people live; only recently have critics started examining microfinance on the African continent.

A study of how an important tool like microfinance impacts the lives of Black people requires Black and diasporic feminist theorizing, as well as interpretative frameworks like intersectionality. The work of Black feminist Patricia Hill Collins (2000) has been central to my understanding of the social economy in the lives of the African diaspora. Diasporic Black feminism pushes for marginalized Black people to develop their own definition of themselves in society. The teachings of Black thinkers who travelled the Americas and beyond – such as Booker T. Washington, Marcus Garvey, and W.E.B. Du Bois – focus on self-reliance, group economics, and independence. This study of microfinance in the Americas, specifically in the Caribbean and among the Black diaspora, can contribute to a knowledge of how we can apply Black and feminist theorizing and intersectionality in the social economy.

The Black race was humiliated during enslavement and colonization for centuries. So it is inevitable that in Caribbean societies today and elsewhere, the African diaspora has been a historically marginalized group. The great Caribbean scholar Sidney Mintz (2010), who often forefronts his own racial and cultural roots in his work, has argued that issues of race, class, and gender have had an intense impact on the lives of Caribbean people. The experience of slavery and colonization continues to affect these very small countries in ways that are distinct from those of larger countries. There is little doubt in the minds of people who know the region, and of people have had to migrate from the region because of racial and class bias, that in order for social change to happen, it will have to be politicized. *Politicized Microfinance* posits that Black people's experiences in microfinance have varied due to different forms of politicizing. There is little dispute that identity and partisan politics trouble the region and interfere in business and society. To overcome the negative aspects of partisanship and clientelism will require socially conscious activism. In places where a people's forebears were tortured, enslaved, and colonized for centuries, any achievement of a just social economy or reversal of the tide of inequality in business and society will require politically conscious people.

The intense class, racial, and gendered politics in the Caribbean have prevented equal access to economic opportunities for people of African descent. Politicized action that inherits the lived experience of those most excluded is thus badly needed. As a Black academic, I am in the process of unlearning aspects of the social economy that are too focused on the Anglo-American perspective. I assert this with a caveat, however: I have found that the French view of the *économie sociale* has resonated more positively because of its boldness in pushing for systemic change in the ways we live. The *économie sociale* in the French tradition is grounded in civil society and works to help excluded people, those routinely overlooked for opportunities. All the same, a Eurocentric perspective on the social economy – often carried out by privileged white people who do not reflect on their own social backgrounds – remains problematic. If social economists are to really think about racialized people, they need to think about politics. Failing to consider the extent to which the social economy is politicized reduces it to a "generic" form – incapable of reacting against the deeply embedded forms of stigma and social exclusion of racialized people. It is time for scholars and practitioners alike to wake up to the pain and suffering of a historically marginalized group – the African diaspora. In *Canada's Economic Apartheid*, African Canadian political scientist Grace Galabuzi (2006) makes the poignant argument that in order for social justice organizations to unravel highly racialized systems, they must not only politicize themselves but also include people of racialized backgrounds in the fight for social justice.

Africans and the people of the diaspora have had a profound effect on alternative economics. The struggle of Black people to find a voice and to create a human economy shows that a non-political approach to the social economy cannot overturn unequal relations in society and business. Black people have been organizing and developing alternative banks and businesses for a long time. While the commercialized form of microfinance does not belong in the social economy, many forms of self-help banking done by the Black diaspora that are people-focused do belong in the social economy. Collective financial groups created by Black people are rooted in indigenous African systems. Healy (2009) has argued that the current one-dimensional form of extreme market fundamentalism needs to be challenged and that this neoliberal economic model is in crisis – which makes it an opportune time to tell the story of collective microfinance by Black people. This type of banking, which puts people first, has been able to inform newer forms of banking, such as microfinance.

We have seen that some microfinance organizations do remain part of the social economy by battling against social and financial exclusion, specifically where Black people organize in a collective manner to help one another – for example, in Haiti and Grenada. But the industry as a whole needs to own up to the fact that commercialized microbanking creates an indebtedness and individualism that separates people and enables local elites to purposely exclude certain groups because of their own political ideas. The politicized nature of banking and the people who work in banking institutions can undermine the fundamental premise of microfinance.

Larry Reed of the Microcredit Summit Campaign (2012) makes the important point that lenders are not all one homogenized type. Microbanking came onto the scene as a collective form of banking, rooted in solidarity circles, to show that business and banking can be done in new ways. This kind of collective banking, which is a deeply held tradition for indigenous African people, flies in the face of commercialized microfinance. Black feminists also note that collective and group economics have been at the core of the African diaspora's survival. This suggests to me that some microlenders are interested in profits while other bankers care about people and development. Given that there are many conscientious and community-oriented microlenders (such as credit unions, *caisses populaires*, and not-for-profits) that co-opt financial services to assist ostracized groups, we cannot reject the entire microfinance industry as a neoliberal tool. The developments in Haiti, and to a lesser extent in Grenada, make it clear that collective microbanking is a way for people to stand up to local elites. These banks are taking risks to reform microfinance to make it more inclusive. The Haitian case in particular is a testimony that lenders who have lived experience and who know the struggles of their people use microfinance as a social movement to react against economic exclusion. Haitian lenders draw on history to bring about social change and argue that they cannot afford to take a back seat.

It is vital to stand up and show that microfinance can be organized in ways that suit its people, regardless of the ideological rhetoric. Haitians are doing precisely this when they use a tool like microfinance to fight for ethics, embedding it in their local activism and in their beliefs about life and business. In some ways, the Black diaspora's co-opting of financial goods in ethical ways can be a lesson for other regions in the world. However, this story also suggests that ideological views may not be right all the time and in every context. One cannot simply plug the neoliberal agenda into every cultural context to explain why microfinance is not effective. To do so would be to undermine the hard work of the African diaspora in using microbanking to uplift its people. Their political resistance in making microbanking useful also exposes the need for politicized action in the sector that engages in business development for racialized people.

Diasporic Black feminists who study oppression see the entanglement of politics and culture in the access to economic opportunity. Thus, creating politicized social action to help people must be part and parcel of development. It is not enough to simply draw a salary and then claim to be helping people in the social economy; instead, people, particularly those of the Black diaspora, need to see development workers and microfinance experts as activists who are politically engaged in the struggle for economic inclusion. The social economy, which includes the so-called revolution in microfinance, has become too sedate. Black people in the diaspora need bankers-to-the-poor who embrace conscientious economics and who challenge the deeply embedded bias in the mindsets of people in the sector. Microfinance should not be about inserting people into unfair economic systems; rather it should be an ethical movement that creates new systems to make sure that marginalized people are included.

Much of microfinance has started to mimic conventional banking. Hiring privileged bankers and financial types to make MFIs profitable cannot bring social change. One of the most impressive financial movements has been the Nigerien Mata Masu Dubara (meaning "women on the move" in Hausa), which involves non-bankers helping local women create village-run banking systems made up of more than 100,000 people. Critics of microfinance could strengthen their argument if they recognized that the power of finance for the poor is defeated by market fundamentalism that ignores cultural politics (Grant 2002). What undermines the goal of inclusive banking is, in fact, cultural and personal politics among bankers. Many bankers-to-the-poor are not thinking about social change due to their own personal biases, and neoliberal politics enables this. The institution needs microfinance bankers who are vested in bringing political change and in questioning how commercialized microfinance operates – bankers who are secure enough that they can draw on indigenous systems.

It is only through studying the Black experience in microfinance that one learns that *politicized microbanking* can also be effective. This is particularly true in formerly enslaved and colonized countries. The culturally distinct lenders in Jamaica, Trinidad, and Guyana have tense interactions with borrowers, who differ from them in terms of class, culture, and sometimes gender. These bankers use politics in ways that deform and limit microbanking, and they can do so because they hide behind the neoliberal rhetoric of making money. Yet they will not engage with certain groups because of their own personal prejudices, even if it makes good business sense to do so (e.g., Guyana, Jamaica, and Trinidad cases). But despite the cultural politics at play in microfinance, there is also evidence within the African diaspora that some politicized bankers are using their power in new ways to assist people. This is also politicized microfinance – except these bankers use their power to uplift the downtrodden groups.

Bankers throughout the region, as well as many cooperative lenders, draw on African traditions to build alternative businesses. Millions of banker ladies in charge of money pools or informal banks make loans available to excluded groups. These informal banks are important because they are locally driven and help people meet their livelihood needs when even microfinance fails to help them. The banker ladies in the region, and the cooperative lenders in Haiti and Grenada, work the way they do because they have lived experience and because they embody the people they work with in terms of racial, class, and educational backgrounds. For example, Haiti's case departs from the others because the bank managers and technical staff have social origins similar to those of the people they work with. These bankers carry out indigenous African banking, either informally or formally, to reach the masses. Banker ladies are often low-income and uneducated women who know full well that they need activism to move ahead; they also live right in the community, experiencing the everyday pain of their comrades. In my view, this form of politicized banking of the African diaspora strives for social progress. In the Black experience, one learns that to be "politicized" does not have to be something that Black people condemn. Politicized microfinance also means that socially conscious microlenders make deliberate decisions to help excluded groups, even when there is danger in doing so. These bankers co-opt microfinance and move it towards conscious economics; however, in doing this, they themselves realize that they have to be politicized in order to confront historically ingrained prejudices and to help the oppressed.

In *Politicized Microfinance*, new themes have emerged that better tell the story of Black people's experiences with microfinance in the Americas. This study offers insights not only for regions of the world with significant African diaspora communities, but also for other marginalized groups or indigenous peoples who experience systemic social and economic exclusion. Wuttunee (2004), for example, has examined the social economy experience for Aboriginal people in Canada, revealing its varied and community-focused nature. Often these ancient indigenous systems have been overlooked; yet these cooperative systems have carried on in spite of the harsh social environment experienced by these indigenous peoples. The African diaspora recognizes the contribution of indigenous economic systems and can relate to Aboriginal indigeneity because of the shared legacy of violent enslavement and/or colonization.

In this closing chapter, I review the contribution of the Black diaspora to the social economy. I have come to understand – and perhaps you have as well – that the current Black social economy offers much in terms of African peoples' engagement with alternative economics. This work contributes to feminist theorizing about the social economy because it presents a Black lens tied to an intersectional interpretative framework. In the remainder of the chapter, I highlight the chief findings of this study and share some key policy considerations for rethinking social exclusion as it pertains both to the Black microbanking experience and to the rest of the sector.

The Black Social Economy in the Americas

Much community organizing among Black people is informal. The coming together to help one another during times of adversity is a certain sign of Black people's commitment to the social economy. In *Take Back the Economy*, Gibson-Graham, Cameron, and Healy (2013) show that diverse economies are grounded in community everywhere. From this feminist understanding, the African diaspora's social economy can be traced back to its slave ancestors, who created markets and communal banks in an era when it was illegal for Black people to do so (St Pierre 1999; Wong 1996; Witter 1989; Mintz 1955). In colonial Jamaica, cooperatives built from the ground up helped citizens agitate for independence. Haitians have engaged in cooperation throughout their country's history and formalized cooperatives at the turn of the twentieth century. African-inspired collectives have dominated life in the Caribbean, especially for marginalized groups. Enslavement and colonization have created racially tiered economic systems in which cultural prejudices (race, class, and gender) are prevalent and cultural politics become part of the decision-making in MFIs. While the case studies of Caribbean microbanking in Jamaica, Haiti, and Guyana reveal that lending unfolds quite differently depending on context and history, all three places have exhibited exclusionary microbanking due to the politicization of individual bankers.

Many well-meaning practitioners and researchers in the social economy and microfinance lack the lived experience of their clients or the people they write about. This matters to Black people. The Black scholar-activists in the Americas I have relied on in this study, such as Gordon Nembhard (2014), Du Bois (1907; 2007[1903]), Gina Ulysse (2007), Njoki Wane et al. (2002) and Patricia Hill Collins (2000), have all made the poignant argument that the Black social and economic experience has been under-studied in terms of its rich contribution to the world. Nothing makes this point better than the UN's current enactment of the International Decade for People of African Descent, which drives home the fact that the major contributions of Black people to humanity have been ignored. In *Politicized Microfinance*, local subtleties in the five cases show cultural and historical variations in microfinance outcomes among Black people. Applying diasporic Black feminist thought within an intersectional framework has served this study well, allowing me to identify the extent to which access to finance is politicized. Furthermore, this "politicized microfinance" can take the socially conscious form of political action to tackle deeply embedded forms of social exclusion in business and society. This can assist the people who work in the social economy, helping them understand the political processes that complicate the disbursement of economic goods. One step forward is to recognize that interconnecting oppressions of class, gender, and race/skin privilege affect microbanking. To counteract identity and partisan politics from within, microbanking will require managers and staff people to politicize themselves – that is, to be actively conscious in a way that can help disenfranchised groups of colour.

Most of the business people in this study, except for those in Haiti and Grenada, did not trust MFIs because of the lenders' exclusionary practices and unwillingness to take risks to help them. Clients' feelings of distrust are reinforced when microfinance managers show prejudice against them, as we observed in the cases of Jamaica, Guyana, and Trinidad. In these countries, microlending reflects the deeply entrenched class, race, and gender prejudices of people in positions of power. The findings also show the importance of the attitudes of microbankers in shaping how resources are distributed. But politics does not have to be oppressive. In fact, as I argue in this study, it takes political courage to confront the personal biases that arise within the social economy. Making investments in economic development is not enough: we need to politicize the work people do in the social economy. Pro-poor financial services focused on grassroots collectives can watch for and check race, gender, and class discrimination. Lenders must be ready to hire staff who know the environment and the people with whom they are working.

The original intent of microfinance was to correct social and market failures that were unfair to certain groups of people – more specifically, to assist the poor who had been shut out by conventional banks (Wilson 2001; Rahman 1999). This idea of turning conventional banking upside down in order to help the excluded was inspiring and has captivated the world. Yet its initial fiery rhetoric has dissipated. The Black diaspora can relate to the bold outing of elitist banks because of their banking experience. In my examination of the Black experience in microfinance, I found microfinance for low-income entrepreneurs to be a highly political topic. Economic and political elites interested in controlling the behaviour of constituents in poor communities try to stymie interactions with these groups. Financial profit has become a priority in commercialized microfinance, and managers have been putting aside the social goals of microcredit as they strive for profits

(Sinclair 2012; Rankin 2001; Harper 1998). Again, this is not happening in every microfinance organization, but where the commercialized trend is strong, actors in the social economy need to take a stand against cultural biases in social finance.

Partisan and identity politics are deeply embedded in targeted economic development programs. Yet cultural and political bias within MFIs is never scrutinized in the social economy. The power dynamics of those in charge of disbursing resources and the race, class, and gender prejudices within lending processes have not been studied. The misuse of power in such social economy adds to the resentment of the masses towards local elites. In the Jamaica, Guyana, and Trinidad cases, ordinary people wanting access to small loans are sceptical of the targeted programs; they see local managers perverting the goals of inclusive microbanking. These managers, knowing the divisions in their own society, have misused microfinance to align with their own prejudices. Local elites corrupt microfinance, backtracking from microfinance goals in ways that lead to the exclusion, or self-exclusion, of legitimate clients. For example, some Jamaican microfinance bankers reward party activists over non-partisan business people, politicizing finance in ways that suit political elites. Privileged people in control of these resources are thus able to redirect microfinance to groups they prefer, thereby reproducing inequalities within the system.

The party and cultural politics of the sector's managers and staff can negatively affect microfinance programs for the poor. In the Jamaican and Guyanese cases, local elites do not follow business practice when they deny eligible business people access to finance because of their own biases. In Trinidad, government-owned microfinance has retarded microcredit development because loans are based on political party support rather than on business qualifications. If the point of commercialized microfinance is to scale up clients, then cultural bias and party politics are impediments to this. MFIs cannot be sustained if personal bias prevents qualified business people from accessing microcredit, as these exclusionary banking practices turn Jamaican, Guyanese and Trinidadian business people towards informal banks, such as partner, box-hand, and *susus*.

In India, where Kim Wilson (2001) has worked for many years in formalized microfinance, the importance of collective self-managed banking groups is recognized, as marginalized groups are able to control access to monies within their own socio-economic group. Around the globe, banker ladies, mainly women from poor areas, create community banks to help comrades excluded from formalized banking systems, including microfinance programs. Ordinary people who recognize the manipulative politics operating in MFIs turn to informal banks because they know and trust the banker ladies running them. I found that business people in low-income communities distrust the local people managing microbanking programs. Choosing a communal bank allows business people to remain independent through enterprise, and this generates a form of resistance from below. Black people are not easily convinced to opt out of banks due to the argument that they are "neoliberal" or commercialized, but they have opted out of these banks because they project a cultural bias against them. For the African diaspora, this move is about taking back banking and focusing on the collective nature of banking that is indigenous to many people of colour. Collective, member-owned models – both formal and informal – determine the sharing of dividends by vote. African diaspora thinkers like Marcus Garvey and W.E.B. Du Bois agree that in order for business enterprise to improve marginalized Black communities, it needs to be collective and focused on helping people of colour. In spite of the push towards a commercialized, neoliberal political environment, collective enterprises persist – especially among the African diaspora. This is a vital finding not adequately addressed by critics of market fundamentalism. It is only when one examines Black experience in microbanking that one discovers that collective microbanking remains very much part of the microfinance environment. To ignore this experience of the African diaspora is to undermine the resistance of Black people in an era of neoliberal politics.

Cultural Bias in the Social Economy

Microfinance, the goal of which was to make microcredit accessible to the entrepreneurial poor, is in reality not easily accessible. In this study, Jamaican lenders were unwilling to acknowledge the role of identity biases, especially race, in the allocation of microloans; whereas in Guyana, lenders admitted their cultural biases without apology. Trinidadian state elites, who run the largest microfinance bank, were aware that patronage was intertwined with their lending processes, which explains why poor Afro-Trinidadians in east Port of Spain are excluded from access to microfinance under the current regime. The cases of Jamaica, Guyana, and Trinidad underline the disconnectedness of the decision-makers from the marginalized people seeking microloans. This divide increases the potential for race, class, and gender biases within microfinance.

In the Jamaican case, exclusionary microfinance takes place because class-identified lenders, who can be partisan, discriminate against certain *hustlas* because of their class (e.g., living location, language, education), race (e.g., skin colour, hair), and gender (e.g., men, women with children by different fathers) as well as partisan politics. Cultural bias is starting to receive attention in mainstream microfinance. In 2015, Joshua Goldstein's blog "Racism is endemic. What role for microfinance?" through the Washington-based Center for Financial Inclusion discussed the growing concern about the prejudice taking root inside MFIs. I have shown that microfinance programs that collude with political actors block the goal of social empowerment for the Black diaspora. Microlenders and political elites legitimize an informal order when they work through Dons because this structure oppresses and limits the freedoms of *hustlas*. Politicized microfinance forces many business people to make calculated decisions to exclude themselves from loan programs to avoid clientelist practices. As a result, *hustlas* turn to partner banks – money pools run by women – to resist the power of Big Men. Partner banks, which reach tens of thousands of people, are a testimony to the tenacity of hard-working business people, who use informal banks to be independent of politics. Those business people who have refused to take on politicized economic resources available to them have engendered positive developments in their communities, and their use of partner banks is what makes their story so compelling.

The Center for Financial Inclusion cited anecdotal experiences of racism in microfinance in Spanish-speaking Latin America, where most managers were white and the borrowers dark-skinned and non-white (ibid.). The Guyana case indicates that powerful racial elites in a pluralistic society have restricted access to finance for Black people. This pluralism is the result of the historical plantation economic system in Guyana, which required African slaves and Indian indentured servants to work the land (Despres 1967). In Guyana, political power over time has resided with certain racial groups, who have been able to oppress other groups. Educated and privileged Indo-Guyanese misuse this multiracial environment to incite conflict between cultural groups as a means to attain power for their own group. In this study, I found that most microlenders (except for one Afro lender, now defunct) were adamant that the financial exclusion of Black people was justified based on their understanding of the business ethics of Afro-Guyanese.

Indo-Guyanese lenders, most of them educated men, perpetuated stereotypes of Afro-Guyanese, which undoubtedly affected their decisions about which loans to make. One prominent Indo-led microfinance lender, when appraising applications, applies a covert married condition that results in the exclusion of Black hucksters, who are less likely to be legally married. As a result of this systematic exclusion, Afro-Guyanese business people have relied on penny banks and box-hands (collective banks) to meet their livelihood needs.

Practitioners and academics need to expose the cultural biases in the social economy. In environments where extreme cultural bias exists, political practice has taken a powerful form that humiliates certain racial groups without support systems. Activism and a deliberate stand against cultural bias are needed, otherwise the social economy becomes a paradox – that is, a place that is supposed to confront inequality but that fails to address the racism that permeates it. This study contributes in this direction by acknowledging the existence of these cultural politics and at the same time taking stock of the ways in which Black people can co-opt financial resources. In Haiti, the banker ladies and the Haitian managers and staff in the collective MFIs, even whitened elites, were politically astute and aware of class and racial conflicts, and they made sure that financial goods were directed to groups who needed them. Diasporic Black feminisms have helped me see that conscious Black activists, banker ladies, and people in the *caisses populaires* have direct knowledge of the lives of the people for whom they organize programs to improve social conditions. This is their mark on the social economy: they are resisting exclusionary practices in order to reach excluded groups. This provides a lesson for microfinance practitioners worldwide, allowing them to see that extreme forms of social exclusion can invigorate microfinance to step up and do its job to combat locally driven cultural bias. But this change will require staff who are politically aware of the inequality in their society and ready to use microfinance as a tool to unravel economic injustice. It will depend on the stamina of the people in the third sector to co-opt financial resource and to react against systemic exclusion in the social economy.

Anti-Male Gender Politics in Microcredit

While at first glance microfinance's focus on women seems to make gendered exclusion impossible, it should be noted that a more commercialized microbanking industry has meant that more men are receiving microloans, not women. In the Caribbean context, female-focused models have been influenced by not-for-profits that have targeted women, such as the Grameen Bank. As a result, Caribbean microfinance has tended to exclude poor men. However, this complicates the living space for the female counterparts of these men. It appears that microfinance programs and methods that have learned and borrowed from abroad fail to take into account the local context. Although Brohman (1995, 130) stresses the importance of programming for the local context, Caribbean lenders to the poor have looked to different cultural milieux to craft their programs – and this often works against Black people. The extrapolation of women-focused financial programs supports the growing literature that women-only microfinance projects exacerbate intra-household conflict between the sexes, as well as conflict among women of the same social group (Ulysse 2007; Tafari-Ama 2006; Miller 1991). In Kingston, the preponderance of women working in MFIs at senior levels and the focus on women as clients do not ensure gender equality. Rather, a gender imbalance has disempowered women and placed many female clients at risk. The resulting violence against women indicates that microfinance that overlooks the context can complicate life for low-income Black women. Moreover, marginalized men who are excluded from microfinance may abandon their families, leaving women overburdened with the family's financial obligations.

Diasporic Black feminism helps us understand identity politics in microbanking. While access to microfinance is not exclusively gender-related (because class and race biases also affect who can access a microloan), anti-male bias does occur in some places. In the Jamaican case, educated women leading microfinance organizations, many of whom are Black, are the main instigators of gendered bias against poor men. Many of the higglers and female business owners I met told me they were not happy that the "fancy" women from uptown (female loan officers) were preventing their male partners, husbands, sons, and brothers from accessing financial services. For change to occur in low-income communities, marginalized Black men must also become part of the development process. The failure to rethink gender in context leaves microbusiness women in these communities disempowered in a conflicted space and facing angry and emasculated men. Jamaican men (potential clients) feel excluded by the educated women in charge of financial programs because these middle-class actors can pick and choose which urban poor can participate in the programs.[1]

Clientelist Microbanking

Party politics and clientelism clearly have a negative effect on microfinance development in Jamaica, Guyana, and Trinidad. The negative outcomes are distinct within the Black Americas because of the contextual realities in each case. The Jamaican case illustrates how microfinance can appear on the surface to be effectively aiding development given that many seasoned female microfinance professionals are engaged in the arena. But on closer examination it becomes evident that microfinance risks reinforcing oppressive structures. Under Jamaica's Big Man politics, economic resources are disbursed unfairly to certain segments of the urban poor, as Dons and members of parliament (MPs) insert themselves in various ways into formal lending projects in the downtown slums to push their own agendas. Educated male Indo-Guyanese lenders are perceived as having close relations with the political elite. These Guyanese lenders also exhibit cultural preferences when approving loans and have embraced the "anyone but Afro-Guyanese" mode of thinking. In Trinidad, the main microfinance agency is state-owned, and political elites are directly involved in making decisions on micro and small loans. In the microfinance industry, bankers cannot claim political neutrality; the MFIs in the region show evidence that partisan politics and political elites have corrupted the allocation process. Indeed, political funds subsidize many microbanking projects in the region; the understanding here is that political supporters will be able to access loans. In all the cases – Jamaica, Guyana, and Trinidad – marginalized Black business people know full well about these political arrangements.

Because of the seepage of formal and partisan politics into Jamaican microfinance, many business people choose to avoid or withdraw from microfinancing. It is likely that the type of clientelist microfinance exposed in the Jamaica case can be found in other diverse developing contexts. Politics is deeply embedded in many microcredit programs, and local managers can respond either by nurturing political manipulation (as seen in Jamaica, Trinidad, and Guyana) or by stemming the biases (as seen in Haiti and Grenada) that interfere with the allocation of microloans. Local people should not be underestimated: they know that their politicians misuse funds and collude with microbankers. In Jamaica, Dons are also involved in microfinance by enabling microfinance retailers to do business in slum communities; indeed, at times the lenders and Dons work together to serve their self-interests. Lenders want security and use the informal order to ensure repayments; Dons control new entrants and manage the residents. *Hustlas* perceive these alliances correctly, and they know that the consequences may be dire for defaulters. Thus, many opt out of microfinance programs, not wanting to be controlled by politicians or gangsters. In this way, they quietly resist politicized microfinance, turning to their own local partner banks.

Political elites and some privileged ethnic groups are powerful enough to shape microfinance programs and to control access to them. They are also aware that "access to finance" can be an important tool for containing and managing dissent. As the Jamaican case illustrates, state involvement in micro-enterprise development is vital because emancipating the urban poor by such means can reduce dependence on political bosses. This sort of independence threatens the politicians. The political actors I met interfered in microfinance because they wanted to be seen as benefactors helping the poor masses. A prime example of this occurred in Haiti after the 2010 earthquake. When a fire broke out in the Croix des Bossales market, then-president René Préval interfered in microfinance by legislating that the *ti machanns* would not have to repay their loans. Managers in the leading MFIs quickly condemned Préval's resort to subsidies, out of fear that politicians' involvement in microfinance would lead to a middle-class takeover of microfinance operations.

Banking and political elites implicate themselves in targeted economic programs that can destroy people's lives. For example, in India in 2010, the suicides of microfinance clients in Andhra Pradesh resulted in increased government regulation to contain commercial lenders – regulation that coincidentally favoured the government's own loan programs (Salmon 2010). In March 2011, Prime Minister Sheik Hasina of Bangladesh ousted Muhammad Yunus, founder and Director of Grameen Bank, because she was aware of the political advantages of controlling microfinance to win electoral support (Roodman 2012a; *New York Times*, 21 March 2011). It is clear that political elites in Jamaica, Guyana, and Trinidad are attuned to the political power they can garner from controlling microfinance to the urban poor.

Political control of the urban poor is a goal that goes beyond the three cases in this study. When local managers capture lending programs and apply their own race, class, or gender biases against people otherwise eligible for them, this compromises the social development aspect of microfinance. Identity and party politics should not determine who gets loans, but intersecting identities (such as race, class, and gender) and partisan politics do affect allocation. The struggle between those who have power and those on the receiving end has been the African diaspora's experience in the Americas. To some extent, microbanking mimics how white masters used to make decisions about their slaves. The degree of power held by individuals within the social economy – that is, within MFIs – is the key variable in explaining Black people's experience in microfinance.

Politicized Microfinance

Examining the economy in relation to society requires people to make bold moves. In *Civilizing Globalization* (2014), Sandbrook and Güven argue that market fundamentalism can be managed through political strategies so that social life is not subordinate to markets. Karl Polanyi (1944) believed that man-made, Western laissez-faire economics was political in its origin – a line of thought that suggests that to undo it will require political action. J.K. Gibson-Graham (1996, 2006) argues that new economic possibilities can be found in the micropolitics of ordinary people but that it will take political will to recognize these actions as changing the oppressive market extremism in business and society.

The Black experience in microbanking reveals that in order for it to assist excluded people, microfinance needs to be politicized in such a way that it advances social progress. Haiti since its inception has experienced political and economic hardships like no other country. It has been challenged by extreme poverty, unforgiving natural disasters, vicious undemocratic regimes, violent political leaders, and intensely racialized class conflicts. Yet the Haitian case in this book stands out, in that it demonstrates that local organizations can actually work to make microbanking people-oriented. Haitian lenders, the *caisses populaires*, have managed to stave off racial and class biases in allocating financing to the country's poorest citizens. This is an exceptional finding, because in general, development aid in Haiti has not been effective. The women sellers, the *ti machanns*, expressed a different attitude towards microlending than the business people in Jamaica and Guyana, who were sceptical of these programs and the people running them. The *ti machanns* embraced microbanking – a difference in attitude that seemed to originate in the fact that microbanking developed in Haiti during periods of extreme hardship. Cruel and oppressive regimes have alienated the *moun andeyo*, leaving them to their own devices, and cooperatives and *caisses populaires* have been important to the local response to that alienation. Managers, who resemble their clients, understand this history and have cultivated lending programs that are radical in this discourse.

Most Haitians access money through informal banks: the *caisses populaires* and the *sols*. Both types of banks are African-inspired *kombits* (collectives) that have persisted under repressive regimes. All of the Haitians I interviewed expressed pride in their cooperatives as well as gratitude for them for helping the poor survive. Lenders have developed financial programs that align with this social context. Haiti's bankers-to-the-poor genuinely understand the lived reality of the people they work with and have absorbed the cultural traits of the *ti machanns* they serve. Many of the bankers themselves come from those social backgrounds, and others have simply embraced these values. Microbankers take a political stand when they declare openly that class discrimination infused with racism marginalizes the masses. The social consciousness of these managers encourages them to use microfinance as a tool for transforming the economic situation of Haiti's poorest citizens. Their approach to Haitian microfinance is inclusive of the masses, and they take serious deadly risks in following it.

The radical rhetoric of "economic democracy" (defined, for me, as closing the widening economic gap between the rich and the *moun andeyo*) espoused by Haitian managers (foreign and local) is absent in Jamaican, Trinidadian, and Guyanese microfinance. Haitian lenders, even whitened elites, were intuitively aware of class and racial conflicts, and despite the stratified social environment, they used financial services in a radical way to benefit those who had been ostracized by political and business elites. Haitian lenders view access to loans as a way to level the playing field for excluded people. This attitude is remarkable given the apartheid-like social structure that exists in the country. It also signals that bringing change in racialized societies involves taking on some degree of risk to challenge the status quo. In Haiti, most lenders are at most one or two generations removed from the people, and this helps them ground their work in practical knowledge. Haitian lenders, including the whitened managers, thus see microfinance as a tool for bringing about economic democracy. This unique stance towards microfinance actually injects the "revolution" back into the microfinance sector, as Haitian cooperative lenders seek to build a consciousness in society about inequality.

Towards Socially Conscious Economics: Building Home-Grown Institutions

People, especially those who cannot fit into mainstream business systems, have turned to home-grown institutions. In *A Postcapitalist Politics*,

Gibson-Graham (2006) has shown that local community economies are everywhere. As early as the sixteenth century, slaves in Haiti (then called Hispaniola) were using *sols* and *gwoupmans* (collectives). These influenced the development of cooperative institutions; indeed, they continue to reach millions of people today. Black cooperative culture has been around for a long time and is deeply embedded in communities as a way to contest political wrongdoings. A weak state, extremely high levels of poverty, and the historical alienation of the *moun andeyo* have all contributed to the rise of collective microfinance for Haitians. It was Karl Polanyi in *The Great Transformation: The Political and Economic Origins of Our Time* (1944) who first pointed out that there is great diversity in how markets operate around the world and that people carry out double-movements alongside an extremist economy. Poor Black entrepreneurs have always had to reorganize market systems for themselves (Bandele 2010; Gordon Nembhard 2014; Du Bois 2007[1903]). Despite a weak and corrupt state, Haitians have a proclivity for democratizing local structures and pooling community resources for the well-being of the community through the *sols*. *Caisses populaires* have met people's needs, illustrating that formalized financial services can succeed by following a cooperative banking model. Similarly, the Grenada case shows that collective action helps direct money in a people-focused way.

Haitian microlenders – Black and local whitened elites as well as foreigners – actively engage in a discourse about economic democracy to correct the social injustices perpetrated by an entitled minority that controls the country's wealth. During my time in the field, I found that many bankers in the region were reluctant to talk about party politics, or gender, race, and class bias in financing; but Haitian microfinance lenders, Black people, local whitened elites, and foreigners were all eager to discuss these issues. It may be that the local staff in microfinance programs, especially in the *caisses populaires*, are drawn from the very communities they serve, and that concepts of economic democracy are not mere rhetoric but a part of the social agenda for these agencies.

Across the region (and elsewhere), millions of people participate in African-inherited informal collective banks. The literature on informal banks is extensive, but while this literature examines people's ingenuity in creating local banking programs, it does not discuss the agency of uneducated Black women in organizing collective banking systems when conventional lenders fail to do so. These collective banks provide financial services to excluded people (or those who are self excluded) and draw on rules and practices that align with the local society and are not regulated by outsiders. Cooperative models share the dividends and profits among their members, and it is the membership that determines how profits are used. The Black women who run the informal banks – banker ladies – operate in a business-like fashion and make sure that members repay their borrowed funds in a timely manner. The cooperative model in microbanking thus presents an alternative way to organize financial services; it is a concrete example of a home-grown model for civilizing markets through collectivity.

Policy Considerations to End Exclusionary Microfinance

People of the marginalized African diaspora want to be able to engage in markets on their own terms, but exclusionary economic programs often make it difficult for them to do so. Exclusionary practices in financial development have different outcomes depending on the context and the local politics. Racial intermingling in the past has led to complex cleavages along class, race, and gender lines. In the Caribbean, the legacy of slavery and racial intermingling has fostered a whitened minority elite that has benefited from its inheritance. In the Caribbean today, many of the rich people are descendants of the planter class, while the majority of people of African ancestry – the landless ones trying to survive in a harsh economic environment – are very dark-skinned Black people. It is true that a significant number of educated Blacks emerged during the post-independence era, but this group has not always assisted the urban poor. Race, class, and partisan politics are very much intertwined in the lives of Black people in the Caribbean region. It is important for social economy organizations to be mindful of this crucial political history, for it determines "who gives" and "who receives" the economic goods.

Eligible business people are often unable to access financing, even through microfinance programs. The present study has shown that deeply embedded systemic discrimination hinders MFIs in Jamaica, Guyana, and Trinidad. However, Haiti's story is different. Despite Haiti's similar legacy of race and class-based politics, the educated Black people in the country are divided: some have used their power to deprive people of basic resources, while others have used their education to advocate for social change. It is Black people from the latter group who have been working in microfinance organizations in Port-au-Prince. These technical managers use their skills to help the marginalized by correcting unfair political conditions and market imperfections. They know the struggles of poor people trying to make better lives because they watched their own mothers and grandmothers struggle as small traders. These Haitian managers view microloan programs as a political tool for emancipating the economically downtrodden masses. The radical rhetoric we hear in Haiti touting microfinance as a tool for change is missing in the other cases. Instead, bankers in Jamaica, Trinidad, and Guyana allow their personal biases to interfere with the allocation of loans, thereby nurturing inequalities.

There are no mechanisms of accountability to expose this deliberate use of identity and partisan politics to harm vulnerable populations. These intermediaries mask their own prejudices as "helping the urban poor," when in fact their approach to handling financial services stigmatizes certain groups and contributes to local conflicts. Jamaican managers and staffs have applied class-based biases infused with racism to allow certain *hustlas* access to financing. The Jamaican case is further complicated by clientelism. Microfinance managers who subscribe to a white ethos and uptown norms, and who are fully aware of the garrison politics downtown, allow partisan politics to take root in these environments. Only *hustlas* who conform to these uptown middle-class value systems are able to access microloans. As a result of the attitudes and actions of the people managing these programs, most business people downtown do not trust microfinance as a tool to help them. Policy changes are needed to counter these covert activities and to ensure that microlending is consistent with social empowerment.

Anti-discrimination policies are absent from the economic development programs that have been established to assist marginalized groups. Bold policies are needed to mitigate cultural bias by ensuring that these programs hire staff who resemble the marginalized groups. Extreme exclusion has been so systematic that there is now a need to target excluded groups and to acknowledge the partisan politics at play. Interestingly, the Haitian case may be the one to instruct the region (and other diverse places) on how to improve outreach and develop inclusive financing for the poor. Very few lenders who understand the context can mitigate the class and racial bias in pro-poor financial programs because of the risks this entails. Yet Haitian managers and staffs take these risks every day. They have learned from the masses how to develop and organize financial products, services, and programs, borrowing from local traditions to meet the livelihood needs of those who have been completely excluded by society. Microfinance is limited in what it can do to transform the social inequalities that pervade Haitian society, but at least Haitians have shown that social economists need to be shaken out of their comfort zones and fight for social and economic change.

I suggest two policy directions to address the issue of exclusionary microfinance: the first concerns partisan politics, and the second concerns the systemic marginalization of certain groups based on identity politics.[2] At the national level, I aim these recommendations at state agencies as well as banks engaged in microfinance to ensure that internalized biases are rooted out of these pro-poor lending institutions. Political and identity bias jeopardizes development investments, as there is a risk of social conflict when prejudices are embedded in financial programs. At the regional level, bilateral and multilateral donor and policy agencies are responsible for exposing social inequalities. Given the historical context of the region, I am aware that what I am proposing will not be easy. In the 1990s, no one thought that social performance management systems could be embedded in microfinance, but socially inclined MFIs are now using these systems. It does not cost policy-makers or bankers anything to have zero tolerance for partisan or identity politics. But it will take political will on the part of bankers.

Partisan politics should be a unit of analysis when microfinance organizations are evaluated. This means that in the annual institutional appraisals there would be a line item for the category of "politics active." If there is evidence of a negative form of politics, then the appraisal should give a low score for performance. Partisan politics will affect the external funds MFIs can receive, because most investors do not want to risk losing their money due to party politicking; but often this category is not documented in the evaluations, or even mentioned. The idea here is that lenders will have to ensure that their institutions are free from partisan politics in order to access capital. In my analysis of the Black experience in the Americas, I have found that partisan politics has hindered microfinance development as a result of clientelism.

These suggested policy reforms, coming out of a deep analysis of the African diaspora's experience in microbanking, are directed towards the policy-makers and practitioners engaging in financial and enterprise development for the wider sector. Too many lenders who are well-versed in best-practice microfinance (Carib Cap website, accessed 23 August 2012) miss the embedded biases that negatively affect financial inclusion. As a result, potential clients and bankers do not trust each other. I found in my fieldwork that except in Haiti and Grenada, most marginalized people of African descent do not trust microbankers.

Personal biases among the staffs of MFIs – biases infused by racism and sexism (including anti-male bias) – are not questioned by state leaders, donors, and investors. The policy changes I put forward for stemming exclusion and assisting excluded groups are merely suggestions, and they cannot take hold if leaders to do not make it a priority to change the mindset from within their institutions. Most of the policy requirements for curbing exclusionary finance to the poor do not cost anything. I have focused on four main areas: research, education and training, privilege, and politicized microfinance.

Advancing research in microfinance. Research should cover the great diversity of lending models, such as cooperatives, the private sector, civil society, and not-for-profits. Ending identity and cultural bias in microbanking will be very difficult. MFIs that claim to be interested in financial inclusion must track who they lend to. Data should be disaggregated by race, location, gender, age, and education in order to understand which segments of the poor are being left out. Research can also document microbanking cases that move towards socially conscious economics. There is a need to focus more on examples of alternative finance and the struggles of certain lenders (e.g., the Haiti case) rather than on commercial microfinance. Indigenous banking options such as cooperatives, ROSCAs, and banker ladies should be counted as part of the microfinance arena.

Increasing political awareness in education. Major microfinance training programs, such as the Boulder Institute of Microfinance, the Microenterprise Development Institute in New Hampshire, and the School of African Microfinance, should offer courses for lenders (especially managers and senior staff) on personal bias and the politics of microfinance. Leaders in MFIs should relocate banks to the communities they serve (e.g., credit unions in Haiti), for this is one way to combat elitism. Another step could be to reverse middle-class bias for the nuclear family. Thus, lenders would not be able to reject borrowers because of their marital status, and single mothers or women with multiple partners would not be treated as a high risk.

Stemming politicized microfinance. Politics should be a unit of analysis when MFIs are being evaluated. To understand whether "politics is active," evaluators need to go beyond technical issues and meet with former clients – who tend to speak their minds freely. MFI evaluations should be managed by the investors or board members. There should be zero tolerance for political donations to capitalize lenders, especially in highly politicized environments. Donors who make contracts with such individuals or organizations are complicit in reproducing inequalities. Any state funds for microfinance should be channelled through an independent institution, and the people in that institution should not be engaged in microfinance. Also, MFIs must not use informal actors (e.g., Big Men, gangsters, Dons) to ensure high repayment rates. A credit bureau can provide an outlet for clients to report partisan or negative forms of microfinance.

Owning privilege. The professionals in the social economy often take their own status in society for granted. All MFIs should adhere to an anti-oppression and anti-racist platform and have policies stating as much. They should also be aware of their own privilege and be ready to hire people who can relate to the class and racial experience of the clients. MFIs should be sensitive to their business location and think about the political implications for the people they target. If staff cannot connect to the lives of the clients, MFIs should be encouraged to innovate, perhaps by partnering with grassroots organizations. In Jamaica, for example, a local not-for-profit called Hope for Children and an MFI called COPE partnered so that the microfinance lender could reach into downtown communities where their staff did not want to go.

Policies to Assist Excluded Groups

If the microfinance industry is to be regarded as "inclusive financing," it needs to address negative forms of politicized microfinance. As this study has shown, many people of African descent experience cultural and partisan bias from bankers-to-the-poor. Business people are discriminated against based on identity and party politics. The Jamaica, Guyana, and Trinidad cases exemplify a negative form of politicized microfinance, and all three have low outreach. Ending the class, gender, and racist biases of lenders will involve changing the mindset of the managers and their staffs, which will not be easy. It will take a new form of politicized behaviour, one that focuses on social progress and on standing up to historically rooted prejudices in society (see the Haitian case in particular). To achieve this goal for inclusive finance, the following three policies can be considered:

Rooting microfinance in culture. Lenders should promote the local vernacular of the masses in microfinance programs and absorb the local culture of the people they serve. One way to do this would be to speak the local dialect, such as patois or Kreyol, in places of business in order to create a welcoming environment for clients and to restore trust between the classes. The use of patois in retail banks could also increase the connection between clients and the staff and managers (Hossein 2009).

Emphasizing lived experience. Managers and staffs should have class and racial/ethnic origins similar to those of the people they are serving. Otherwise the cultural biases of lenders will result in biased policies, such as the "marriage condition" in the Guyana case. Bankers who can connect to their clients can cultivate better relations with them. Managers and loan officers should have similar social backgrounds to their clients and should be trained to respond to those clients' needs. Hiring managers and staffs who have lived experience of the community would make clients more comfortable. Finally, the board representation in MFIs should include people who know this social background and are ready to take on an activist orientation.

Rethinking gender politics in banking. Greater gender equality and cultural awareness would reduce the stigma of banking programs targeting the poor. Targeting microfinance at women can in some ways assist them, but in other ways it burdens women, for it forces them to repay the debt while leaving men with the option not to do so. Evidence that young Black men from ghettos are being ostracized suggests that marginalized men, not just women, need to be targeted for finance. Moreover, the Jamaica case showed that, given the low male literacy rates in downtown areas and men's sensitivity about this issue, it is important to provide private rooms where loan officers can help them read applications. Finally, more loans to family-owned businesses could help balance gender relations.

Conclusion

Microfinance institutions and the professionals who work in them are not neutral. The lending decisions people make are highly political. For many Black people, banking can be a harrowing experience, and this is exacerbated if they are marginalized. MFIs were intended to be a means for Black people in the Caribbean region to access the monies they need for their livelihood. But these banks have low outreach and are not well-liked by low-income groups in the region. Indeed, people of the African diaspora view microfinance with suspicion, mainly because many of them have been subjected to identity and partisan politics through these institutions. The distribution of political power among certain groups and not others in microfinance has led to exclusion, and it is only by examining the Black experience in microfinance that we can see how politicized it is. Yet politicized microbanking is not *always* restrictive; it can also be emancipatory in the social and business lives of Black people.

Microfinance was reinvented to be a "revolution" of sorts to help excluded groups.[3] In this book I have examined the role of microbanking in the lives of Black people in a new way – by capturing the Black experience in microfinance and analysing lending processes within an intersectional framework. Prior to this work, practitioners, investors, and academics seemed largely oblivious to the systemic prejudice that lurks within microfinance programs. Hubris exists not only among the advocates, but also among the best of critics, who apply anti-neoliberal rhetoric without understanding the cultural lay of the land. There is evidence that many people are co-opting microfinance. Thus, we cannot lump all microfinance into the categories of commercialized and ineffective. Such a conclusion would be contested by feminists like J.K. Gibson-Graham (2003), who have made it abundantly clear that ordinary people everywhere are forming caring economic collectives.

The Black diaspora is one such community: its members are co-opting microfinance in ways that work for them. The ancestors of the African diaspora were brutally enslaved to assist European capitalist development. That is why their descendants respond in deeply personal ways to any project that would profit from them. African people, in Africa and in the diaspora, have found ways to co-opt the banking system, especially through cooperation. Collective institutions are important to historically oppressed people everywhere, and the African diaspora is no exception. I carried out this study knowing that people concerned about Black people's inequality need to scrutinize those who are engaged in the social economy who are claiming to help Black lives. The social economy and the motives of the individuals who make a living within the third sector are seldom questioned. The rhetoric coming out the social economy and the microfinance industry seems to come from good people; however, these people need to own up to their privilege.

Making a difference in the lives of people of African descent means including them; failing to do so makes alternative economics less about Black people. We need to showcase diverse economies, for commercialized microbusiness is not effective, nor is it the only way to do business (Healy 2009). Given the current problems with commercialized microfinance, the significance of my book is that it captures the experience of Black people in microfinance, as well as various effects of politicized microfinance on their lives. I take my cues from Gibson-Graham's (1996) "smashing up" of the concept of capitalism as a blanket definition of the economy; in this book, I have smashed up what is meant by "politicized microfinance." The discrimination embedded in microfinance is a reflection of the societal, political, racial, and class hierarchies in the MFIs I studied. This kind of exclusionary microfinance is politicized in a negative form. This book represents a first attempt to explore the impact of the attitudes of managers and staffs involved in microlending and to address the issue of politicization in microbanking.

In this closing chapter, I have argued that in Jamaica and Guyana, and to a lesser extent in Trinidad, the cultural and party politics of lenders have generated conflicts and led to the exclusion of certain business people. Each of the cases of a negative form of politicized microfinance had a very different outcome, which tells us there is not one experience for Black people in microbanking. Politicized microfinance can also refer to people within microfinance who are taking bold steps to help excluded groups.

African business traditions have influenced the development of cooperation and group economies in the Americas. In Haiti, most technicians in microfinance are drawn from the same (or similar) social class background as the people they serve and are able to influence how the microfinance sector is organized. The traditional systems of *gwoupmans* and *kombit* exhibit strong democratic processes, even though patrimonial political elites have failed to ensure lasting democracy at the national level. As Haitian scholar Robert Fatton (2007, 222) explains, the poor who suffered under authoritarian regimes have created their own "home-grown version of democracy." It is this kind of daring political action in the social economy that has made microfinance matter. African people who have long been alienated by the state and the private sector have turned inward to create their own collective systems to help one another. This is very much part of the cooperative and social economy story. We need to deliberately insert politics into microbanking if we are to fight for social justice for marginalized Black people. The banker ladies across the region are a testimony to this kind of courage, for they have long constituted a deliberate counter-movement that is quietly rejecting commercialized banks and offering up community-rooted financial services. Jamaicans turn to local systems when a clientelist system has shaped microfinance allocation. Similarly, Trinidadian and Guyanese people have turned to their own *susu* and box-hand banks to carry out business when they are excluded from banks.

Social economy and financial development programs are not neutral entities: they are deeply wedded to their political environments, as historical experience has shaped the way economic resources are shared in society. In the Black Americas, bankers-to-the-poor have the power to either replicate inequalities against subsets of the urban poor who do not conform to their views or to use politics to upset the status quo.

There is a need for a more ethical and engaged social economy. This will be no easy task given that the social structure has been arranged in such a way that it continually discriminates against marginalized people, especially of African descent. Making this change will require courageous people to be activist in orientation; it will also require politicized banking so that the people involved think about the oppressed. In closing, the people of the African diaspora are showing, through their diverse economies, that another world is possible – one that is people-owned and rooted in cooperation. A more ethically engaged social economy would allow us to reorganize business in society and possibly contribute to social transformation for Black people.

Appendix

Description of the downtown communities in the Jamaica Case

Community	Maxfield Park	Arnett Gardens	Rosetown (Lower)*	Whitfield Town	Tivoli Gardens	Denham Town
Election results	PNP (61.48%)	Trench Town PNP (88.15%)		PNP (91.49%)	West Kingston JLP (86.16%)	
Population	5,103	10,201	2,642	12,172	4,405	8, 345
Level of violence	High	High	Very low/none	High	Low	Moderate
Main forms of violence	Intra-party, gangs, police	Gangs, Multiple Dons, Party Factions	NA	Gangs, police	Police, Don	Petty theft
Access to state resources	None	High	Low	Low	High	Low
External support	Very low	High	Moderate–high	Very low	Low	Low
Community and social organizations	Norman Manley High (shift school) School, Lift Up Jamaica	Arnett Gardens FC, Boys' Town, Charlie Smith High School, HEART training centre, the Trench Town, Reading Centre and Boys' Town, AIR, many Christian churches	Rose Town Benevolent Society, Community library, HCDC, Information Affairs and Crisis Task Force (I-Act) Peace Management Institute (PMI)	HCDC-COPE	Tivoli Gardens Community Center, Day care, Presidential Click, (Don), Edward United Youth Club	

Continued

Community	Maxfield Park	Arnett Gardens	Rosetown (Lower)*	Whitfield Town	Tivoli Gardens	Denham Town
Access to microfinance	Low	High	Very low	Very low	High	High
Active microlenders in slums in this study	JNSBLL, Partner, Michaels Investment, Kris an Charles, Orion	COKCU-AIR, CCCUL, JNSBLL, MEFL, Partner, Dons	HCDF-COPE, Access, Partner, Orion	HCDF-COPE, Partner	Don, Partner, JNSBLL, MCL, Nation Growth, First Union, Worldnet, Kris an Charles	JNSBLL, MCL, MEFL, Nation Growth, First Union, Don, Partner

*Lower Rosetown is a JLP stronghold but it is part of Trench Town constituency represented by a PNP MP Omar Davies.

Sources: Population data from STATIN 2001. The 2007 election results from www.jamaicaelections.com/general/2007/index.php. Most community profile data taken from various SDC reports 2007 to 2009 and the Jamaica Information Services(JIS): http://www.jis.gov.jm/newsletter/archive/jan2009/jan30/index.htm. Information on Lower Rosetown's organizations taken from http://www.princes-foundation.org/index.php?id=291 and Information Affairs and Crisis Task force (I-ACT) pamphlet (an organization created two years ago by Melbourne Absolam) to target inner-city youths between 7 and 18 years old.

Notes

Preface

1 I use Quarter, Mook and Armstrong's (2009) definition of the social economy.
2 See Kamat (2002) and Ferguson (2001) for discussions about politicization and depoliticalization within the development of Southern countries.
3 The literature includes: Sinclair's *Confessions of a Microfinance Heretic*; Roy's *Poverty Capital*, Karim's *Microfinance, and Its Discontents*; Harper et al.'s *What's Wrong with Microfinance?*; Roodman's *Due Diligence*; and Bateman's *Confronting Microfinance*.
4 The informal banks I discuss are rotating savings and credit associations (ROSCAs), an ancient tradition engaged in mostly by women. ROSCAs are also known as self-help groups and are not linked to illicit or private lenders in any way.

Chapter 1

1 Many conferences have recognized microfinance as an important intervention: Programme of Action of the World Summit for Social Development (1975); Beijing Declaration and Platform for Action of the Fourth World Conference on Women (1995); Programme of Action for the Least Developed Countries for the Decade 2001–2010; and International Conference on Financing for Development in 2002.
2 MDGs emerged from the Millennium Declaration, Resolution 57/266 of 20 December 2002.

3 While the terms "microcredit," "microbanking," and "microfinance" are used interchangeably in the literature, this study deals with "microcredit," very small loans made to the entrepreneurial poor (Midgley 2008, 468). The more modern term "microfinance" includes loans, savings, remittances, insurance, and business consultation services.

4 In 1976, Muhammad Yunus, who was then an economics professor at the University of Chittagong, revived the concept of microloans with a personal loan of $27 to a group of 42 women stool makers in rural Bangladesh, which succeeded (Bennett 2009; Yunus 2007a; *Credit where Credit Is Due 2000*; Harper 1998; Counts 1996). In 1983, Yunus formally launched the Grameen Bank to give marginalized rural women access to finance (Sengupta and Aubuchon 2008, 10; Harper 1998, 33; Counts 1996, 34; Wahid 1994, 2).

5 Obama declared a new partnership among the IDB, the US Overseas Private Investment Corporation (OPIC), and the Inter-American Investment Corporation (IIC), for a new Microfinance Growth Fund for the Western Hemisphere. See http://www.whitehouse.gov/the_press_office/The-United-States-and-the-2009-Summit-of-the-Americas-Securing-Our-Citizens-Future.

6 eBay's founders created in November 2005 the Omidyar-Tufts Microfinance Fund (OTMF) with USD$100 million. See http://www.tufts.edu/microfinancefund. Bob Pattillo of Atlanta, Georgia, operates the Rockdale Foundation, the Gray Ghost Microfinance Fund, and Gray Matters Capital. See more at http://www.grayghostventures.com.

7 Several IDB projects support microenterprise projects: ATN/ME-1089-RG Carib Cap project; ATN/ME-10342-JA, which assists rural lending expansion of MEFL in Jamaica; and ATN/ME-10862-JA.

8 Books that support the microfinance sector include the following: Drake and Rhyne's *The Commercialization of Microfinance: Balancing Business and Development* (2002), Yunus's *Banker to the Poor: Micro-lending and the Battle against World Poverty* (2007a), and Klobuchar and Cornell Wilkes's *The Miracles of Barefoot Capitalism: A Compelling Case for Microcredit* (2003).

9 I recognize that formalized microfinance institutions are not the same as informal banks, but the idea of lending to low-income self-employed persons is a historically established concept in the Caribbean.

10 The Jamaican term "higgler" dates back to the colonial period, when women traders brought agricultural goods from the country to the towns (Ulysse 2007; Witter 1989). Most Jamaican business people I interviewed

called themselves *hustlas*, and those in higher-level retailing referred to themselves as higglers.

11 In Navajas and Tejerina's IDB report (2006) examining 23 countries in the LAC region including Jamaica, Guyana, and Haiti, Haiti emerges as a potential microfinance leader.

12 The rankings were as follows: Jamaica (100), Guyana (114), and Haiti (149).

13 *The Gleaner* (April 2009) reported that one-third of Jamaicans live in squatter dwellings with no title. The *Jamaica Survey of Living Conditions for 2007* reported a decline in poverty, but this seemed to be reversing after the 2008 financial crisis.

14 On 12 January 2010, Haiti experienced a 7.0 magnitude earthquake that left 300,000 people dead and 1.5 million displaced and living in tent cities (GOH 2010, 2). This event affected data collection in September 2010 and August to October 2011.

15 Stakeholders include civil society experts, bankers, activists, policy experts, and academics.

16 Kingston slums for this study were selected based on the following: high incidence of poverty, party stronghold, relatively good access to the community, and a large pool of small business people.

17 In Guyana, the term "dougla" refers to a mixed-race person of East Indian and African ethnicity (Gibson 2005, 69; St Pierre 1999, 133).

18 See the comments of Carolyn Cooper of the University of the West Indies on "Language Politics," about the relationship between patois and social class in Jamaica, in *The Gleaner*, 15 November 2009, A9: http://old.jamaica-gleaner.com/gleaner/20091115/cleisure/cleisure3.html.

19 An all-male focus group was held in Trench Town on 22 August 2009, and another one at Tivoli Gardens on 25 August 2009 (suggestion made by "Bling").

20 The Jamaican comedienne Miss Kitty coined the term "Fluffy" to refer to plus-size women.

21 In October 2010, the Ministry of Commerce and several government agencies were operating out of tents, portables, and trailer-like structures.

22 Smaller libraries with good MFI reports are housed at the Small Business Association of Jamaica, the Agency for Inner City Renewal (AIR), and Development Options Limited, and in the office of Claremont Kirton, Economics Department at UWI/Mona.

23 A Guyanese academic and journalist with *Kaieteur News*, Freddie Kissoon, was reportedly attacked and fired from the university for statements against the state (*Kaeiteur News*, 27 January 2012).

Chapter 2

1 Burrowes (1984, 26) refers to this racialized economic environment in the Guyana case as a "colour pyramid," where whites are at the pinnacle of economic might, and "field hands," made up of Indian and African labourers, are at the bottom.

2 Figueroa and Sives (2003, 65) define a "garrison" as a "political stronghold or veritable fortress completely controlled by a party," adding that "any significant social, political, economic or cultural development within a garrison can only take place with tacit approval of the leadership of the dominant party."

3 Smith (1964, 27) argued that offspring by slave women and white men had an "intermediate status" that ranked them better-off than slaves.

4 In today's Jamaica, maroons like Nanny and Cudjoe are celebrated for their resistance to slavery.

5 The author recognizes that historians debate the role of the maroons once they were settled in the highlands and that some were not receptive of runaway slaves.

6 Rodney (1981, 31–33) documents the recurring slave revolts, which created problems with productivity for the white planters.

7 Mars (1995, 171) says that the state places a high premium on ethnic partisanship.

8 The term "browning" refers to light-skinned or mixed-race Jamaicans, who often are well-educated and belong to the upper middle class. I use the term "light-skinned" reluctantly, but it is the only term to describe the blatant colour codes in these contexts.

9 In the Jamaican and Haitian cases, I employ the term "dark-skinned" to refer to people with African physical features. The terms "Afro-Jamaicans" and "Black Haitians" are complex, and pigmentation and class are often aligned with these variations in skin colour.

10 Major parties in Jamaica were linked to the trade union movements: Bustamante's Labour Party (later known as the JLP) was linked to the Industrial Trade Union, and Manley's PNP was tied to the National Workers' Union.

11 Marcus Garvey remains an important political figure for underprivileged Black youth, as witnessed at Liberty Hall on Duke Street in downtown Kingston.

12 Rastafari, a faith that developed in Jamaica in the 1930s, has spread to most Caribbean countries. Rastafari is a cultural and political movement and a way of life infused with Judeo-Christian teachings; it considers Ethiopia's Emperor Haile Selassie (1930–36 and 1941–74) to be God incarnate, or *Jah*.

13 This section draws a lot on my article titled "'Big Man' Politics in the Social Economy: A Case Study of Microfinance in Kingston, Jamaica," forthcoming in *Review of Social Economy* (see Hossein 2015).

14 The term "small man" is used in both Jamaica and Guyana to refer to a poor person who depends on the "big man" – the wealthy person – to ensure that his basic needs are met. In Guyana the term also refers specifically to poor persons of Black, Indian, or *dougla* (mixed) ethnicity (fieldwork, Kingston, Jamaica, 2009; Georgetown, Guyana, November 2009, March–April 2010).

15 In *Going Home to Teach* (2006, 89–99) Anthony Winkler argues that being Black is less a colour and more a way of being in which one's class also denotes colour. In other words, poor Blacks may view a rich and educated dark-skinned Jamaican not as Black like them because of the class distinction (this issue will come up again in chapter 3).

16 Gray (2004, 179) notes that the PNP's Tony Spaulding built housing for supporters in Arnett Gardens.

17 See Wong (1996), Witter (1989), Harrison (1988), Katzin (1959), and Mintz (1955) for work on higglers. A more recent study by Freeman (2001, 1021) examines the new role of the "suitcase trader" (i.e., higgler).

18 Keith and Keith (1992) point out that UWI academics have criticized the near-white complexion of capitalists and heads of state agencies.

19 Opposition Leader Simpson-Miller (2009) is the MP for South St Andrew (which includes Whitfield Town and some of Maxfield Park, included in this study).

20 Online stories in *The Gleaner* going back to 2001 discuss relations between Dons and politicians. See http://www.jamaica-gleaner.com/gleaner/20091207/lead/lead10.html and http://www.jamaica-gleaner.com/gleaner/20010514/news/news1.html), and Ian Boyne's piece, http://mobile.jamaicagleaner.com/20090517/focus/focus1.php.

21 See more at the *Jamaica Observer*, a leading national paper: http://www.jamaicaobserver.com/news/Taxpayer-tab-for-Manatt – Dudus – Enquiry-soon_8146902.

22 Perry Henzell and Trevor Rhone's *The Harder They Come* (1973) and recent films such as *Shottas* (2002) and *Third World Cop* (1999) show the ties between criminals from the downtown communities and political and business elites. Nordisk's film by Asgar Leth, *Les Chimères de Cité Soleil* (2007), shows the warring gangs allegedly set up under Aristide.

23 *The Garrison: A Place Governed by Its Own Laws*, a novel by Jamaican writer Sean Harris, gives insights into the informal power structures in the Kingston slums.

24 For Tivoli Gardens drug lords' various activities, including contracts from the state, see http://www.timesonline.co.uk/tol/news/world/us_and_americas/article7135596.ece.

25 I acknowledge Laurent Dubois's (2004, 5–6) point about simplifying colour categories in Haiti and his use of *gens de couleur*, whom he calls "free-coloreds," who were lighter in skin colour and educated.

26 Vodun, or voodoo, is a traditional religion practised by many Haitians and often functions as a signifier of class. See *Voodoo and the Church in Haiti* (1998).

27 Robinson (2007, 6) argues that the United States supported the Haitians against the French because the Haitians had helped the Americans arrange the Louisiana Purchase with France.

28 L'Ouverture used Noiriste philosophy to mobilize the Africans and Haitian-born against the French colonizers. Some historians have noted that L'Ouverture, a freed slave, himself owned slaves. Also, review *The Black Jacobins: Toussaint L'Ouverture and the San Domingo Revolution* by Trinidadian C.L.R. James (1989) for an account of Haiti's revolution.

29 Fatton (2002) uses the term *politiques du ventre* (politics of the belly) to characterize corruption in Haitian politics.

30 See Girard's (2010) historical review of the American presence in the island since 1986.

31 It is noted that the groundswell of support for Aristide came from the masses.

32 Informal banks are referred to as rotating and credit savings associations (ROSCAs); see chapter 1.

33 Girard (2010, 109–11) argues that the Black power ideas raised by both Duvaliers were a "sham" because both father and son married mulatto women.

34 Graham Greene's (1965) *The Comedians* is an account of the regime's violence under Papa Doc.

35 Girard (2010, 185) notes that Dominique was killed on 3 April 2000. The Demme film *The Agronomist* (2003) suggests that Dominique's murder was political because he criticized Aristide's changed politics.

36 USAID has had, since 1995, a pro-market agenda to liberalize the economy. This refers specifically to the USAID project Program for the Recovery of the Economy in Transition (PRET). From 2000 to 2005, USAID financed the project Financial Services Network for Entrepreneurship Empowerment (FINNET), which had a budget of USD$10.3 and was managed by the private, for-profit sub-contractor Development Alternatives Inc. (DAI), which currently manages enterprise projects (MSME and HI FIVE) for USAID.

37 *Chimères* is a French word meaning "phantom" or "ghost."

38 Hallward (2010, 161) is sceptical about the accusations that Aristide created a violent paramilitary force.
39 Robinson (2007) argues that Aristide was kidnapped and forced into exile by US President George W. Bush. However, Haitian scholar Fatton (2007, 206) argues that Aristide's re-election (2000) was different, as he clamped down on opposition and his government was corrupt. See also Haitian scholar Alex Dupuy's work on the Aristide's regime in *The Prophet and Power* (2007).
40 Gangs have transitioned into various roles: some are paid assassins, others are linked to the narcotics business, and others extort protection money from businessmen. A few gang retirees have formed *groupuscules* (cliques) and carry out local projects funded by international NGOs. Viva Rios, a Brazilian NGO, has a former *tet du pon* (gang boss) managing its project "Honor and Respect for Bel Air" (interview at INURED, 5 October 2010).
41 Kean Gibson (2005, 10–11) found that since 1992 there has been a steady population decline of Afro-Guyanese and contends that Afro-Guyanese do not identify with being Black and will choose the mixed-race category because of the current politics.
42 See Smith's (1964, 29) work on the plantation economy and the staggered race and social structure.
43 In 1914, the BGB became the foreign-owned bank Royal Bank of Canada.
44 The Small Business Credit Initiative (SBCI) closed down in 1997 due to management issues (Tejerina and Navajas 2006, 2).
45 Horowitz (1985) argues that most states are divided by identity, and he cites Guyana's and Trinidad's political parties, which use race/ethnicity to mobilize votes.
46 Dawn Holder, an Afro-Guyanese lawyer, has stated that Indian regions are favoured by economic inputs from the PPP state; this perpetuates the exclusion of Afros (Spotlight television show, 22 April 2010).
47 An academic and journalist had excrement thrown in his face, allegedly for his criticisms of the president. See *Stabroek News* for information on this incident: http://www.stabroeknews.com/2010/news/stories/05/25/columnist-hit-with-bowl-of-faeces.Because of such incidents, I have been diligent about protecting sources, because the state's retribution tactics are well known locally.

Chapter 3

1 Stakeholders include civil society experts, microfinance managers and staff, community activists, policy experts, and academics.

2 The EESJ Jamaica Survey of Living Conditions (2008) cites twelve micro/small-enterprise lenders, but I speculate that there are at least 40 lenders in Kingston.

3 I do not count those who claim to venture downtown to visit a gallery, or who partake in a dancehall "passa passa" or enjoy "Old Hits" on Sundays at Raetown, as engaging in lived experiences.

4 These numbers are area codes that refer to a garrison community in downtown Kingston.

5 About 42 per cent of the managers (32) disagreed that class or racial discrimination takes place against poor business people in marginalized areas.

6 Collins and colleagues (2009) find that the poor do head accounting with accuracy.

7 In the Jamaica case, 37 per cent of those interviewed (86 out of 233) had from two to five children, and 20 per cent (46 out of 233) had more than five.

8 Ahmed (2008) discusses how male exclusion in Bangladesh hurts women's empowerment by not including "high-minded" (supportive) men in the process.

9 Residents from Tiger Bay are being relocated as part of a state plan to revitalize the businesses in the downtown core areas and housing schemes, such as Para Faite Harmony and Diamond.

10 Nettles (1995, 438) claims that Black women are more likely to be on their own than Indian women.

11 Participant observation at Demerara Bank confirmed that staff are mainly Indo-Guyanese; also, it was run (like IPED) by an Indo-Guyanese, Pravinchandra Dave, in 2010.

12 See Rahman (1999, 68) concerning the use of a hidden transcript by Grameen Bank to exclude male clients.

13 A report published by McGarrell (2010) analysing Guyana's micro and small-enterprise sector failed to mention the influence of racial bias on the allocation of resources. McGarrell finds that micro and small enterprise is a high priority for the state, but gives no evidence as to what this support is. The 2010 budget only allocated about USD $75,000 to the entire small business sector (in previous years the allocation was only USD $7,500). The IMF and Bank of Guyana also published a report (Rizavi and Ganga 2006), which found that microfinance goes to the rural areas (where the Indo-Guyanese mostly reside).

14 See the *Stabroek* article (2010) for more information on the GSBA at http://www.stabroeknews.com/2010/business/05/14/whither-the-guyana-small-business-association.

15 Globe Trust, an investment company founded by an Afro-Guyanese, was liquidated in October 2009. See more on the fall of Globe Trust in the *Stabroek* paper: http://www.stabroeknews.com/2010/stories/05/05/liquidator-signals-%E2%80%98beginning-of-end%E2%80%99-for-globe-trust.

16 *Pourri* and *poulari* are Indo-Caribbean vegetarian snacks and popular among all Guyanese.

17 This section on state-managed microfinance is discussed in greater detail in a forthcoming article (Hossein 2015b).

18 I use the first part of the country's name, Trinidad.

19 Poverty figures can be political in Trinidad and Tobago. The more recent poverty rate issued by the Ministry of People and Social Development, from 2005, is 16.5 per cent (interview, 20 June 2013).

20 See more about NEDCO at its website: http://www.nedco.gov.tt

21 There was a Laventille Initiative (Barataria), but there was no branch (interview, NEDCO, senior manager, 18 June 2013).

22 In both Trinidad and Guyana, a *dougla* is a mixed-race person of East Indian and African ethnicity (St Pierre 1999, 133).

Chapter 4

1 When I ran a village bank in West Africa, I screened loan applications from business people, and am trained in screening people's eligibility for a micro-loan.

2 There is a need to explore the use of private firms governed by the money-lending act. There seemed to be a high demand for these institutions, and I did not find any of them to be linked to politicians. In addition, many of them seemed less "development savvy" and from lower socio-economic backgrounds than those professionals in the MFIs.

3 The CDF program staff at the Office of the Prime Minister (OPM) confirmed that under the rubric "Economic Enablement and Social and Human Development," politicians use CDF to capitalize microloan programs. Senior CDF managers confirmed that CDF is now J$20 million per MP; 5 October 2009. See Arthur Hall's article in *The Gleaner* on 25 September 2009.

4 CDF monies earmarked for local development duplicate the work of agencies like the Social Development Commission (SDC) and the Jamaica Social Investment Fund (JSIF), which are already active in marginalized areas. See more in "Bad News: Parallel Institutions Competing with the SDC," *Jamaica Observer*, 26 October 2010. See also http://www.jamaicaobserver.com/news/Bad-news – Parallel-institutions-competing-with-the-SDC_8089335.

5 St Andrew Western is a PNP constituency where CCCUL (a credit union) plans to be active because of a personal contact with the MP. This MP provides CDF to CCCUL.
6 Communities in this study fit the definition of "garrison" – that is, they are strongholds controlled by a political party (Figueroa and Sives 2003; Harriott 2003; Munroe 1999; Stone 1980, 1986, 1994).
7 Stone (1980, 1994) argues that wealthy Jamaicans have been viewed suspiciously by the poor as not wanting the "small man" to move out of poverty.
8 Although microfinance staff were reluctant to admit their political party to me in interviews, it was easy for me in a small society like Kingston to learn of people's political activism in national newspapers and through direct conversations with business people.
9 The banking term "moral hazard" refers to loss of profits when neutrality is compromised (e.g., through political interference).
10 Information revealed during a consulting assignment to a microfinance retailer, which was being appraised by Micro Rate, an American firm, 28 September 2009.
11 This section draws heavily on Hossein 2014b.

Chapter 5

1 In November 2005, the eBay founders created the Omidyar–Tufts Microfinance Fund (OTMF) with US$100 million. See www.tufts.edu/microfinancefund. Atlanta, Georgia's, Bob Pattillo operates the Rockdale Foundation, Gray Ghost Microfinance Fund, and Gray Matters Capital. See more at http://www.grayghostventures.com.
2 The term monopolistic capitalism refers to the definition by Samir Amin (2013).
3 Greene's book *The Comedians* (1965) provides insight into the horrors of the Tonton Macoutes terror under François Duvalier. See Marquis (2007), which focuses on the Papa Doc regime.
4 Girard (2010, 196) notes that the scandal unfolded in 2002, but my fieldwork verified it was in 2000.
5 I recognize that this view may be contested by non-cooperative lenders.
6 Cooperatives are regulated by Audit, Inspection et Formalité: Les federations de Caisses Populaires (10 July 2002).
7 CIDA awarded $20 million to DID to provide technical assistance services to Le Levier (field trip, October 2011).

8 This figure is conservative: KNFP finds that registered cooperative lenders reach 300,000 people, and a USAID report (2008) finds that 245,000 access microfinance. The numbers of unregistered lending groups are not captured in either report.
9 State supervision of formal banks, including the *caisses populaires*, is carried out by the Banque de la République d'Haïti (BRH) and the Ministère d'Economie et de la Finance (MEF). Credit unions are also supervised by the CNC.
10 Law 14 (November 1980) of the BRH regulates all banks (Kerlouche and Joseph 2010).
11 USAID projects, Financial Networks for Entrepreneurial Empowerment (FINNET), and Haiti Micro and Small and Medium Enterprises (HMSME), supported the non-cooperative microfinance sector significantly. See Hossein 2012, 2014b.
12 Much of this section was reprinted with permission from the *Review of Black Political Economy*.
13 A "penny bank" is an organized savings plan, usually run by a religious entity.

Chapter 6

1 A business person, "Hogman," mentioned that it was "women's time" and that was why microfinance was going to females and not to hard-working men like him. He argued that to curb crime, microfinance managers needed to "think man" (i.e., include males in their programs) (interview in Kingston, Jamaica, August 2009).
2 Some of the suggestions are taken from a policy report (JA-T1042) completed for the IDB and the Office of the Prime Minister in Jamaica, October 2009.
3 Ferguson (2001) speaks to the depoliticalization of people to bureaucratic control. This is why I stress that microfinance would be made more accountable to the borrowers if people power were injected into it.

Bibliography

Acacia, Michel. 2006. *Historicité et Structuration Social en Haiti*. Port-au-Prince: Bibliotheque Nationale d'Haiti.

The Agronomist. 2003. 91 minutes. Dir. Jonathan Demme. Think Films.

Ahmed, Fauzia. 2008. "Microcredit, Men, and Masculinity." *NWSA Journal* 20(2) (Summer): 122–55.

Al-Jazeera. 2010. "Extraditing Cokes." http://www.youtube.com/user/AlJazeeraEnglish#p/search/4/CLrb28fn_mo

Amin, Samir. 2013. *The Implosion of Contemporary Capitalism*. New York: Monthly Review Press.

Amnesty International. *Annual Report: Guyana 2010*. http://www.amnestyusa.org/research/reports/annual-report-guyana-2010

–. *Annual Report: Haiti 2012*. http://www.amnesty.org/en/region/haiti/report-2012

Ardener, Shirley, and Sandra Burman, eds. 1996. *Money-Go-Rounds: The Importance of Rotating Savings and Credit Associations for Women*. Oxford: Berg.

Armendáriz, Beatriz, and Jonathan Morduch. 2007. *The Economics of Microfinance*, 2nd ed. Cambridge, MA: MIT Press.

Armendáriz, Beatriz, and Nigel Roome. 2008. "Gender Empowerment via Microfinance in Fragile States." *ULB Institutional Repository* 2013/14347, CEB Working Paper No. 08/001, Université Libre de Bruxelles. 1–25.

Bakan, Abigail B. 1990. *Ideology and Class Conflict in Jamaica: The Politics of Rebellion*. Montreal and Kingston: McGill-Queen's University Press.

Bandele, Ramla. 2008. *Black Star: African American Activism in the International Political Economy*. Champaign: University of Illinois Press.

–. 2010. "Understanding African Diaspora Political Activism: The Rise and Fall of the Black Star Line." *Journal of Black Studies* 40(4): 745–61. http://dx.doi.org/10.1177/0021934708318622

Barriteau, Eudine. 1998. "Theorizing Gender Systems and the Project of Modernity in the Twentieth-Century Caribbean." *Feminist Review* 59 (Summer): 189–210.

Barriteau, Eudine, and Alan Cobley. 2006. *Enjoying Power: Eugenia Charles and Political Leadership in the Commonwealth Caribbean*. Kingston: University of the West Indies Press.

Barrow-Giles, Cynthia. 2002. *Introduction to Caribbean Politics*. Kingston: Randle.

Bateman, Milford. 2010. *Why Doesn't Microfinance Work? The Destructive Rise of Local Neoliberalism*. London: Zed.

–. 2011. *Confronting Microfinance: Undermining Sustainable Development*. Sterling: Kumarian Press.

Bateman, Milford, and Ha-Joon Chang. 2012. "Microfinance and the Illusion of Development: From Hubris to Nemesis in Thirty Years." *World Economic Review* 1: 13–36.

Bedford, Kate. 2009. *Developing Partnerships: Gender, Sexuality, and the Reformed World Bank*. Minneapolis: University of Minnesota Press.

Benería, Lourdes. 2003. *Gender, Development, and Globalization: Economics As If All People Mattered*. New York: Routledge.

Benjamin, Russell, and Gregory Hall. 2010. *Eternal Colonialism*. Lanham: University Press of America.

Bennett, Drake. 2009. "Small Change: Does Micro-lending Actually Fight Poverty?" *Boston Globe*, 20 September. http://www.boston.com/bostonglobe/ideas/articles/2009/09/20/small_change_does_microlending_actually_fight_poverty

Bennett, George W. 1875. *An Illustrated History of British Guiana*. Georgetown: Compiled from various authorities.

Bernal, Richard L. 1994. "Recent Developments in the Hemisphere: Their Implications for Jamaica." In *Jamaica: Preparing for the Twenty-First Century*, ed. Patsy Lewis. 211–41. Kingston: Randle.

Besson, Jean. 1996. "Women's Use of ROSCAs in the Caribbean: Reassessing the Literature." In *Money-Go-Rounds: The Importance of Rotating Savings and Credit Associations for Women*, ed. Shirley Ardener and Sandra Burman, 263–89. Oxford: Berg.

Best, Michael, and Robert Forrant. 1994. "Production in Jamaica Transforming Industrial Enterprise." In *Jamaica: Preparing for the Twenty-First Century*, ed. Patsy Lewis, 53–97. Kingston: Randle.

Bissessar, Ann Marie, and John Gaffar La Guerre. 2013. *Trinidad and Tobago and Guyana: Race and Politics in Two Plural Societies*. New York: Lexington.

Black, Clinton Vane de Brosse. 1965. *Story of Jamaica, from Prehistory to the Present*, rev. ed. London: Collins.

Bonitto, Brian. 2008. "Of Politics and 'Politricks.'" *Jamaica Gleaner*, 12 November.

Bowen, Glenn A. 2005. "Challenges and Opportunities for the Caribbean Countries in an Era of Globalization." *Chicago Policy Review* 9(1) (Fall): 25–37.

–. 2007. "The Challenges of Poverty and Social Welfare in the Caribbean." *International Journal of Social Welfare* 16(2) (April): 150–8. http://dx.doi.org/10.1111/j.1468-2397.2006.00453.x

Brathwaite, Edward. 1971. *The Development of Creole Society in Jamaica, 1770–1820*. Oxford: Clarendon.

Bridge, S., B. Murtagh, and K. O'Neil. 2009. *Understanding the Social Economy and the Third Sector*. London: Palgrave MacMillian.

Brody, Alyson, Martin Greenley, and Katie Wright-Revolledo, 2005. *Money with a Mission: Managing the Social Performance of Microfinance. Bourton-on-Dunsmore*. UK: ITDG. http://dx.doi.org/10.3362/9781780440873

Brohman, John. 1995. "Universalism, Eurocentrism, and Ideological Bias in Development Studies: From Modernisation to Neoliberalism." *Third World Quarterly* 16(1): 121–40.

Bronfman, Alejandra. 2007. *On the Move: The Caribbean Since 1989*. New York: Zed.

Bruck, Connie. 2006. "Millions for Millions." *The New Yorker*, 30 October, 62–73. http://www.newyorker.com/archive/2006/10/30/061030fa_fact1

Burrowes, Reynold A. 1984. *The Wild Coast: An Account of Politics in Guyana*. Cambridge, MA: Schenkman.

Casimir, Jean. 1993. *Haiti et ses elites: l'interminable Dialogue de Sourds*. Port-au-Prince: Université d'Etat d'Haiti.

Castor, Suzy. 2006. "Conclusion – la difficile sortie d'une longue transition." In *Haiti: Hope for a Fragile State*, ed. Yasmine Shamsie and Andrew Thompson, 111–28. Waterloo: Wilfrid Laurier University Press.

Castor, Suzy, Herold Jean François, Gerald Mathurin, and Christian Rousseau. 2010. "Les impacts du tremblement de terre du 12 janvier 2010." *CRESFED Recontrer*, 22–3 July.

CDB (Caribbean Development Bank). 2010. "Biennial Social Development Report 2010."

CGAP (Consultative Group to Assist the Poor). 2006. *Graduating the Poorest into Microfinance: Linking Safety Nets and Financial Services*, No. 34.

–. 2010. *Consumer Protection Regulation in Low-Access Environments: Opportunities to Promote Responsible Finance*, No. 60. https://www.cgap.org/sites/default/files/CGAP-Focus-Note-Consumer-Protection-Regulation-in-Low-Access-Environments-Opportunities-to-Promote-Responsible-Finance-Feb-2010.pdf

Chalmers, Geoffrey, and Mark Wenner. 2001. Working Paper: "Microfinance Issues and Challenges in the Anglophone Caribbean." Washington: Inter-American Development Bank.

Charles, Christopher. 2002. "Garrison Community as Counter Societies: The Case of the 1998 Zeeks' Riots in Jamaica." *Caribbean Journal of Psychology* 1: 30–43.

Chauvet, Max E. 2010. "12 janvier 2010: tremblement du terre en Haiti. 35 seconds." *Le Nouvelliste*, 21 February.

Les chimères de Cité Soleil. 2007. Dir. Asgar Leth. Nordisk Film Productions.

Chowdri, Siddhartha H., and Alex Silva. 2004. "Downscaling, Institutions, and Competitive Microfinance Markets: Reflections and Case Studies from Latin America." Unpublished policy document by Calmeadow.

Christen, Robert Peck. 2001. "Commercialization and Mission Drift: The Transformation of Microfinance in Latin America." CGAP Occasional Paper No. 5. www.cgap.org.

Chua, Amy. 2003. *World on Fire: How Exporting Free Market Democracy Breeds Economic Hatred and Global Instability*. New York: Random House.

Clementi, Cecil. 1939. *A Constitutional History of British Guiana*. New York: Macmillan.

Collier, Paul. 2007. *The Bottom Billion: Why the Poorest Countries Are Failing and What Can Be Done about It*. Oxford: Oxford University Press.

Collins, Daryl, Jonathan Morduch, Stuart Rutherford, and Orlanda Ruthven. 2009. *Portfolios of the Poor: How the World's Poor Live on $2 a Day*. Princeton: Princeton University Press.

Collister, Keith. 2008. "Creating a World without Poverty – Yunus." *Jamaica Observer*, 13 June. http://www.jamaicaobserver.com.

Colloque sur la microfinance, 28–29 September 2010. Speakers included Clermont, Fleurstin, François, Ministère de la Économie. Port-au-Prince, Haiti.

Cooper, Carolyn. 2009. "Language Politics." *The Gleaner*, 15 November, A9. http://old.jamaica-gleaner.com/gleaner/20091115/cleisure/cleisure3.html.

Cooperative Republic of Guyana. 1970. Georgetown: Guyana Lithographic.

Counts, Alex. 1996. *Give Us Credit: How Muhammad Yunus's Micro-Lending Revolution Is Empowering Women from Bangladesh to Chicago*, 1st ed. New York: Random House.

Credit Where Credit Is Due. 2000. Dir. Bruce Ashley. Bullfrog/Television Trust for Environment, BBC Worldwide.

Crenshaw, Kimberlé. 1991. "Mapping the Margins: Intersectionality, Identity Politics, and Violence against Women of Colour." *Stanford Law Review* 43(6): 1241–99. http://dx.doi.org/10.2307/1229039

CSFI (Center for the Study of Financial Innovation). 2008. *Microfinance Banana Skins 2008: Risk in a Booming Industry*. New York.

–. 2011. *Microfinance Banana Skins 2011: Losing Its Fairy Dust*. New York.

Daley-Harris, Sam. 2004. *State of the Microcredit Summit Campaign: Report 2004*. Washington: Microcredit Summit Campaign.

–. 2005. *State of the Microcredit Summit Campaign: Report 2005*. Washington: Microcredit Summit Campaign.

–. 2006. *State of the Microcredit Summit Campaign: Report 2006*. Washington: Microcredit Summit Campaign.

Dalton, Henry. G. 1885. *History of British Guiana*. 2 vols. London and Georgetown.

Daly, Vere. 1974. *The Making of Guyana*. Oxford: MacMillan Caribbean.

Davis, G. Ovid. 1979. "Counting Small Local Economic Activity and a Comparative Analysis of Financial Performance of Private Business in Guyana." Management Studies Department, University of Guyana.

Despres, Leo A. 1967. *Cultural Pluralism and Nationalist Politics in British Guiana*. Skokie: Rand McNally.

Develtere, Patrick. 1993. "Cooperative Movements in the Developing Countries: Old and New Orientations." *Annals of Public and Cooperative Economics* 64(2): 179–208. http://dx.doi.org/10.1111/j.1467-8292.1993.tb01389.x

Dichter, T.W. 1996. "Questioning the Future of NGOs in Microfinance." *Journal of International Development* 8(2): 259–69. http://dx.doi.org/10.1002/(SICI)1099-1328(199603)8:2<259::AID-JID377>3.0.CO;2-7

Dichter, Thomas, and Malcolm Harper. 2007. *What's Wrong with Microfinance?* Warwickshire: Intermediate Technology. http://dx.doi.org/10.3362/9781780440446

Drake, Deborah, and Elisabeth Rhyne. 2002. *The Commercialization of Microfinance: Balancing Business and Development*. Bloomfield: Kumarian.

Du Bois, W.E.B. 1907. *Economic Co-operation among Negro Americans*. Atlanta: Atlanta University Press.

–. 2007[1903]. *The Souls of Black Folk*. Minneapolis: Filiquarian Publishing.

Dubois, Laurent. 2004. *Avengers of the New World*. Cambridge, MA: Harvard University Press.

Duncan, Clem. 1990. "Small Business Development in Guyana." In *Small Scale Enterprises and Development in Guyana*, ed. Frank Long, 17–39. Turkeyen: University of Guyana.

Duncan-Waite, Imani, and Michael Woolcock. 2008. Working Paper No. 46: "Arrested Development: The Political Origins and Socio-Economic Foundations of Common Violence in Jamaica." Brooks World Poverty Institute and University of Manchester, June.

Dunford, Christopher. 2009. "Credit Unions and Rural Banks Reaching Down and Out to the Rural Poor through Group-Based Microfinance." *Enterprise Development and Microfinance*. 20(2): 107–124. http://dx.doi.org/10.3362/1755-1986.2009.012

Dupuy, Alex. 1996. "Race and Class in the Postcolonial Caribbean: The Views of Walter Rodney." *Latin American Perspectives* 23(2) (Spring): 107–29. http://dx.doi.org/10.1177/0094582X9602300207

–. 2007. *The Prophet and Power: Jean-Bertrand Aristide, the International Community, and Haiti*. Lanham: Rowman and Littlefield.

–. 2010. "Commentary beyond the Earthquake: A Wake-Up Call for Haiti." *Latin American Perspectives* 37(3): 195–204. http://dx.doi.org/10.1177/0094582X10366539

Economist Intelligence Unit. 2008. "2008 Microscope on the Microfinance Business Environment in Latin America and the Caribbean." Commissioned by the IDB. October.

Eisenstadt, S.N., and L. Roniger. 1984. *Patrons, Clients, and Friends*. Cambridge: Cambridge University Press. http://dx.doi.org/10.1017/CBO9780511557743

Elahi, Khandakar, and Constantine P. Danopoulos. 2004. "Microcredit and the Third World." *International Journal of Social Economics* 31(7): 643–54. http://dx.doi.org/10.1108/03068290410540855

ESSJ (Economic and Social Survey Jamaica). 2008. Kingston: Planning Institute of Jamaica (PIOJ).

Ewing, Adam. 2014. *The Age of Garvey: How a Jamaican Activist Created a Mass Movement and Changed Global Politics*. Princeton: Princeton University Press. http://dx.doi.org/10.1515/9781400852444

Fanon, Frantz. 1967. *Black Skin, White Masks*. New York: Grove.

FAO (Food and Agriculture Organization). 2008. "Country Profiles: Rural Poverty in Haiti." http://www.ruralpovertyportal.org/web/guest/country/home/tags/haiti

Farmer, Paul. 1994. *The Uses of Haiti*. Monroe: Common Courage.

Fatton, Robert. 2002. *Haiti's Predatory Republic: The Unending Transition to Democracy*. Boulder: Lynne Rienner.

–. 2006. "The Fall of Aristide and Haiti's Current Predicament." In *Haiti: Hope for a Fragile State*, ed. Yasmine Shamsie and Andrew Thompson, 15–24. Waterloo: Wilfred Laurier University Press.

–. 2007. *The Roots of Haitian Despotism*. Boulder: Lynne Rienner.

Ferguson, J. 1997. *In Focus: Eastern Caribbean: A Guide to the People, Politics, and Culture*. New York: Interlink Books.

–. 2001. *The Anti-Politics Machine*. Minneapolis: University of Minnesota Press.

Few, April L. 2007. "Integrating Black Consciousness and Critical Race Feminism into Family Studies Research." *Journal of Family Issues* 28(4): 452–73. http://dx.doi.org/10.1177/0192513X06297330

Ffrench, Sean. 2008. "Funding Entrepreneurship among the Poor in Jamaica." *Social and Economic Studies* 57(2): 119–48.

Figueria, D. 2010. *The Politics of Racist Hegemony in Trinidad and Tobago*. Bloomington: Universe.

Figueroa, Mark, and Amanda Sives. 2003. "Garrison Politics and Criminality in Jamaica: Does the 1997 Election Represent a Turning Point?" In *Understanding Crime in Jamaica: New Challenges for Public Policy*, ed. Anthony Harriott, 63–88. Kingston: University of the West Indies Press.

Freeman, Carla. 2001. "Is Local:Global as Feminine:Masculine? Rethinking the Gender of Globalization." *Signs* 26(4): 1007–37. http://dx.doi.org/10.1086/495646

Freire, Paulo. 2010. *Pedagogy of the Oppressed*, 30th ed. New York: Continuum International.

"Gafsons Industries Celebrates 60 Stellar Years of Service." 2011. *Kaietur News*, 11 December.

Galabuzi, Grace-Edward. 2006. *Canada's Economic Apartheid: The Social Exclusion of Racialized Groups in the New Century*. Toronto: Canadian Scholars' Press.

Gardner, W.J.A. 1971. *History of Jamaica: From Its Discovery by Christopher Columbus to Year 1872*. London: Cass.

Garner, Steve. 2008. *Guyana 1838–1985: Ethnicity, Class, and Gender*. Kingston: Randle.

Gatehouse, Jonathon. 2006. "Interview with Nobel-Prize Winner, Muhammed Yunus: On Bankrolling, Beggars and Fighting Terrorism." *Maclean's*, 27 November, 16–18.

Geertz, Clifford. 1962. "The Rotating Credit Association: A Middle Rung in Development." *Economic Development and Cultural Change* 10(3): 241–63. http://dx.doi.org/10.1086/449960

Gentle, Eileen. 1989. *Before the Sunset*. Montreal: Marquis.

Gibson, Kean. 2005. *Sacred Duty: Hinduism and Violence in Guyana*. Georgetown: Group Five.

–. 2006. "The Dualism of Good and Evil and the East Indian Insecurity in Guyana." *Journal of Black Studies* 36(3): 362–81. http://dx.doi.org/10.1177/0021934704273908

Gibson-Graham, J.K. 1996. *The End of Capitalism (as We Knew It): A Feminist Critique of Political Economy*. Oxford: Blackwell.

–. 2003. "Enabling Ethical Economies: Cooperativism and Class." *Critical Sociology* 29(2): 123–61. http://dx.doi.org/10.1163/156916303769155788

–. 2006. *A Postcapitalist Politics*. Minneapolis: University of Minnesota Press.

Gibson-Graham, J.K. Jenny Cameron, and Stephen Healy. 2013. *Take Back the Economy: An Ethical Guide for Transforming our Communities*. Minneapolis: University of Minnesota Press.

Girard, Philippe. 2010. *Haiti: The Tumultuous History – from Pearl of the Caribbean to Broken Nation*. New York: Palgrave Macmillan.

Goetz, Anne Marie, and Rina Sengupta. 1996. "Who Takes the Credit? Gender, Power, and Control over Loan Use in Rural Credit Programs in Bangladesh." *World Development* 24(1): 45–63. http://dx.doi.org/10.1016/0305-750X(95)00124-U

Goldstein, Joshua. 2015. "Racism Is Endemic. What Role for Microfinance?" Center for Financial Inclusion. http://cfi-blog.org/tag/racism

GOG (Government of Guyana). 2002. Georgetown: Bureau of Statistics Census.

–. 2004. *Small Business Act No. 2*.

GOH (Government of Haiti). 2010. *Action Plan for National Recovery and Development of Haiti: Immediate Key Initiatives for the Future*. March.

Gordon Nembhard, Jessica. 2011. "Microenterprise and Cooperative Development in Economically Marginalized Communities in the US." In *Enterprise, Deprivation, and Social Exclusion: The Role of Small Business in Addressing Social and Economic Inequalities*, ed. Alan Southern, 254–77. New York: Routledge.

–. 2014. *Collective Courage: A History of African American Cooperative Economic Thought and Practice*. College Park: Pennsylvania State University Press.

–. 2015. "Guyana Opposition Wins Election in First Change of Government for 23 Years." *The Guardian*, 15 May.

Gordon Nembhard, Jessica, and Valerie Ooka Pang. 2003. "Ethnic Youth Programs: Teaching about Caring Economic Communities and Self-Empowered Leadership." In *Critical Race Theory Perspectives on the Social Studies*. ed. Gloria Ladson-Billings, 171–97. Charlotte: Information Age Publishing.

Grant, Colin. 2009. *Negro: The Rise and Fall of Marcus Garvey*. London: Vintage.

Grant, William, and Hugh Allen. 2002. "CARE's Mata Masu Dubara (Women on the Move) Program in Niger: Successful Financial Intermediation in the Rural Sahel." *Journal of Microfinance* 4(2): 189–216.

Gray, Obika. 2003a. "Baddness–Honour." In *Understanding Crime in Jamaica: New Challenges for Public Policy*, ed. Anthony Harriott, 13–48. Kingston: University of the West Indies Press.

–. 2003b. "Rogue Culture or Avatar of Liberation: The Jamaican Lumpenproletariat." *Social and Economic Studies* 51: 1–33.

–. 2004. *Demeaned BUT Empowered: The Social Power of the Urban Poor in Jamaica.* Kingston: University of the West Indies Press.

Greene, Graham. 1965. *The Comedians*. London: Penguin.

Greenidge, Carl. 1981. *The State and Public Enterprises in Guyana*. Georgetown: University of Guyana,.

–. 2001. *Empowering a Peasantry in a Caribbean Context: The Case of Land Settlement Schemes in Guyana, 1865–1985*. Kingston: University of the West Indies Press.

Guinnane, Timothy. 2001. "Cooperatives as Information Machines: German Rural Credit Cooperatives, 1883–1914." *Journal of Economic History* 61(2): 366–89. http://dx.doi.org/10.1017/S0022050701028042

Gulli, H., and M. Berger. 1999. "Microfinance and Poverty Reduction: Evidence from Latin America." *Small Enterprise Development* 12: 55–67.

Gunst, Laurie. 2003. *"Born Fi Dead": A Journey through the Yardie Underworld.* Edinburgh: Canongate.

Haitian Truth. 2011. "Prominent Haitian Banker Gunned Down." 13 June. http://www.haitian-truth.org/prominent-haitian-banker-gunned-down

Hallward, Peter. 2010. *Damming the Flood: Haiti and the Politics of Containment.* London: Verso.

Handa, Sudhanshu, and Claremont Kirton. 1999. "The Economies of Rotating Savings and Credit Associations: Evidence from the Jamaican 'Partner.'" *Journal of Development Economics* 60(1): 173–94. http://dx.doi.org/10.1016/S0304-3878(99)00040-1

The Harder They Come. 1973. Dir. Perry Henzell and Trevor Rhone. Kingston: Island Records.

Harper, Malcolm. 1998. *Profit for the Poor: Cases in Microfinance.* London: Intermediate Technology Publications. http://dx.doi.org/10.3362/9781780440910

Harper, Malcolm, and Sukhwinder Singh Arora, eds. 2005. *Small Customers, Big Markets*. New Delhi: Teri. http://dx.doi.org/10.3362/9781780440965

Harriott, Anthony. 2003. *Understanding Crime in Jamaica: New Challenges for Public Policy*. Kingston: University of the West Indies Press.

–. 2008. *Bending the Trend Line: The Challenge of Controlling Violence in Jamaica and the High Violence Societies of the Caribbean*. Kingston: University of the West Indies Professorial Inaugural Lecture. Arawak Monograph Series.

Harris, Sean K. 2009. *The Garrison: A Place Governed by Its Own Laws.* Bookfetish.

Harrison, Faye V. 1988. "Women in Jamaica's Informal Economy: Insights from a Kingston Slum." *New West Indian Guide* 62(3–4): 103–28. http://dx.doi.org/10.1163/13822373-90002040

Harvard School of Public Health. 2011. "MINUSTAH: Keeping the Peace, or Conspiring Against It? A Review of the Human Rights Record of the United Nations Stabilization Mission in Haiti, 2010–2011." October.

Healy, S. 2009. "Economies, Alternative." In *International Encyclopedia of Human Geography*, vol. 3. ed. R. Kitchin and N. Thrift, 338–44. Oxford: Elsevier. http://dx.doi.org/10.1016/B978-008044910-4.00132-2

Heinl, Robert Debs, and Nancy Gordon Heinl. 2005. *Written in Blood: The Story of the Haitian People, 1492–1995*. Rev and expanded ed. by Michael Heinl. Lanham: University Press of America.

Hill Collins, Patricia. 2000. *Black Feminist Thought: Knowledge, Consciousness, and the Politics of Empowerment*. 2nd ed. New York: Routledge.

Hintzen, Percy C. 1989. *The Costs of Regime Survival: Racial Mobilization, Elite Domination, and Control of the State in Guyana and Trinidad*. Cambridge: Cambridge University Press. http://dx.doi.org/10.1017/CBO9780511571008

Holden, Paul. 2005. *Implementing Secured Transactions Reform in Jamaica: Issues and Policy Options*. Kingston: Enterprise Research Institute.

Honig, Benson. 1998a. "What Determines Success? Examining the Human, Financial, and Social Capital of Jamaican Microentrepreneurs." *Journal of Business Venturing* 13 (5): 371–94. http://dx.doi.org/10.1016/S0883-9026(97)00036-0

–. 1998b. "Who Gets the Goodies? An Examination of Microenterprise Credit in Jamaica." *Entrepreneurship and Regional Development* 10(4): 313–34. http://dx.doi.org/10.1080/08985629800000018

–. 2000. "Small Business Promotion and Microlending: A Comparative Assessment of Jamaica and Israeli NGOs." *Journal of Microfinance* 2: 92–110.

Hope, Donna. 2006. *Inna di Dancehall*. Kingston: University of the West Indies Press.

Hope, Kemp Ronald. 1985. *Guyana: Politics and Development in Emergent Socialist State*. Oakville: Mosaic.

Horowitz, Donald L. 1985. *Ethnic Groups in Conflict*. Berkeley: University of California Press.

Hossein, Caroline Shenaz. 2009. "Access and Microfinance in Kingston, Jamaica: Perspectives from Inna di Yard." Report # JA-T1042. IDB. 71 pages.

–. 2012. "The Politics of Microfinance: A Comparative Study of Jamaica, Guyana, and Haiti." PhD diss., University of Toronto.

–. 2013a. "The Black Social Economy: Perseverance of Banker Ladies in the Slums." *Annals of Public and Cooperative Economics* 84(4): 423–42.

–. 2013b. "Using a Black Feminist Framework: A Comparative Study of Bias against Female Entrepreneurs in Caribbean Micro-Banking." *Intersectionalities: A Global Journal of Social Work Analysis, Research, Polity, and Practice* 2 (April): 51–70.

–. 2014a. "The Exclusion of Afro-Guyanese in Micro-Banking." *European Review of Latin America and Caribbean Studies* 96 (April): 75–98.

–. 2014b. "Haiti's *Caisses Populaires*: Home-Grown Solutions to Bring Economic Democracy." *International Journal of Social Economics* 41(1): 42–59.

–. 2014c. "The Politics of Resistance: Informal Banks in the Caribbean." *Review of Black Political Economy* 41(1): 85–100.

–. 2015. "Government-Owned Micro-Banking and Financial Exclusion: A Case Study of Small Business People in East Port of Spain, Trinidad and Tobago." *Canadian Journal for Latin American and Caribbean Studies* 40(3): 393–409.

–. 2016 (In press). "'Big Man' Politics in the Social Economy: A Case Study of Microfinance in Kingston, Jamaica." *Review of Social Economy*.

Howard, David. 2005. *Cities of the Imagination*. Kingston: Signal.

Hulme, D. 2000. "Is Microcredit Good for Poor People? A Note on the Dark Side of Microfinance." *Small Enterprise Development* 11(1): 26–8. http://dx.doi.org/10.3362/0957-1329.2000.006

Human Rights Watch. 2004. "Aristide Should Uphold Rule of Law." February. https://www.hrw.org/news/2004/02/13/haiti-aristide-should-uphold-rule-law

In the Sky's Wild Noise. 1983. Automedia and the Victor Jara Collective.

Inward Hunger: The Story of Eric Williams. 2011. Savant Limited. http://035d8fd.netsolhost.com/WordPress/documentary-projects/inward-hunger

Jamaica Living Conditions Survey. 2007. Kingston: STATIN/PIOJ.

Jamaica Gleaner. n.d. Various issues.

Jamaica Observer. n.d. Various issues.

James, C.L.R. 1989. *The Black Jacobins: Toussaint L'Ouverture and the San Domingo Revolution*, 2nd rev. ed. New York: Vintage.

Johnson, Bill. 2008. "Report of Survey Research Conducted for JN Small Business Loans Ltd." Survey Research Ltd. January.

Johnson, Susan, and Ben Rogaly. 1997. *Microfinance and Poverty Reduction*. Oxford: Oxfam.

Kabeer, Naila. 2001. "Conflicts over Credit: Re-evaluating the Empowerment Potential of Loans to Women in Rural Bangladesh." *World Development* 29 (1): 63–84. http://dx.doi.org/10.1016/S0305-750X(00)00081-4

K'adamwe, K'nife, Allan Bernard, and Edward Dixon. 2011. ""Marcus Garvey the Entrepreneur? Insights for Stimulating Entrepreneurship in Developing Nations." *76 King Street* 2: 37–59.

Kah, Jainaba M.L., Dana L. Olds, and Mahmmadou M.O. Kah. 2005. "Microcredit, Social Capital, and Politics: The Case of a Small Rural Town – Gossas, Senegal." *Journal of Microfinance* 7(1): 119–49.

Kaieteur News. n.d. Various issues.

Kamat, Sangeeta. 2002. *Development Hegemony: NGOs and the State in India*. Oxford: Oxford University Press.

Karim, Lamia. 2008. "Demystifying Micro-Credit: The Grameen Bank, NGOs, and Neoliberalism in Bangladesh." *Cultural Dynamics* 20(1): 5–29. http://dx.doi.org/10.1177/0921374007088053

–. 2011. *Microfinance and Its Discontents: Women in Debt in Bangladesh*. Minnesota: University of Minnesota Press. http://dx.doi.org/10.5749/minnesota/9780816670949.001.0001

Katzin, Margaret Fisher. 1959. "The Jamaican Country Higgler." *Social and Economic Studies* 8(4): 421–40.

Keith, Nelson W., and Novella Z. Keith. 1992. *The Social Origins of Democratic Socialism in Jamaica*. Philadelphia: Temple University Press.

Kerlouche, Joachim, and Nancy Joseph. 2010. "Impacts de la microfinance sur l'emanicipation des femmes de la commune de Saint-Marc." Thesis, Quisqueya University, Port-au-Prince.

Khan, Sana. 2009. "Poverty Reduction Efforts: Does Microcredit Help?" *SAIS Review* 2: 147–57.

Kissoon, Freddie. 2010a. "Arrival and Enigma: Fascism and the Guyanese East Indian Mind." *Kaieteur News*, 5 May.

–. 2010b. Lecture: "East Indian Support for Elected Dictatorship in Guyana: The Role of Class Formation." University of Guyana, Georgetown, 13 May.

Klak, Thomas H., and Jeanne K. Hey. 1992. "Gender and State Bias in Jamaican Housing Programs." *World Development* 20(2): 213–227. http://dx.doi.org/10.1016/0305-750X(92)90100-A

Klobuchar, Jim, and Susan Cornell Wilkes. 2003. *The Miracles of Barefoot Capitalism: A Compelling Case for Microcredit*. London: Kirk House.

KNFP (Konsey Nasyonal Finansman Popilè). 2008. Unpublished and untitled report about informal cooperatives. Port-au-Prince.

Lashley, Jonathan. 2004a. *Microfinance in the Eastern Caribbean and Delivery Options*. Barbados: SALISES/University of the West Indies.

–. 2004b. "Microfinance and Poverty Alleviation in the Caribbean: A Strategic Overview." *Journal of Microfinance* 6(1): 83–94.

–. 2006. "Enterprise Development and Poverty Alleviation in Dominica: The Role and Motivations of Eugenia Charles." In *Enjoying Power: Eugenia Charles and Political Leadership in the Commonwealth Caribbean*, ed. Eudine Barriteau and Alan Cobley, 214–39. Kingston: University of the West Indies Press.

Ledgerwood, Joanna. 2013. *Microfinance Handbook*. Washington: World Bank.

Ledgister, F.S.J. 1998. *Class Alliances and the Liberal Authoritarian State: The Roots and Post-Colonial Democracy in Jamaica, Trinidad, and Surinam*. London: Africa World.

Littlefield, E., Jonathan Morduch, and Sayed Hashemi. 2003. "Is Microfinance an Effective Strategy to Reach the Millennium Development Goals?" *CGAP Focus*, Note 24.

Long, Frank. 1990. *Small Scale Enterprises and Development in Guyana*. Turkeyen,: University of Guyana.

Lorde, Audrey. 1984. *Sister Outsider*. Trumansberg: Crossing Press.

Maclean, Karen. 2010. "Capitalizing on Women's Social Capital? Women-Targeted Microfinance in Bolivia." *Development and Change* 41(3): 495–515. http://dx.doi.org/10.1111/j.1467-7660.2010.01649.x

Maguire, Robert. 1997. "From Outsiders to Insiders: Grassroots Leadership and Political Change." In *Haiti Renewed: Political and Economic Prospects*, ed. Robert Maguire, 154–66. Washington: Brookings Institution.

–. 2006. "Assisting a Neighbour: Haiti's Challenge to North American Policy-Makers." In *Haiti: Hope for a Fragile State*, ed. Yasmine Shamsie and Andrew Thompson, 25–36. Waterloo: Wilfrid Laurier University Press.

Majeed, Halim. 2005. *Forbes Burnham: National Reconstruction and National Unity (1984–1985)*. New York: Global Communication.

Malkin, Elisabeth. 2008. "Microfinance's Success Sets Off Debate in Mexico." *New York Times*, 5 April.

Mann, Michael. 2008. "American Empires: Past and Present." *Canadian Review of Sociology* 45(1): 7–50. http://dx.doi.org/10.1111/j.1755-618X.2008.00002.x

Mansru, Basdeo. 2005. *The Elusive El Dorado: Essay on the Indian Experience in Guyana*. Lanham: University Press of America.

Marquis, John. 2007. *Papa Doc: Portrait of a Haitian Tyrant*. Kingston: LMH.

Mars, Perry. 1995. "State Intervention and Ethnic Conflict Resolution: Guyana and the Caribbean Experience." *Comparative Politics* 27(2): 167–86. http://dx.doi.org/10.2307/422163

Marshall, Catherine, and Gretchen Rossman. 2006. *Designing Qualitative Research*, 4th ed. London: Sage.

Martin, Tony. 1983. *Marcus Garvey, Hero: A First Biography*. Dover: The Majority.

Massiah, J. 1983. *Women as Heads of Households in the Caribbean*. Paris: UNESCO.

Mathews, Lear K., and George K. Danns. 1980. *Communities and Development in Guyana: A Neglected Dimension in Nation-Building*. Mimeo. Georgetown: University of Guyana.

Matin, Imran, David Hulme, and Stuart Rutherford. 2002. "Finance for the Poor: From Microcredit to Microfinancial Services." *Journal of International Development* 14(2): 273–94. http://dx.doi.org/10.1002/jid.874

Maxwell, Joseph. 2005. *Qualitative Research Design: An Interactive Approach*, 2nd ed. London: Sage.

Mayoux, Linda. 1999. "Questioning Virtuous Spirals: Microfinance and Women's Empowerment in Africa." *Journal of International Development* 11(7): 957–84. http://dx.doi.org/10.1002/(SICI)1099-1328(199911/12)11:7<957::AID-JID623>3.0.CO;2-#

McCoy, Jennifer L. 1997. "Introduction: Dismantling the Predatory State." In *Haiti Renewed: Political and Economic Prospects*, ed. Robert Rotberg, 1–27. Washington: Brookings Institution.

McFarlane, Carmen. 1997. "The 1996 Micro and Small Enterprise Sector Survey, Jamaica." *STATIN*, September.

McGarrell, Claudeville. 2010. Report for the Government of Guyana: "Action Plan: A Small Sector Consultancy and Action Plan: Support for Competitive Programme (1751/SFGYD)." 30 September.

McLeod Arnopoulos, Sheila. 2010. *Saris on Scooters: How Microcredit Is Changing Village India*. Toronto: Dundurn.

Meeks, Brian. 2001. *Caribbean Revolutions and Revolutionary Theory: An Assessment of Cuba, Nicaragua, and Grenada*. Kingston: University of the West Indies Press.

Members of Parliament List. 2007. Jamaica, October.

Microfin. 2002. *Microfinance in the Caribbean*. Trinidad and Tobago: Port of Spain. 14 March. http://www.microfin.org

MIDA (Micro Investment Development Agency). n.d. Annual Report: "Facilitating Growth, Development, and Sustainability of the Micro Sector for 15 Years: 2006–2007." Kingston.

Midgley, James. 2008. "Microenterprise, Global Poverty, and Social Development." *International Social Work* 51(4): 467–79. http://dx.doi.org/10.1177/0020872808090240

Midy, Franklin. 2010. *Haiti: tutelle furtive, colère sociale manifeste*. CRESFED Recontrer, nos. 22–3 (juillet).

Miller, Errol. 1991. *Men at Risk*. Kingston: Jamaican.

Mintz, Sidney. 1955. "The Jamaican Internal Marketing Pattern: Some Notes and Hypotheses." *Social and Economic Studies* 4(1): 95–103.

–. 2010. *Three Ancient Colonies: Caribbean Themes and Variations*. Cambridge, MA: Harvard University Press.

–. 2011. *Pratik: Haitian Personal Economic Relationships*, 1–15. Open Anthropology Cooperative Press.

MIX (Microfinance Information Exchange). 2006. *Country Profiles*. www.mixmarket.org

–. 2007. *Championship League 2007: Latin America and Caribbean 100*. www.mixmarket.org

Mohammed, Patricia. 2000. *The Construction of Gender Development Indicators for Jamaica*. Kingston: PIOJ/CIDA/UNDP.

Montasse, Emmanuel. 1983. *La gestion strategique dans le Cadre du développement d'Haiti au moyen de la coopérative, Caisse d'Epargne et de Credit*. Port-au-Prince: IAGHEI, UEH.

Montgomery, R. 1996. "Disciplining or Protecting the Poor? Avoiding the Social Costs of Peer Pressure in Micro-Credit Schemes." *Journal of International Development* 8(2): 289–305. http://dx.doi.org/10.1002/(SICI)1099-1328(199603)8:2<289::AID-JID368>3.0.CO;2-2

Moore, Brian L. 1987. *Race, Power, and Social Segmentation in Colonial Society*. New York: Gorodon and Breach.

–. 1995. *Cultural Power, Resistance, and Pluralism: Colonial Guyana, 1838–1900*. Montreal and Kingston: McGill-Queen's University Press.

Morduch, Jonathan. 1999. "The Microfinance Promise." *Journal of Economic Literature* 37 (4): 1569–614. http://dx.doi.org/10.1257/jel.37.4.1569

–. 2000. "The Microfinance Schism." *World Development* 28(4): 617–29. http://dx.doi.org/10.1016/S0305-750X(99)00151-5

Mosley, P., and D. Hulme. 1998. "Microenterprise and Finance: Is There a Conflict between Growth and Poverty Alleviation?" *World Development* 26(5): 783–90. http://dx.doi.org/10.1016/S0305-750X(98)00021-7

Mullings, Beverley. 2005. "Women Rule? Globalization and the Feminization of Managerial and Professional Workspaces in the Caribbean" *Gender, Place, and Culture* 12(1): 1–27. http://dx.doi.org/10.1080/09663690500082745

Munroe, Trevor. 1999. *Renewing Democracy into the Millennium: The Jamaican Experience in Perspective*. Kingston: University of the West Indies Press.

Nath, Dwarka. 1950. *A History of Indians in British Guyana*. London: Nelson.

National Coalition for Haitian Rights. 2012. http://nchr.org/nchr/hrp/archive/jeannot3.htm

Navajas, Sergio, Mark Schreiner, Richard L. Meyer, Claudio Gonsalvez-Vega, and Jorge Rodriguez-Meza. 2000. "Microcredit and the Poorest of the Poor: Theory and Evidence from Bolivia." *World Development* 28(2): 333–46. http://dx.doi.org/10.1016/S0305-750X(99)00121-7

Navajas, Sergio, and Luis Tejerina. 2006. "Microfinance in Latin America and the Caribbean: How Large Is the Market?" Report titled Sustainable Development Department Best Practices Series, No. MSM-135. Washington: Inter-American Development BankIADB.

Nettleford, Rex, ed. 1989. *Jamaica in Independence: Essays on the Early Years.* Kingston: Heinemann Caribbean.

Nettles, Kimberly D. 1995. "Home Work: An Examination of the Sexual Division of Labor in the Urban Household of the East Indian and African Guyanese." *Journal of Comparative Family Studies* 26(3): 427–41.

–. 2007. "Becoming Red Thread Women: Alternative Visions of Gendered Politics in Post-Independence Guyana." *Social Movement Studies* 6(1): 57–82. http://dx.doi.org/10.1080/14742830701251336

Niger-Thomas, Margaret. 1996. "Women's Access to and the Control of Credit in Cameroon: The Mamfe Case." In *Money-Go-Rounds: The Importance of Rotating Savings and Credit Associations for Women*, 95–111. Oxford, UK: Berg.

Nkofi, Accabre. 2007. *Rebirth of the Blackman*. Georgetown: IB.

Le Nouvelliste. n.d. Various issues.

NYT (New York Times). n.d. Various issues.

N'Zengou-Tayo, Marie-José. 1998. "*Fanm se poto mitan*: Haitian Woman, The Pillar of Society." *Feminist Review: Rethinking Caribbean Difference* 59(1): 118–42. http://dx.doi.org/10.1080/014177898339497

Panton, David. 1993. *Jamaica's Michael Manley: The Great Transformation, 1972–1992*. Kingston: LMH.

Paquin, Raphael, and Jose Brax. 2006. *Histoire d'Haiti: 1492–2004*, 2nd ed. Port-au-Prince: Haiti souvenirs mémoires d'un siècle.

Paravisini-Gebert, L. 1997. "Decolonizing Feminism: The Home-Grown Roots of Caribbean Women's Movements." In *Daughters of Caliban: Caribbean Women in the Twentieth Century*, ed. C.L. Springfield, 3–17. Bloomington: Indiana University Press.

Payne, Anthony J. 1994. *Politics in Jamaica*. Kingston: Randle.

PBS (Public Broadcasting System). n.d. Various articles and broadcasts.

Pierre, Mathias. 2011. *The Power of a Dream: One Man's Determination to Pursue His Ideals*. Port-au-Prince: Create Space.

PIOJ (Planning Institute of Jamaica). 1997. "National Committee on Political Tribalism." Kingston, Jamaica. Unpublished, government report.

Polanyi, Karl. 1944. *The Great Transformation: The Political and Economic Origins of Our Time*. Boston: Beacon Press.

Poto mitan: Haitian Women, Pillars of the Global Economy. 2008. Prod. Tet Ansanm. http://www.potomitan.net

Premdas, Ralph R. 1995. *Ethnic Conflict and Development: The Case of Guyana*. Hampshire: Ashgate.

Quarter, Jack, Laurie Mook, and Ann Armstrong. 2009. *Understanding the Social Economy: A Canadian Perspective*. Toronto: University of Toronto Press.

Raghunandan, Moolchand, and Balraj Kistow. 1998. "The Cooperative Movement in the Midst of Economic Chaos: The Guyanese Experience." *Journal of Small Business Management* 36(2): 74–8.

Rahman, Aminur. 1999. "Micro-Credit Initiatives for Equitable and Sustainable Development: Who Pays?" *World Development* 27(1): 67–82. http://dx.doi.org/10.1016/S0305-750X(98)00105-3

Ramharack, Baytoram. 2005. *Against the Grain: Balram Singh Rai and the Politics of Guyana*. Port of Spain: Chakra.

Rankin, Katherine. 2001. "Governing Development: Neoliberalism, Microcredit, and Rational Economic Women." *Economy and Society* 30(1): 18–37. http://dx.doi.org/10.1080/03085140020019070

–. 2002. "Social Capital, Microfinance, and the Politics of Development." *Journal of Feminist Economics* 8(1): 1–24. http://dx.doi.org/10.1080/13545700210125167

Rapley, John. 2003. ""Jamaica: Negotiating Law and Order with the Dons." *NACLA Report on the Americas* 37: 2–25.

–. 2006. "The New Middle Ages." *Foreign Affairs* 85(3): 95–103. http://www.jstor.org/stable/10.2307/20031970?origin=crossref 0

Reed, Larry. 2012. "A Too-Generalized Look at Microfinance." *Washington Post*, 14 March. https://www.washingtonpost.com/opinions/a-too-generalized-look-at-microfinance/2012/03/13/gIQANqjcCS_story.html

Reinert, Kenneth A., and Jon E. Voss. 1997. "Rural Grassroots Organizations in Haiti: A Case of Wanted Potential." *Development in Practice* 7: 65–9.

Rhyne, Elizabeth, and Maria Otero. 2006. "Microfinance through the Next Decade: Visioning the Who, What, Where, and When and How." Paper commissioned by the Global Microcredit Summit.

Richfield and Pace Investments Limited. 1994. *Report on the Micro and Small Business Sector in Jamaica*. (unpublished).

Rizavi, Saquib, and Gobind Ganga. "Microfinance Sector and Poverty Alleviation in Guyana: A Overview" (draft version). Annual Monetary Studies Conference, 31 October to 3 November 2006. Barbados.

Robinson, M. 2001. *The Microfinance Revolution: Sustainable Finance for the Poor*. Washington: World Bank. http://dx.doi.org/10.1596/0-8213-4524-9

Robinson, Randall. 2007. *An Unbroken Agony: Haiti, from Revolution to the Kidnapping of a President*. New York: Perseus Group.

Robotham, Don. 2000. "Blackening the Jamaican Nation: The Travails of a Black Bourgeoisie in a Globalized World." *Identities* 7(1): 1–37.

–. 2003. "Crime and Public Policy in Jamaica." In *Understanding Crime in Jamaica: New Challenges for Public Policy*, ed. Anthony Harriott. Kingston: University of the West Indies Press.

Rodney, Walter. 1981. *A History of the Guyanese Working People, 1881–1905*. Baltimore: Johns Hopkins University Press.

–. 1982. *How Europe Underdeveloped Africa*. Washington: Howard University Press.

–. 1996. *The Groundings with My Brothers*. London: Bogle L'Ouverture.

Rogaly, Ben. 1996 "Microfinance Evangelism, Destitute Women, and the Hard Selling of a New Anti-Poverty Formula." *Development in Practice* 6(2): 100–12.

Roodman, David. 2012a. *Due Diligence: An Impertinent Inquiry into Microfinance*. Washington: Center for Global Development.

–. 2012b. "Microcredit Doesn't End Poverty, Despite All That Hype." *Washington Post*, 8 March. https://www.washingtonpost.com/opinions/microcredit-doesnt-end-poverty-despite-all-the-hype/2012/01/20/gIQAtrfqzR_story.html

–. 2012c. "Think Again: Microfinance." *Foreign Policy* 1 (February): http://foreignpolicy.com/articles/2012/02/01/think_again_microfinance?page=0,2

Rotberg, Robert. 1997. *Haiti Renewed: Political and Economic Prospects*. Cambridge, MA: World Peace Foundation.

Roy, Ananya. 2010. *Poverty Capital: Microfinance and the Making of Development*. New York: Routledge.

Rutherford, Stuart. 2000. *The Poor and Their Money*. New Delhi: DFID/Oxford University Press.

Ryan, S. 2013a. "Welfare and Poverty in Laventille." *Trinidad Express*, 7 September. http://www.trinidadexpress.com/commentaries/Welfare-and-poverty-in- Laventille-222830601.html

–. 2013b. "Some Causes of Poverty in East Port of Spain." *Trinidad Express*, 29 May. http://www.trinidadexpress.com/commentaries/Some-causes-of-pov erty-in-East-Port-of-Spain-209435071.html

Saint-Gérard, Yves. 2004. *Haiti 1804–2004: Entre mythes et réalités*. Paris: Felin.

St Pierre, Maurice. 1999. *Anatomy of Resistance: Anticolonialism in Guyana 1823–1966*. London: MacMillan Education.

Salmon, Felix. 2010. "The Lessons of Andhra Pradesh." *Reuters*, 18 November. http://blogs.reuters.com/felix-salmon/2010/11/18/the-lessons-of-andhra-pradesh

Sandbrook, Richard, and Ali Burak Güven. 2014. *Civilizing Globalization, Revised and Expanded Edition: A Survival Guide*. New York: SUNY Press.

Sandbrook, Richard, Marc Edelman, Patrick Heller, and Judith Teichman. 2007. *Social Democracy in the Global Periphery: Origins, Challenges, Prospects*. Cambridge: Cambridge University Press. http://dx.doi.org/10.1017/CBO9780511491139.

Sandford, Gregory, and Richard Vigilante. 1984. *Grenada: The Untold Story*. New York: Madison.

Schomburgk, Robert H. 1970[1840]. *A Description of British Guiana*, 1st ed. London: Cass.

Schreiner, Mark. 2002. "Aspects of Outreach: A Framework for Discussion of the Social Benefits of Microfinance." *Journal of International Development* 14(5): 591–603. http://dx.doi.org/10.1002/jid.908

Scott, James. 1972. "Patron–Client Politics and Political Change in Southeast Asia." *American Political Science Review* 66(1): 91–113. http://dx.doi.org/10.2307/1959280

–. 1977. *The Moral Economy of the Peasant: Rebellion and Subsistence in Southeast Asia*. New Haven: Yale University Press.

Scott, Michael. 2007. "The Politics of Public Sector Transformation in Guyana." *Transition* 37 (December): 40–89.

SDC (Social Development Commission). 2007–8. *Community Profiles: Denham Town, Tivoli Gardens, Arnett Gardens, Maxfield Park, Rosetown, Whitfield Town*.

Seidman, Irving. 2006. *Interviewing as Qualitative Research: A Guide for Researchers in Education and the Social Sciences*. New York: Teachers College Press.

Sengupta, Rajdeep, and Craig P. Aubuchon. 2008. "The Microfinance Revolution: An Overview." *Federal Reserve Bank of St. Louis Review* 90(1): 9–30.

Shamsie, Yasmine. 2006. "The Economic Dimension of Peace-Building in Haiti: Drawing on the Past to Reflect on the Present." In *Haiti: Hope for a Fragile State*, ed. Yasmine Shamsie and Andrew Thompson, 37–50. Waterloo: Wilfrid Laurier University Press.

Shottas. 2002. Dir. Cess Sivera. Kingston: Access Pictures.

Shragge, Eric, and Jean-Marc Fontan. 2000. *Social Economy: International Debates and Perspectives*. Montreal: Black Rose.

Sinclair, Hugh. 2012. *Confessions of a Microfinance Heretic*. San Francisco: Berrett-Koehler.

Singh, Jai Narine. 1996. *Guyana: Democracy Betrayed: A Political History, 1948–1993*. Kingston: Kingston Publishers.

Sives, Amanda. 2002. "Changing Patrons, from Politician to Drug Don, Clientelism in Downtown Kingston Jamaica." *Latin American Perspectives* 29(5): 66–89. http://dx.doi.org/10.1177/0094582X0202900505

–. 2010. *Elections, Violence, and the Democratic Process in Jamaica: 1994–2007*. Kingston: Ian Randle.

Small Business Development Trust (SBDT). 2006. Annual Report. Kingston, Jamaica.

Smartt-Bell, Madison. 2007. *Toussaint Louverture: A Biography*. New York: Vintage.

Smith, Phil, and Eric Thurman. 2007. *A Billion Bootstraps: Microcredit, Barefoot Banking, and the Business Solution for Ending Poverty*. New York: McGraw-Hill.

Smith, Raymond T. 1964. *British Guiana*. London: Oxford University Press.

Sookdeo, Harold. 1997. "Small Business Financing: An Examination of the Financing of Small Firms in Guyana 1985–1995." Masters thesis, Durham University.

Sookraj, R. 2010. "Kamla Came from Humble Beginnings." *Trinidad and Tobago Guardian*, 26 May. http://m.guardian.co.tt/archives/news/general/2010/05/26/kamla- came-humble-beginnings

Stabroek News. n.d. Various issues.

–. 2010. "President Jagdeo receives United Nations Environment Programme (UNEPS) Champion of the Earth award." 23 April. http://www.stabroeknews.com/2010/archives/04/23/president-jagdeo-receives-unep-champion-of-the-earth-award

STATIN (Statistical Institute of Jamaica). 2008. *Labour Force*. Kingston.

Statistics Bureau of Guyana. n.d. Various reports.

Steele, Beverley. 2003. *Grenada: A History of Its People*. London: Macmillan Caribbean.

Stoby, Es. 1931. *British Guiana Centenary Yearbook 1831–1931*. Georgetown.

Stone, Carl. 1980. *Democracy and Clientelism in Jamaica*. New Brunswick: Transaction.

–. 1986. *Class, State, and Democracy in Jamaica*. New York: Praeger.

–. 1994. "The Jamaican Party System and Political Culture." In *Jamaica: Preparing for the 21st Century*, ed. Patsy Lewis, 132–148. Kingston: Randle.

Storey, D.J. 2004. "Racial and Gender Discrimination in the Micro-Firms Credit Market? Evidence from Trinidad and Tobago." *Small Business Economics* 23(5): 401–22. doi:10.1007/s11187-004-7259-0.

Stotzky, Irwin. 1997. *Silencing the Guns in Haiti: The Promise of Deliberate Democracy*. Chicago: University of Chicago Press.

Szeftel, Morris. 2000. "Clientelism, Corruption, and Catastrophe." *Review of African Political Economy* 85 (September): 427–41.

Tafari-Ama, Imani. 2006. *Blood, Bullets, and Bodies: Sexual Politics below Jamaica's Poverty Line*.

Tejerina, Luis, and Sergio Navajas. 2006. "Microfinance in Latin America and the Caribbean: Connecting Supply and Demand." In *IDB report*, 1–48. Washington: IDB Sustainable Development Department.

Tennant, David. 2008. *Policy Report for the Jamaican MSME Sector*. PSDP/GOJ/EU.

Terborg-Penn, Rosalyn. 1995. "Through an African Feminist Theoretical Lens: Viewing Caribbean Women's History Cross-Culturally." In *Engendering History: Caribbean Women in a Historical Perspective*, ed. Verene Shepherd and Brigid Brereton, 3–19. London: Currey.

Third World Cop. 1999. Dir. Christopher Browne. Kingston: Palm Pictures.

Thomas, Clive Y. 1988. *The Poor and the Powerless: Economic Policy and Change in the Caribbean*. New York: Monthly Review Press.

Thomas, Deborah A. 2004. *Modern Blackness: Nationalism, Globalization, and the Politics of Culture in Jamaica*. Durham: Duke University Press. http://dx.doi.org/10.1215/9780822386308

Trotz, Alissa D. 2004. "Between Despair and Hope: Women and Violence in Contemporary Guyana." *Small Axe* 8(1): 1–20. http://dx.doi.org/10.1215/-8-1-1

Trouillot, Michel-Rolph. 1995. *Silencing the Past: Power and the Production of History*. Boston: Beacon.

Tucker, Michael, and Winston Tellis. 2005. "Microfinance Institutions in Transition: Fonkoze in Haiti Moves toward Regulated Banking Status." *Journal of Microfinance* 7(2): 101–25.

Ulysse, Gina A. 2007. *Downtown Ladies: Informal Commercial Importers, a Haitian Anthropologist, and Self-Making in Jamaica*. Chicago: University of Chicago Press.

UN. 2011. International Year for People of African descent. Retrieved 17 November 2015 from: http://www.un.org/en/events/iypad2011/

UNCDF (United Nations Capital Development Fund). 2003. *Haiti Companion Report: Impact Assessment 2003*.

UNDP. 2009. Human Development Index Report. http://hdr.undp.org/sites/default/files/reports/269/hdr_2009_en_complete.pdf

UN (United Nations). 2003. General Assembly Meeting, 23 July. A/58/179

UN Human Development Report. 2008. Jamaica.

USAID (US Agency for International Development). 2008. "Recensement sur l'Industrie de la Microfinance Haïtienne: 2007–8." In Contract # GEG-1-04-02-00011-00. Port-au-Prince: Strategic Management Group.

UWI (University of the West Indies). 2006. "Survey of Family-Owned and Women-Owned Businesses." Final Report (April). Kingston: Mona School of Business.

Van Staveren, Irene. 2015. *Economics after the Crisis: An Introduction to Economics from a Pluralist and Global Perspective*. New York: Routledge.

Verrest, Hebe. 2013. "Rethinking Micro-Entrepreneurship and Business Development Programs: Vulnerability and Ambition in Low-Income Urban Caribbean Households." *World Development* 47: 58–70. http://dx.doi.org/10.1016/j.worlddev.2013.02.016

Vonderlack-Navarro, Rebecca. 2010. "Targeting Women versus Addressing Gender in Microcredit: Lessons from Honduras." *Journal of Women and Social Work* 25(2): 123–34. http://dx.doi.org/10.1177/0886109910364356

Von Stauffenberg, D. 2000. "Microfinance in the English Caribbean." Barbados: Caribbean Development Bank.

Voodoo and the Church in Haiti. 1998. Dir. Bob Richards. Nine Morning Productions.

Wahid, Abu N.M. 1994. "The Grameen Bank and Poverty Alleviation in Bangladesh." *American Journal of Economics and Sociology* 53(1): 1–15. http://dx.doi.org/10.1111/j.1536-7150.1994.tb02666.x

Waller, Gary, and Warner Woodworth. 2001. "Microcredit as Grass Roots Policy for International Development." *Policy Studies Journal: The Journal of the Policy Studies Organization* 29(2): 267–82. http://dx.doi.org/10.1111/j.1541-0072.2001.tb02091.x

Wane, Njoki, Katerina Deliovsky, and Erica Lawson. 2002. *Back to the Drawing Board: African Canadian Feminisms*. Toronto: Sumac.

Washington, Booker T. 2013[1910]. *Up from Slavery: An Autobiography*. Delhi: Ratna Sagar.

Wells, Jennifer. 2010. "Lovely's Haiti: Small Loans, Big Trouble." *Toronto Star*, 3 December. http://www.thestar.com/news/world/2010/12/03/lovelys_haiti_small_loans_big_trouble.html

Westley, Glenn. 2005. "*Microfinance in the Caribbean: How to Go Further.*" Technical paper series. Washington: IADB Sustainable Development Department.

White, Timothy. 2000. *Catch a Fire: The Life of Bob Marley*. New York: Holt.

Whyte, Barrington. 2001. "A Micro and Small Enterprise (MSE) Sector Lending Strategy for Credit Union Movement in Jamaica." Kingston: Jamaican Cooperative Credit Union League.

Williams, Eric. 2004[1944]. *Capitalism and Slavery*. Chapel Hill: University of North Carolina Press.

Wilson, Kim. 2001. "The New Microfinance: An Essay on the Self-Help Group Movement in India." *Journal of Microfinance* 4(2): 217–46.

Wilson, Leon C., Letroy Cummings, and Brenda Marshall. 2007. "Economic Stress and Well-Being in Urban Guyana: A Microanalysis." *Transition* 37 (December): 90–116.

Winkler, Anthony C. 2006. *Going Home to Teach*. Oxford: Macmillan.

Witter, Michael. 1989. "Higglering/Sidewalk Vending: Informal Commercial Trading in Jamaican Economy." Department of Economics Occasional Paper No. 4. Kingston, Jamaica: University of West Indies, Mona campus.

Wong, David. 1996. "A Theory of Petty Trading: The Jamaican Higgler." *Economic Journal* 106 (435): 507–18. http://dx.doi.org/10.2307/2235264

World Bank. 2009a. Jamaica at a Glance.

–. 2009b. Jamaica Population Data. http://data.worldbank.org/country/jamaica

–. 2011. http://data.worldbank.org/country/jamaica

–. 2013. Trinidad and Tobago data. http://data.worldbank.org/country/trinidad-and-tobago

Wuttunee, Wanda. 2004. *Living Rhythms: Lessons in Aboriginal Economic Resilience and Vision*. Montreal and Kingston: McGill–Queen's University Press.

Young, Allan. 1958. *The Approaches to Local Self-Government in British Guiana*. London: Longman.

Young, Robin, and Lauren Mitten. 2000. *Cadre juridique et normes de performance pour la microfinance: quelques enseignements pour Haiti*. Port au Prince: PRÊT/DAI and KNFP.

Yunus, Muhammad. 1994. "Does the Capitalist System Have to be the Handmaiden of the Rich?" Eighty-Fifth Rotary International Convention, Taipei. 1–8.

–. 1998. "Poverty Alleviation: Is Economics Any Help? Lessons from the Grameen Bank Experience." *Journal of International Affairs* 52: 47–65.

–. 2007a. *Banker to the Poor: Micro-lending and the Battle against World Poverty*. New York: Public Affairs.

–. 2007b. "What Is Microcredit?" Grameen Bank. 28 September. www.grameen-info.org/bank/WhatIsMicrocredit.htm

–. 2010. *Building Social Businesses: The New Kind of Capitalism That Serves Humanity's Most Pressing Needs*. New York: Public Affairs.

Zanotti, Laura. 2010. "Cacophonies of Aid, Failed State Building, and NGOs in Haiti: Setting the Stage for Disaster, Envisioning the Future." *Third World Quarterly* 31(5): 755–71. http://dx.doi.org/10.1080/01436597.2010.503567.

Index